My Work in Sport Psychology

Second Edition

Burt Giges M.D.

ISBN: 1532843801
ISBN 13: 9781532843808
Library of Congress Control Number: 2016908567
CreateSpace Independent Publishing Platform
North Charleston, South Carolina

Acknowledgements

I am very fortunate to have a wife and two daughters who have consistently encouraged and supported me throughout my entire professional life. They also have been very helpful in my writing, frequently serving as editors, offering suggestions and making corrections that improved the quality of the writing.

In addition, I want to express my deep appreciation to my close professional colleagues, Al Petitpas, Judy Van Raalte, and Britt Brewer at Springfield College. They have been my mentors, consultants, co-authors, editors, and personal supporters. They have also helped me become more visible in the sport psychology community by inviting me to deliver keynote addresses and producing videos demonstrating my work.

My gratitude extends to several other professional colleagues who, from the beginning of my career in sport psychology, served as good friends, helped me get started, stimulated me to move forward, invited me to present my work at conferences or write a chapter, and supported my participation in other professional activities. Warmest thanks to Jack Lesyk, Ken Ravizza, Mark Andersen, Sean McCann, Gloria Balague, and Michael Sachs.

Special thanks to my good friend Gail Staal for a cover picture that eloquently captures self-reflection in the moment.

Table of Contents

Preface to the Second Edition

Although I had thought about publishing a second edition to "My Work in Sport Psychology," the real stimulus to do so came from Dr. Kate Hays' review of the first edition (*The Sport Psychologist*, 2015, 29, 156-157). Dr. Hays expressed the hope that a second edition would include full text reproductions of articles and book chapters I had written.

In response to her suggestion, this Second Edition will include five chapters, four journal articles, and two book reviews that were originally published elsewhere.

In addition, I decided to include the dates, locations, and names of co-presenters of the 70 presentations I have given at various universities, meetings and conferences. Many of the lectures and workshops were repeated at different locations around the country.

I hope you enjoy reading them as much as I enjoyed writing and presenting them.

Preface to the First Edition

The idea of writing a book about my work has been with me for several years. The stimulus to convert that idea into reality came from two important milestones – my 25th anniversary in the field of sport psychology and my 90th birthday later this year. To create a more permanent work, this book is a printed form of the website I established in 2010. In addition to describing my philosophical perspective, the book contains commentary on two controversial issues in the field, as well as the lectures and workshops I have presented to graduate students and professionals around the country. The workshops and lectures in outline form are the notes from which the actual presentations were made.

Part I

Introduction

Philosophical Perspective

Although originally trained as a clinician, with a background in medical research, I've come to see myself more as an educator. This change involved a shift from the medical model of illness and disease to a growth and development model, in which problems are seen as the result of learned thinking patterns. The goal of my work with athletes and others is to help them change those patterns that contribute to distressed feelings or troublesome behavior and to remove the barriers to their optimal functioning. My focus is primarily on present-day experiences, because of my assumption that current patterns of thinking and feeling often prevent past negative experiences from receding into the background. In addition, I am particularly interested in the language a person uses, because it not only expresses present thoughts and feelings, but also contributes to their development.

I believe that what we learned in the past can be changed by what we learn in the present.

* * *

Excerpts

I have included these excerpts in the introduction because they capture the essence of my thinking about important issues in my professional and personal life.

From an interview, AASP Conference, October 2001
(Conducted by Artur Poczwardowski)

What I'm looking for in my work with athletes is a very modest goal for every session – something that can help them make a small shift in how they see their own situation. It's what I work towards – it doesn't have to happen. If the goal is modest enough, it can be a first step that can help point them in the right direction.

I like to see beginnings. They can build confidence, because the person has their own experience in that first step. I think that's one of the essential elements of change: the realization that you can begin a change process. Most people are focused on outcome, end-result, and there's a big difference to go from where they are now to where they want to be. But it's not such a big step to go from where they are now to almost where they are now. This beginning small step helps them see they already know how to change.

One of the things I don't enjoy when I'm consulting is getting lost, losing focus. And it happens in many interviews. At some point in the interview, I lose it. It can happen if something that's said leads me to disconnect from the other person, or if I decide not to pursue something. And what I usually do to help me get it back, is to ask the person what's going on for them right now, as a way of helping me re-connect to their experience in the moment.

It's ok to start working with someone who doesn't trust you. That is where they are. Too early a trust is probably not trustworthy. If somebody trusts you before they've had much to do with you, it's probably a fantasy, a wish, or an idealization of you.

If you have too fixed an idea of what you can do for someone, you might miss creative opportunities to do something different.

I was once asked by a woman in a group "Why don't you get frustrated if we don't improve?" I said, "Because my primary satisfaction comes from what I do, not from what you do." And she said, "Don't you care about us?" And I replied, "Yes I do, but you asked why I don't get frustrated."

* * *

From an interview, AASP Newsletter, 21, 1, 2006, p. 5-6

AASP: What advice do you have for students entering the field?

BG: To borrow from Zen teaching: When being a student, just be a student. Be as fully a student as you can be. Soak up new information, whether it matches your prior ideas or not. Be open to differences as an expansion of your knowledge, rather than a threat to your beliefs. Learn from teachers, coaches, books, journals, fellow students, athletes, and especially from your own experience.

Being an excellent student is different from being an excellent consultant, teacher, or researcher. As a student, your excellence is in your dedication and commitment to learning, and in your acceptance of what you have not yet learned or cannot yet do.

Be mindful of your long-term development as a professional, and consider every step of the way as preparation for the next step.

* * *

From the chapter, Removing Psychological Barriers: Clearing the way in *Doing Sport Psychology*, 2000, *17-31*

The growth model includes focusing on developing one's potential, giving prominence to here-and- now experience, encouraging risk-taking behavior, and highlighting choices and responsibility. A basic assumption of the model, as applied in sport psychology, is that athletes inherently have the capacity for optimal functioning, and would be able to do so if nothing were in the way. Removing psychological barriers is an approach that helps release potential and can be seen as "clearing the way." Present functioning and here-and-now experience are the starting points of intervention.

In the process of synthesizing the several influences on my present work, there are three guiding principles that help me integrate the concepts and apply them in consultation with athletes: (a) examining present psychological experience, (b) listening carefully to language, and (c) using "entry points" to help remove psychological barriers.

* * *

From the AASP Newsletter, 11, 3, 1996, p. 24, 27

An important distinction must be made, however, between therapy in a clinical context and intervention in sport performance. In the world of sport, sometimes the symptom *is* the problem.

Whatever underlying issues there may be, they are not necessarily the focus of the work. Even the presence of some diagnostic entity does not determine the appropriate intervention. It may not be why the athlete came for help; and sometimes, relieving the symptom removes the problem. I have seen this happen with runners whose performance was impaired by anxiety, anger, self-doubt, or loss of confidence, motivation, or concentration. In such instances, when the symptoms were dealt with directly, no further exploration (of deeper issues) was required *(AASP Newsletter, 11, 24).*

* * *

From the Conference on Counseling Athletes, "Winning in Sport and Life," Springfield College, June 21-23, 2002

The essence of winning is "I feel good about myself." The essence of losing is "I don't feel good about myself." So then the question becomes "Can this essence of feeling good about myself be obtained in other ways?"

In our culture, failure is not a description, it is a judgment. Failure carries the implication that we are not good enough.

When something is in the way of your excellence, when there is a barrier to your performance, can it be changed, or removed?

What's in your environment or experience that needs to be recognized, set aside in some way, and eventually transcended?

* * *

From the Workshop on Change

When people say, "I'll never change," what do they mean? They might mean, "I'll never be able to change my behavior or my feeling." They don't usually mean, "I'll never change my awareness." And they may not realize that a change in awareness is often the first step in changing other aspects of their experience. It can be seen relatively early in the change process, and can be the beginning of a realization that they can change.

When people have difficulty deciding which of two alternatives to choose, it is often helpful to have them imagine that they have already decided on one. It doesn't matter which one they do first. Have them live for the next few days or hours (depending on the situation) as if that is what they are going to do. Ask them to pay attention to what feelings, thoughts, and wants come in to their awareness. Then have them switch to the other choice, and live with that one for the same amount of time. Then have them compare and discuss the two experiences. Usually, they will be able to recognize the one that is stronger.

* * *

From the Workshop on Self-Awareness for Sport Psychology Practitioners

Self-awareness provides an opportunity for change. Most often, we become aware of a problem behavior after it occurs. When this happens, we may say "I see that I did that." With a commitment to change and repeated awareness of the behavior, awareness begins to occur earlier. When it is present during the behavior, we may say "I see that I am doing that right now." With additional time and practice, awareness moves earlier in time, until it is present before the undesired behavior occurs. At this point, we can say "I see that I am about to do that." When awareness precedes the behavior, a choice can be made to behave differently. This is an opportunity for change and is represented by the statement "I can do it differently."

Everything we do is connected to something we want.

What we want is not only what we don't have.

When a person answers a question with "I don't know," they may mean "I don't know, so let's go on to something else." You may be able to help them change that to, "I don't know, so let's look further to find out."

Part II

Commentary

AASP Newsletter, 11, 3, 1996, p. 24

Clinical and Sport Psychology

In a recent discussion on the Internet (Listserv. sportpsy), some recommendations were made to a runner about how to deal with anxiety during competition. A few contributors reacted to these ideas with concern about suggestions being offered without having more background information from the person seeking assistance. Such caution is both understandable and reasonable. It derives from clinical training, and is based on the theory that symptoms (i.e., anxiety) are expressions of deeper problems. Offering techniques to deal with these symptoms, therefore, would be premature, without knowing more about the underlying problems.

An important distinction must be made, however, between therapy in a clinical context and intervention in sport performance. In the world of sport, sometimes the symptom *is* the problem. Whatever underlying issues there may be, they are not necessarily the focus of the work. Even the presence of some diagnostic entity does not determine the appropriate intervention. It may not be why the athlete came for help; and sometimes, relieving the symptom removes the problem. I have seen this happen with runners whose performance was impaired by anxiety, anger, self-doubt, or loss of confidence, motivation, or concentration. In such instances, when the symptoms were dealt with directly, no further exploration (of deeper issues) was required.

I believe that experienced, creative practitioners can recognize this possibility, and offer relevant, effective interventions, which may, however, deviate from traditional theory and practice. Theory-based practice is an essential part of education and training. Experienced-based practice sometimes presents a challenge to originally learned theory, and then requires courage and careful reflection. A theory about what is so is not the same as what is so. The Eastern mystic knows the "the finger pointing the way is not the way." A more Western expression of that thought is, "The map is not the territory."

To hold one's practice too strictly to a theoretical position may narrow the ability to consider other approaches. Sometimes a careful follow-up of an intervention may reveal unexpected lasting benefit from what seemed initially to be "first aid." In other situations, where no such benefit is obtained, or when recurrences continue to interfere with performance, underlying difficulties might then be addressed.

* * *

AASP Newsletter, 10, 1, 1995, p. 24

Clinicians and Educators

Recently there has been increasing interest and discussion, both in the literature and at conferences, of the appropriate education, training, and experience necessary for sport psychology practice, as well as the legal and ethical issues involved.

In the early years after training, the differences between the clinical and educational consultant in sport psychology seem many, the similarities few. What we are, clinician or educator, seems synonymous with what we know and what we do. Our professional discipline seems to define us. We have been educated, trained, and licensed. We have credentials. We are educators, counselors, therapists. There are books that describe our unique identities and support and reinforce our separateness. And so we stand tall. We have status, rights, and privileges. And with those rights and privileges, a territory begins to be defined. Others, without similar status and credentials, may not enter this territory.

And so it was 35 years ago, when I began my residency in psychiatry. I was one of the physicians. All others were called "ancillary personnel," implying a subsidiary position. In the hospital setting, psychologists did testing not treatment. Nurses, social workers and other therapists each had their function and their place, lower to be sure than the physicians. Whatever anxiety there was about our territory being invaded by others was often expressed as part of our concern for patients or desire to maintain professional standards. As if these were the exclusive properties of physicians. They weren't then, and they aren't now. Any professional discipline can have clients as their concern and professional standards as their guidelines. And of course, any can also zealously guard the boundaries or their territory.

It's still going on. In our own organization, vigilance is still maintained over who has the right to do what psychotherapists do. Of course, we must protect our citizens from untrained or unscrupulous practitioners. That's true in every area of professional practice. It is interesting to note, however, that while therapists and counselors may be educators, educators may not be therapists or counselors, unless they have obtained the proper credentials. *But, is helping someone learn new behavior or change their thinking, considered education, counseling, or therapy?* I believe it is part of each and all three. Therefore, it can be done by an educator, counselor, or therapist who has acquired the necessary knowledge, skill, and experience to do so.

Furthermore, when one discipline tells another what it may not do, an implicit hierarchy develops which can breed resentment and create antagonism and distance. This can be intensified when referral is viewed as a one-way street, from those perceived as less skilled to those seen as more skilled. Referral can, however, be in both directions, if there is mutual respect for each other's special knowledge and ability.

Fortunately, all is not lost. What we know and what we do need not be limited to what we call ourselves. What we do derives from multi-dimensional considerations. It is at least a blend of what we have learned – from teachers, colleagues, clients, books, journals, etc. – and what we created from our own experience. What we do also depends on our own thoughts, feelings, needs, and wants. Hopefully it also derives from the people we are trying to help, the situations we deal with, the focus of the work, and the techniques we use.

As time passes, if we remain open to influence by our current experience, the sharp differences between us may decrease, the commonalities increase. Knowledge can be acquired that was not part of our original training. Others can do this too. As we learn more, we can do more; and hopefully we can avoid the pitfall of holding what we learned originally as superior to what others learned later. If we do this, then the professional discipline which defined us will not restrict us.

So continue to learn. And keep on learning. Soak up new information. Listen to differentness as an expansion of your knowledge rather than a threat to your beliefs. Be mindful of how your own feelings and wants influence your beliefs and behavior. And follow your own path to excellence.

Part III

Lectures

AASP Presidential Address 2007

Last year, when Jean Williams called to ask if I would be interested in being a candidate for President-Elect, I asked, "Why me?" She politely avoided telling me that they couldn't get anyone else, and she said, "For your perspective and wisdom." It worked. I can tell you about my perspective, but I'll leave it to others to decide about wisdom.

In thinking about this Presidential Address, I asked myself, "What's the purpose of it?" My answer was: to give each president an opportunity to discuss what he or she sees as important: for those we serve, for sport psychology, or for AASP itself. For this address, I chose to focus on our own organization; and the challenge this presented for me was how to do it.

About 12 years ago, Ken Ravizza invited me to speak to his students at Cal State Fullerton. At that time, I had been working for a few months on the draft of my AASP Keynote Address "How People Change." So I decided to test it out with them. When I was about half-way through the presentation, Ken interrupted me and said, "Burt, it's not you. We can read that stuff in any sport psychology text. We want to hear about your experience." That's my buddy Ken. You recognize him?

After recovering from being crushed, I spent the next few months rewriting it, making it more personal. In the end, he was right because it turned out just fine. Over the years, Ken's advice to me has always worked out well. From that experience, I decided to use the same personal approach for this Presidential Address, and discuss some issues that are especially important to me.

My older daughter, who is a psychologist, also gave me some advice. In responding to my concern that the address would not be long enough, she said, "Dad, what you often say in one sentence is worth a paragraph; so use paragraphs for your presentation." This is the paragraph version.

My very first involvement in sport psychology was 50 years ago, during my psychiatric residency. I was team physician to a high school football program, and I learned a lot about coach stress, sport injury, and parent involvement. My first connection to AASP didn't come until over 30 years later. It was a very meaningful and personal experience. At the age of 65, I had begun to wind down my activities, with somewhat mixed feelings. AASP and sport psychology created a wonderful opportunity for a new beginning. And in the past 18 years, AASP and I have grown up together. During these years, I've worked with athletes, coaches, and others who, although not primarily athletes, were seriously involved in sport participation and competition. More than a dozen different sports were involved, including some less common ones, such as fencing, badminton, luge, and straight pool. I learned a lot more about sport, about consulting, and about myself. One surprising lesson for me was that the sports I knew best were not my most effective consultations.

AASP, too, has grown both in size and complexity. We have some 15 Committees and 15 Special Interest Groups. We now have members from over 30 different countries, representing almost 15% of our membership. We also have an International Relations Committee, and a Distinguished International Scholar Award. There have been qualitative changes as well as quantitative, with the addition of the Rees Management Group, Centennial Conferences, a public relations firm, and a professional web designer.

I want to tell you about where I am with AASP today. At the outset, I want to acknowledge and emphasize that the scope of AASP is much more than my connection, interests, and initiatives. The specifics I will focus on today are only a small part of the breadth and depth of AASP's mission and commitment to a science-based and ethical approach to research and practice. Jack Lesyk captured both the essence and scope of AASP by identifying our goal as the "improvement of physical and mental health and well-being through sport and exercise" (www.appliedsportpsych.org). Our new website is an excellent description of the complexity of our organization.

What is important to me is that we become the strongest organization we can be; and I think that the strength of an organization comes from the strength of its members. But when you think about it, what does strength mean for members? I think it means being the best we can be in how we are members; and if we do that, then AASP will be the best it can be. So, how can we achieve this goal? Well, one way is to have our process become our goal; that is, to improve how we go about doing what we do.

There is a Sufi story about a Golden-Haired Lion, in which the Disciple says to the Master, "Master, when lions seize upon an opponent, be it rabbit or elephant, they make exhaustive use of their power. Where does this power come from?" The Master nods and replies, "It comes from putting forth one's whole being, in which nothing is kept in reserve, nothing goes to waste. When you perform in this way, you too can be a golden-haired lion." Can we use any part of that teaching as members of AASP?

George Bernard Shaw once wrote, "By the time I die, I want to be all used up." When I first read this, it didn't sound like such a good idea. As I reflected more on it, I came to realize that what he was saying was that he wanted to have given all his ability and energy to the way he lived his life.

Among Zen teachings, there is one that says, "When walking, just walk; when sitting, just sit." In other words, whatever you do, do fully, in the present, with your whole being. To supplement that profound message, there's a wise and whimsical story of a Korean Zen Master, who repeatedly admonished his students, "When eating, just eat! When reading, just read!" One day, his attendant walked in on him while he was eating breakfast, and there he was reading a newspaper at the very same time. "Master," he exclaimed, "You always teach us 'When eating, just eat! When reading, just read!' What is the meaning of this?" To which the Master replied, "Yes. It is true that I always teach you 'When eating, just eat! When reading, just read!' And now I am teaching you 'When eating and reading, just eat and read!"

Can we apply that to ourselves as members? When being a member, just be a member. What would be involved? It would certainly include awareness, dedication, commitment, and energy. As members, what would that actually look like? It would mean caring how AASP goes about doing what it does, and then contributing to its improvement. That might include any of the following actions:
- becoming a member of a committee; (15)
- joining a special interest group (SIG); (15)
- nominating candidates for the Executive Board;
- voting when it's time to vote (less than 20% of members vote);

- finding out how you could run for office;
- suggesting or creating something that AASP needs and doesn't have;
- working toward changing something AASP does to make it better;
- adding new ideas to this list, and getting involved in initiating them

Another element that could increase the strength of our Association is member connectedness – something like what cohesion is for a team. This means we would:
- pull together toward common goals;
- support each other by listening with an open mind;
- communicate in ways that accept our differences even when we disagree;
- work toward resolving whatever problems interfere with our performance.

In my Position Statement as candidate for President-Elect last year, I mentioned some specific issues that are important to me, and it is my hope that we can work on these together. AASP is now 21 years old, and if we extend Erik Erikson's ideas on development to apply to our association, then one of our tasks as we enter early adulthood is to master the challenges of intimacy.

So the first issue I want to address is the relationship between psychologists and sport scientists. Over the past 18 years, this relationship has shown continuing evidence of strain. We are surviving, but perhaps not thriving. Many members know about it, and talk about the differences in perspective and practice; but little attention has been given to the relationship between the professions. How to heal the rift has not been directly addressed. It is a challenging task to know even how to begin. Where and when could we do it? Who would initially be involved? Given the time constraints, differences in our training, and separateness of our lives, what would be a first step? Because our Annual Conference is the one time we are all together, a beginning could be Invited Symposiums at our AASP conferences. Dialogue between the professions could focus on this question, "Can we heal our relationship if we still disagree?" The structure and participants in this effort need to be worked out; therefore, a Committee on Professional Relations will be established to address this challenge. Its mission will be to address the problem, plan the symposiums, and make specific recommendations about how to continue the dialogue. The Committee will include members of both professions, and will be chaired by Past-President Len Zaichkowsky.

The second issue I mentioned was increasing the connection between students and professionals. Students are the future of our organization. Adapting Erickson's teachings again, one of our tasks is to guide the next generation. To enrich the experience of our student members would serve both student and professional members of AASP. It will increase learning opportunities for both groups; provide more involvement of students in AASP activities; increase students' exposure to mentoring; and give them a close-up view of different types of applied work.

One important way to accomplish this enrichment is to organize structured opportunities for greater contact between students and experienced professionals. One such opportunity is the "Think Tank" weekend. Bob McGowan organized them on the East Coast, and I attended two of them in 1994 and 1996. Ten years later, Ken Ravizza organized one on the West Coast. My co-candidate for President-Elect, Artur Poczwardowski, wrote about the West Coast experience in *The Sport Psychologist* last year. Other such meetings could be scheduled at the AASP Annual Conference, and at the Student Regional Conferences throughout the year. A Committee on Student Development will, therefore, be created to organize and develop this program. The Committee would include professional and student members of AASP, and Artur Poczwardowski will serve as its Chair.

Because students represent about 40% of our membership, with only one student representing them on the Executive Board, I have proposed that an additional student representative be added to the Board. The functions of the Executive Board Student Representative have grown in number and complexity, including supervision of the regional student representatives from seven regions. These regional representatives have recently been much more involved in developing new programs to improve the operation of AASP.

An increase to two student representatives on the Executive Board would be consistent with encouraging members to become more involved in AASP functions. Two student representatives on the Board will also provide increased opportunities for mentoring future members of the leadership pool. This change would involve a Constitutional amendment, and it is my hope that you will approve it when it is presented at the business meeting.

In addition, with the help of the Executive Board Student Representative, we are planning to improve communication with the Regional Student Representatives, and increase their involvement in AASP by keeping them better informed about our committees and Special Interest Groups. We hope this will improve their ability to help students and other members of AASP understand the purpose and function of these groups, and create the possibility of greater participation in them.

My next idea focuses on direct services to coaches by interested members of AASP. Although much has been written in the sport psychology literature about helping coaches in their work with individual athletes and teams, there is very little about helping coaches with their own needs.

Coaches face similar challenges to those experienced by athletes, such as performance, time management, transition, health, family, and personal issues. However, the needs of coaches before burnout occurs have not received the attention they deserve. AASP has an excellent opportunity to provide leadership in this area. To address this need, I am proposing that our members offer workshops to coaches around the country. These workshops would differ from most coaching education programs in that they would focus on the coaches themselves. The workshops could be free-standing or through existing coaching organizations.

There are many such organizations at all levels of sport participation, including high school, college, national, regional, and local groups. In addition, various sport coaching associations, as well as youth services groups, such as Little League and Pop Warner could be contacted. If coaches benefit from these workshops, their interest in providing similar services to their athletes could increase. A Committee on Services for Coaches will, therefore, be established to develop this program, and monitor its effectiveness on an ongoing basis. Many AASP members have considerable experience in coaching, and the Committee will tap into this expertise, by including those who are or have been coaches, consultants who have worked with coaches and others with a special interest in this area. Gloria Balague, with extensive experience with coaches, will be the Chair.

There is one other change I would like to make. I have proposed that the Performance Enhancement/Intervention Focus Area name be changed to Performance Psychology Focus Area. Although initially intended as a description of professional help, the term Performance Enhancement has changed. Our culture has pre-empted the term, and in the media and in the minds of many, "performance enhancement" has taken on the meaning of using artificial or chemical means to improve performance.

The other half of the term PE/I, 'Intervention,' can be done for purposes other than enhancement; and is not only applicable to performance. Health and Exercise Psychology, and Social Psychology are also involved with interventions.

The new name would clarify that there are more issues in performance than just enhancement. Performance Psychology would identify an area of research and practice, similar to Health Psychology, Exercise Psychology, and Social Psychology. The newer term is widely accepted, and courses in "Performance Psychology" are now being taught in many universities in the U. S., Australia, and the United Kingdom.

Some concern has been expressed about how coaches and athletes will see and understand this change, in view of studies exploring coach and athlete attitudes about sport psychology, and why services aren't used more often. Because of misperceptions of the word psychology, many practitioners describe their work with coaches and athletes emphasizing mental skills training and/or performance enhancement, not psychology. This need not change.

The proposed name change is to identify and clarify an area of our work, in the same way we use the terms Social Psychology, Health Psychology, and Exercise Psychology. It is not necessary to use this term to describe what we actually do with teams, athletes and coaches. For example, when we are involved with team cohesion and communication, we don't usually bring in the term Social Psychology. Similarly, when we are working with athletic injury and rehabilitation, we don't usually talk about Health Psychology.

As an example, when we do performance work and mental skills training, we do not need to actually use the term Performance Psychology. It is primarily to describe the body of knowledge from which we draw our applied techniques and interventions. This proposed change will require a Constitutional amendment, and will also be presented at the business meeting for a vote by the membership. Again, I hope that you will vote in favor of it.

One final issue that will require a membership vote for a Constitutional amendment involves the position of Science and Education Division Head. This position was assigned many responsibilities when the Executive Board was restructured in 2001. To improve the effectiveness of this Division, the Board is now proposing that the position of Division Head be divided into two: one responsible for the development of Conference program, and a separate one for oversight of Focus Area Committees and Special Interest Groups. The Board considers this change an essential element in the plan to increase the importance of these committees and SIGS, and to improve their functioning.

I began this address on a personal note, and I want to end on another one. As you will hear in a moment, "note" is the appropriate word. I mentioned earlier that my first reaction to being asked if I would run for President-Elect was to ask, "Why me?" At the same time, I asked myself a very different kind of question, "Why am I taking on such responsibility at this time in my life?" My response was very similar to my first contact with AASP. I was again being offered a new beginning. Beginning is good, especially at the age of 82, when so many things are ending. So you will see why the article I am about to read is so inspiring to me. Written six years ago by a reporter for the Houston Chronicle, it captures the essence of what it means to be all that you can be.

"On Nov. 18, 1995, Itzhak Perlman, the renowned violinist, came on stage to give a concert at Lincoln Center in New York City. If you have ever been to a Perlman concert, you know that getting on stage is no small achievement for him. He was stricken with polio as a child, has braces on both legs, and walks with the aid of two crutches. To see him walk across the stage one step at a time is quite something. He walks slowly, sometimes painfully, yet majestically, until he reaches his chair. He sits down, slowly puts his crutches on the floor, undoes the clasps on his legs, tucks one foot back, and extends the other foot forward. Then he bends down, picks up his violin, puts it under his chin, nods to the conductor to begin, and proceeds to play. By now, the audience is quite used to this ritual. They sit quietly while he makes his way across the stage to his chair. They remain reverently silent while he undoes the clasps on his legs. They wait patiently until he is ready to play.

On this particular occasion, just after he began playing the first few bars, one of the strings on his violin snapped. It went off like gunfire, and you could hear it across the room. There was no mistaking what that sound meant. There was no mistaking what he might have to do. Some people who were there that night thought to themselves: "He might have to get up, put the clasps on again, pick up his crutches, and limp his way off stage. Then he has to find another violin, or find another string for this one, or wait for someone to bring him one."

He didn't do any of those things. Instead, he closed his eyes, waited a moment, and then signaled the conductor to begin again. The orchestra began, and he picked up just where he had left off. Of course, anyone knows that it is impossible to play a symphonic work with just three violin strings. I know that, you know that, but that night Itzhak Perlman refused to know that. You could see him modulating, recomposing, and changing the piece in his head. At one point, it sounded like he was re-tuning the strings, to get sounds from them they had never made before. And he played with more passion, power, and purity than many who were there had ever heard before.

When he finished, there was a moment of awesome silence in the room. Then people rose to their feet and cheered. There was an extraordinary outburst of applause from every corner of the auditorium. We were all cheering and screaming, doing everything we could to show how much we appreciated what he had done. Here was a man who has prepared all his life to make music on a violin with four strings, who all of a sudden, in the middle of a concert, found himself with three. And the music he made that night with three strings was more beautiful, more sacred, and more memorable than any that he made with four strings. He smiled, wiped the sweat from his brow, raised his bow to quiet us, and said in a pensive, reverent tone, "You know, sometimes our task is to find out how much music we can still make with what we have left."

What a powerful lesson that can be! It can, in fact, be a way of life, not just for an artist with a disability, but for us all at any age. Perhaps our task, in this fast-changing, bewildering world, is to make music, at first with all that we have; and then, when that is no longer possible, to make music with what we have left."

AASP Keynote Address, "How People Change", 1995

When Al Petitpas first called to ask if I would be interested in being keynote speaker, my delight and excitement were tinged with some anxiety and trepidation. I felt like the kid on the bench when the coach yelled, "Giges, get in there!" Although I have been studying change for 40 years and have made important career and personal changes, the invitation seemed a bit intimidating. But having learned a little about stress, I realized I could see it more as a challenge than a threat. So here I am -- challenged! I feel very honored and appreciative for the opportunity to deliver this keynote address.

Since I will be speaking for an hour my presentation will be divided in two parts, with a brief pause for comments and questions at the halfway point, and a longer discussion period at the end.

To begin, I would like to ask for your assistance. Would you for a few moments shift from being part of an audience to being an individual participant? If you are willing to answer a few questions in the privacy of your own thoughts, would you now please close your eyes. No need to relax or get comfortable.

Now, think of an important change that you have made in your life. What motivated you to make that change? Were you seeking enjoyment/satisfaction, or moving away from something uncomfortable? Was it some of both, as is often the case? What helped you make the change? What made it difficult? How did you finally get yourself to do it?

Now, shift to thinking of an important change you are currently considering. If there is none, imagine one you would like to make. What seem to be the reasons to do so? What are your reasons not to? If you were to guess right now what decision you'll make, which would it be? What do you think about the choice you made? And how do you feel having made it?

Would you now open your eyes. Sometimes, we can clarify which choice to make by what I call "decision by sound." Imagine that you have decided to make the change. Think of a sound you could express that matches that decision. If we were working one-to-one, I would ask you to actually make the sound out loud. Now imagine that you decided not to make the change; and again think of a sound that matches this decision. By comparing the two sounds, you may discover which choice you would really prefer.

These questions are intended to give you a small personal glimpse of some elements of the process of change I'll be discussing.

The changes we make are obviously connected to motivation, choices and barriers. But, how do people change? What are the requirements, considerations, and elements of change? And how can we as professionals help other people change?

It depends on whom you ask. Imagine the different responses you'd get about how people change from an anthropologist, a chemist, the clergy, a physicist, a molecular biologist, or a psychologist. Even among psychologists, the response would depend on whether their orientation was behavioral, psychoanalytic, existential, social, or cognitive. To give you some idea of my own perspective, I'll present a highly condensed summary of my professional background, with a footnote of personal reflections.

After graduating from medical school, I was initially involved in medical research, and made my first career change when I shifted from research to medical practice. At that time, I also began a personal psychoanalysis. Later, I changed direction again and entered training in psychiatry, accompanied by another go at psychoanalytic treatment. Five years after my psychiatric residency, I took a position in mental health administration, and conducted a part-time private practice. My growing interest in gestalt therapy, transactional analysis, and group process resulted in my leaving the administrative position. I finally arrived at my current perspective, which is cognitive/affective, about 15 years ago.

During this evolution, I gradually shifted from the medical model to a growth and developmental model, seeing most problems not so much as illness or disease, but more the result of learning and training. So, although originally trained as a clinician, I've come to see myself more as an educator. I use the term cognitive/affective both to emphasize thinking as the major source of feelings, and to give importance to emotions as the significant link between our thoughts and our behavior.

As I reflect on each of these career changes, I see that most were attempts at external solutions to internal problems. For example, I made the first change, from research to practice in medicine, because of a sense of isolation and loneliness despite having reached what I thought was my goal. The second change, into psychoanalytic psychiatry, was related to an unsatisfactory ending to my first analysis, and to a need to learn more about myself. The third change, to gestalt therapy, transactional analysis, and group therapy, emerged from a decreased sense of aliveness as an individual analytic psychotherapist and mental health administrator.

The final change to a cognitive/affective orientation was significantly different. It seemed to represent personal growth rather than restlessness. Confirmation of this comes from a sense of being "at home," that is, "where I belong" professionally, and from the fact that after 15 years, I'm still here. And as part of a lifelong interest in sport, and a continuing search for stimulation, I became actively involved in sport psychology five and a half years ago.

So much for background. I'll approach the subject of change from five aspects: 1) the content of change, that is, what can be changed; 2) the timing of change, that is, when does it occur and is there a sequence involved; 3) the process of change, that is, how does it occur and are there prerequisites for it; 4) resistance to change, that is, the barriers and obstacles, the "why not" of change; and 5) how we as practitioners can help others achieve the changes they seek. I'll focus on intentional change rather than change which occurs as a consequence of normal development or external and environmental factors. I will also draw from the writings of others to give a broader perspective to my discussion.

First, the content of change. What can be changed? We usually think in broad categories, mostly changing behavior, and also changing feelings, thoughts or wants. Within each of these categories, however, there are many specific examples of what can be changed. For instance, we can change awareness, expectations, habits, values, goals, viewpoint, attitudes, opinions, judgments, intentions, choices, decisions, beliefs, directions, or commitment. Foremost, we can change the importance we give to any one of these specific examples.

In my work with one woman, I noticed how much importance she gave to avoiding feeling uncomfortable. She was quite reluctant to experiment with new behavior, whether it was to change her schedule, express herself more assertively, or do something differently than she had before. After prolonged and persistent work about the importance of being in charge of herself, she announced one day, "You know, I could give less importance to feeling comfortable and more to feeling good about myself!" For her, this was a very significant change, even before she did it. Subsequently, it affected how she faced new difficulties, much less as the victim of others' reactions.

We can also change situations, such as job, career or residence, and we can change our communication and our relationships. In relationships, a most important change could be in the meaning we give to others' comments or behavior. How often has feeling hurt been the result of how we interpreted someone else's behavior? We frequently react as if someone's behavior or expression of feeling is a measure of our own worth.

My favorite illustration of this is the hurt one fellow felt when he leaned forward to kiss his girlfriend and she turned away. His hurt was instantaneous. If we were able to stop time, we might observe the following sequence of thoughts: "She doesn't want to kiss me; she no longer loves me; I must not be lovable; I'm less worthwhile; I feel hurt." Immediately after she turned away, however, she sneezed, then turned back and kissed him lovingly. He then realized that it was his interpretation of her turning away that had caused his hurt. Turning away had merely been the trigger.

In examining what can be changed, it is very helpful to give importance to beginning or partial change. Picture the injured athlete who thinks only of final recovery and return to competition. He/she might discount the significance of the beginning of movement in an injured leg, and be frustrated or disappointed with an apparent lack of progress. Only after the trainer describes the significance of this early change is it appreciated as a good beginning to rehabilitation. If limited by all or none, either/or thinking, meaningful early change may be overlooked. And if one is too narrowly focused on changing behavior or feelings, a change in viewpoint may go unnoticed. Yet, this beginning change might be a critical component of reaching one's goal.

A competitive middle distance runner began having a problem when, after leading the pack, she would drop out if someone passed her late in a race. In our work together, she described feeling intense shame at the moment of being passed, as a result of viewing herself as unworthy in that instant. After clarifying, exploring, and modifying this negative viewpoint, guided imagery was used to provide a chance for her to re-experience the race. In the fantasy, she was able to picture herself again being passed, but this time without feeling shame, and without dropping out. In actual competitions subsequent to this work, there were no recurrences of the problem. What had changed were her awareness and her view of herself, and these led to changes in her feeling and her racing behavior.

For a psychiatrist, particularly one trained in psychoanalytic psychotherapy, this was an astounding experience. How can important things happen so quickly? Doesn't it take years to get profound change? It was difficult to let go of a long-standing belief I had, that depth of work correlated with length of time. Since she was willing and open to do so, we went as deeply as I knew how to help her go in two sessions. She was able to do that, benefit from it, and then put it to work.

A humorous illustration of how difficult it is to change people's beliefs is the story of the man who believed he was dead. This delusion is called Cotard's Syndrome. Everyone tried to convince him he wasn't dead, but he held to his belief that he was. Finally, his physician thought he would outsmart him. "Do dead men bleed?" he asked. "No," said the man. "Dead men don't bleed." Whereupon the physician made a small cut in the man's finger and it bled. Triumphantly, the doctor said, "There, what do you say to that?" The man hesitated a moment and finally said, "Oh! I guess dead men do bleed!" An interesting paradox in this anecdote about people not changing is that although the man didn't change his belief about being dead, he did change his belief about dead men not bleeding. I think this illustrates that if we look only for one particular change, we may miss another less dramatic one.

A very intense golfer who wanted to improve his golf score became so angry when he played poorly that he would throw his golf ball into the woods. After a while, he began breaking his golf clubs, and it was at this point he decided to seek help. He felt ashamed, out of control, and was quite critical of himself for his behavior. In discussing his passion to do well, I also noted his strong desire to learn more about his game. With this in mind, I suggested that his golf ball could be viewed as his teacher. Whenever he hooked or shanked a shot, his ball would inform him that something needed correction. And he was actually pleased when I portrayed his golf clubs as his allies, who could help him make the necessary corrections. Following these discussions, which took only a few sessions, there was a significant shift in his attitude toward the ball and his clubs. He accepted my suggestion to have a silent dialogue with his clubs during a game, about how to make use of what the ball was teaching them. There was a marked decrease in his anger and frustration, and he no longer threw golf balls or broke clubs. His attitude, feeling, behavior and enjoyment had changed. All this, despite the fact that his golf handicap remained exactly the same!

When people say, "I'll never change," what do they mean? They might mean, "I'll never be able to change my behavior or my feeling." They don't usually mean, "I'll never change my awareness." And they may not realize that such a change is often the first step in changing other aspects of their experience. In fact, Fritz Perls, the founder of gestalt therapy, said, "Awareness is curative." Even if it's not, it's a very significant element in most changes that can be seen relatively early in the change process, and can be the beginning of a realization that they can change.

This occurred in the case of a runner who was intensely anxious on returning to competition after taking a year off to complete his graduate study. He was not aware that the major source of his worry was how he would look to others. In the hotel room set aside for the team to relax before competition, we were able to clarify this. With the goal of decreasing his anxiety, I guided him through imagery of running all alone in the empty stadium. When he was fully into it, I suggested that other runners would be doing the same thing, that is, running their own race alongside him, and that spectators would be drifting into the stadium. He was able to run his own race, not distracted by others on the track or in the stands. When we then discussed the imagery, he said he had not realized how much his fear was about not looking good. Now that he was aware of it, it seemed to have less of a grip on him.

Incidentally, in the actual race that night, he came in dead last. The coach was quite surprised, however, that the runner did not react with his usual sullenness at finishing so poorly. Instead, he had rejoined his teammates in good spirits. His increased awareness seemed to have helped him change his feeling and his behavior.

The next part of my discussion pertains to the timing of change. When is change most likely to occur? Does it occur in some sequential pattern? James Prochaska and colleagues have done extensive studies about people changing. They list five stages of change, which they call pre-contemplation, contemplation, preparation, action and maintenance. I won't describe these in detail, but will mention that within these stages, a number of processes are involved in changing problem behaviors. The authors also emphasize a spiral pattern of repeating cycles, each bringing movement closer to the desired goal. Their work is quite thoughtful, as they present a trans-theoretical approach crossing traditional boundaries.

As an individual practitioner, however, I have some of the same reservations that I had with Kubler-Ross' stage theory of reactions to terminal illness. Change often doesn't happen in discrete stages, or even in the sequence described. And data drawn from large group studies are not specifically applicable to one individual. The value of such information is in the study of phenomena and processes, rather than the understanding of what is happening in any one person. The work of Ronald Lippitt and colleagues is of interest in this regard. In their seminal book, The Dynamics of Planned Change, published almost 40 years ago, they state that, although there is no fixed progression of steps in the change process, there does seem to be a directional flow, with different elements being more important than others, and occurring at different times in various situations. With this in mind, they do suggest that change usually begins with awareness.

Several authors have emphasized the importance of awareness. In his book How People Change, Allen Wheelis writes that freedom to change is based on an awareness of alternatives and ability to choose. Our own Ken Ravizza, in his chapter "Increasing Awareness for Sport Performances," in the book Applied Sport Psychology, edited by Jean Williams, believes that awareness is the first step in raising self-control in sport participation. And Eric Hoffer, the noted longshoreman philosopher, in his book The Ordeal of Change, describes that change involves choice, and awareness creates the opportunities for choice. Lippitt and colleagues also emphasize that in addition to being aware of a situation or problem, it is important to clarify its nature, be specific in its definition, and perhaps even explore its causes.

Of course, change may occur without knowledge of the origins of or reasons for a problem. Sometimes unpleasant feelings alone are motivation enough to initiate change. Unfortunately, in such instances, when the discomfort subsides, this type of motivation may not be sufficient to sustain a commitment to continue the change process. Motivation to change can also be stimulated by an unrewarding situation or an ineffective solution, as well as by a longing for satisfaction or enjoyment. Both the player who usually sits on the bench and the starter who wants to improve his batting average may be eager to bring about change.

Goals become intentions. Intentions can lead to action, depending on one's readiness and ability to change. Readiness is determined in part by the presence or absence of barriers, and hinges on the balance between motivation to change and the forces opposing it.

One runner was aware that he was training excessively and sought help to change this pattern. At the same time, he had started a new job, which required a lot of traveling and many night hours. He was also under pressure from his parents to "make something of his life." Because he was not ready to make the training changes he wanted, he dropped out of running. When I saw him over a year later, he said he was thinking about returning, and almost felt ready to do so. In this instance, the forces opposing change were stronger than the motivation to change his training patterns.

One's perception of ability to change is influenced by how difficult the task appears. This often means how difficult it seems to complete the task of changing. It may not mean how difficult it is to initiate change. If one is able to initiate it, then continuing may not be as difficult as imagined. And if this is true, completion may be less difficult than anticipated. This process is commonly known as "one step at a time," for which there is an Eastern mystical proverb, "The longest journey begins with one step."

Ability to change can be developed by identifying needed skills and proceeding to learn them. Martin Seligman, in his most recent book, "What You Can Change and What You

Can't," states that we can make major changes throughout adulthood, if we know the ways of changing that actually work. The "What" in his title "What You Can Change..." refers to certain diagnostic conditions that may or may not be changed by different treatments. In this particular book, he is not really discussing how people change. Seligman also believes that an adult's ability to change is less related to childhood environment and trauma than is usually described.

My own view is that adults' ability to change depends more on how they view and treat themselves in the present, without diminishing the importance of early experience. In fact, I believe we can perpetuate early trauma and past environment by continuing to do now what was done to us in earlier years. Fortunately, what we learned in the past is subject to change as a result of what we can learn in the present. Wheelis pointed out that we first learn skills for survival, and then later interpret many situations as if they were survival issues. Fortunately, such an interpretation can be changed, allowing us to live more fully in the present.

A self-critical runner reprimanded herself when she didn't win, or perform up to her expectations; or if she sustained an injury, or ran fewer miles per week than planned. In our work together, she came to understand that these situations were not the explanation for her self-criticism, but rather that self-criticism was a pattern of thinking she had learned in the past. It could not be trusted as a reliable evaluator of her present ability, effort or worth. With additional work, she became better able to allow that critical voice to recede into the background of her thinking, and free herself from the grip of disapproval that had begun with her father.

As mentioned before, awareness creates the possibility for alternatives, and thereby can lead to change in existing patterns or in creating new ones. It leads the way to making new choices and new decisions. At times, it is desirable to try out new behavior before a commitment to continue is affirmed. Lippitt and colleagues also emphasize the importance of maintenance, that is, stabilizing and reinforcing the changes made. They stress the need for practice, as well as for a willingness to tolerate frustration. For change to continue, they note that feedback is desirable, since it can help someone see that change has begun, even if the end result is not yet in sight. And behavioral change is more likely to be maintained if there are concurrent changes in perception or attitude. Important lasting change, they also point out, may even involve overcoming other people's resistance to it. Finally, they predict that best results are obtained when a specific change can be generalized to other areas of one's functioning; for example, when improvement in an athlete's relationship with family is extended to sport life with teammates, or social life with friends.

To summarize, in order to change, it helps to know where you are (what is the situation or problem), how you got there (what are the causes), where else you can be (what are options and alternatives), where you want to be (what are goals and intentions), how to get there (what are needed skills, choices and decisions), and how to stay there (issues of maintenance and reinforcement).

At this point, I would like to pause to allow for comments or questions, and then resume the second half of my presentation.

Having discussed the content of change and its timing, I'll now talk about the process of change. First, I want to point out that as a process, changing is fundamentally similar to staying the same. Let me repeat that...as a process, changing is fundamentally similar to staying the same. How can that possibly be? How can changing be similar to staying the same? I'll try to explain the apparent contradiction. Paul Wachtel, in the book How People Change, Inside and Outside Therapy, edited by Rebecca Curtis and George Stricker, makes the point that any pattern of behavior requires continued reinforcement. From that I conclude that staying the same is an active, on-going practice. Therefore, it is not too different from changing, which is also an active, on-going practice. What is different is the content of the practice.

Staying the same means continuing to respond in the same way as before. Changing implies responding in a different way than before. Therefore, since people know how to stay the same, they already know how to change. The question is whether the right conditions exist to respond with a different content than before.

In the same book, Curtis writes that the role of affect is primary, that is, that change is affect driven. In her view, the desire to experience positive affect or avoid negative affect is the central motivating force to change; and that a belief that change is possible is helpful but not required. In another chapter, Allen Cooper and Joel Cooper state that change will occur if people become aware of their attitudes, have good reason to question them, and allow themselves to reconsider their position.

Some authors list specific requirements in order for change to occur. Wheelis believes that effort and will are required. Hoffer writes that change requires opportunity, self-confidence and independence. What these authors consider prior requirements, however, are themselves qualities that can be changed. Effort, will, self-confidence and independence can be acquired if they aren't already present; and such acquisition would itself constitute change.

In his book, Grow or Die, George Land considers that part of making a change is a willingness to be changed. He sees it both an active and passive process; that is, not only that we do something, but also that we allow something to happen to us. If we take in new information, for example, our original learning may be challenged. To do this, therefore, involves a willingness to experience some discomfort. In allowing what is new to influence our belief system, we are already changing, and at the same time creating an opportunity for additional change.

If change is understood as moving beyond one's usual boundaries, then what lies outside is unfamiliar, perhaps even unknown. For many, this unfamiliarity is uncomfortable, perhaps even perceived as dangerous. If high priority is given to avoiding emotional discomfort, change will be more difficult. If, however, we can tolerate the discomfort, the path to change remains open. Although Hoffer believes that we can never be fully prepared for that which is entirely new, it may be possible to be well prepared for the process of change, even if the content isn't known.

Gestaltists view change as part of a process of organismic self-regulation, in which something important, called "figure," emerges from the background of our experience. If it is satisfied, it recedes from the foreground, and something else emerges. This process usually continues again and again, with different elements emerging and receding. If, however, what has become figure is not satisfied, it remains in the foreground, the flow is interrupted, change does not occur, and stasis results. The healthy process of emerging and receding figures is illustrated in the following vignette.

Imagine that you have been walking in the desert for several hours. You reach an oasis, are aware of an overpowering thirst, so you drink until quenched. It is then that you realize that your neck is burning from the sun, and needs immediate attention. After applying a soothing lotion, you then notice a blister on your foot, which you proceed to take care of. At this point, you become aware of how exhausted you are, and decide to take a short rest. After resting, you awake feeling very satisfied about having spent your energy to the fullest.

Each of these situations: thirst, sunburn, blister, and fatigue could become problems if not attended to, and interfere with rest or satisfaction.

I will now discuss resistance to change. What inhibits, interferes with or discourages change? What are the barriers or obstacles? What makes change difficult at times? Why are some things more difficult to change than others? What might account for the differences? Descriptively, resistance to change is adherence to existing patterns, whether they are of thinking, feeling, behaving, or wanting. One reason for resistance is that change involves loss. At the very least, we lose the familiar way of responding. Hopefully, what is gained after the change will be sufficiently valuable to warrant the loss.

Change is often defended against because it isn't "natural." What's considered "unnatural" may really only be unfamiliar. Wheelis makes the point that what may look like our nature is really our past choices that became familiar. He also states that we sometimes use what we have been in the past to avoid what we can be in the future. He believes that who we have become is our identity not our destiny. This is a key element in change: how we currently perceive ourselves need not remain fixed, unless of course we are determined that it shall be so.

Several authors have described different aspects of resistance. George Land sees resistance to change as a protective device to ensure that change is integrative growth, reflecting the strength of connections we made during our lives. Lippitt and colleagues point out that whatever factors caused the original problem often contribute to the difficulty removing it. Wheelis views resistance as patterns of thinking or behaving that reinforce themselves by automatic repetition, and become part of one's identity. He also believes that if responsibility for change is attributed to others, what we are left with that is ours is resistance.

Hoffer describes significant change as a crisis in self-esteem, calling upon us to prove ourselves once again. The common elements in each of these views are the threat to existing patterns and the effort to prevent their alteration. So if a particular change is too much, or occurs too soon or too fast, resistance will be intensified to maintain the status quo.

A steeplechase runner was repeatedly urged by the coach to ease up on the number of miles he was running every day. The runner was reluctant to do so. He believed that if he did, he'd be less powerful during competition. If he didn't build up his stamina, he thought, he might not be able to finish strong. He ignored the coach's recommendation and continued training hard and secretly. Instead of increasing his strength, he was draining it. At race time, although he said he felt fine, his early pace seemed sluggish, and he landed each stride more heavily. About halfway through the race, he had difficulty clearing one barrier, but persisted. Finally, he hit the next barrier hard, fell and injured both his leg and his hand. Unfortunately, he had resisted the suggested change in training because he believed it to be a threat to his success.

Let's examine in more detail some specifics regarding threats to existing patterns. Resistance to change may be caused by what we think, what we feel, or what we want. Some typical resisting thoughts are: change is not important; it won't solve the problem; it won't even help; if it does work, it won't last; and it won't prevent the problem from recurring; or it will be a mistake, and the consequences will be worse than the original problem, all examples of negative or pessimistic thinking.

Among feelings that cause resistance, the most prominent is fear. Some specific fears are fear of failure; fear of criticism, disapproval or judgment; fear of inadequacy; and fear of responsibility or independence. Anger frequently interferes with change, either because of defiance or retaliation. If change is someone else's agenda, it can trigger rebelliousness, even if the original initiative was one's own. If you haven't personally experienced this, ask someone who began to diet, and then was pressured by a parent or spouse to keep losing weight. It's very difficult to do something you want to do when someone else is telling you to do it.

Other feelings that may contribute to reluctance to change are guilt, if you believe another person may be hurt; shame or embarrassment, if an unpleasant trait may be revealed; or sadness, if change involves a significant loss. Resistance can also occur if a competing want exists that seems more important than change at the moment. An example would be the one I gave earlier of the runner who wanted help with training too much, but wanted more to spend his time and energy n his new job, so he dropped out of running. A want to avoid discomfort can also be stronger than a want to seek satisfaction. Consider the athlete who eagerly wants to play, but because of fear of not doing well, says, "I don't want to play today." To avoid fear, he/she may avoid playing.

So, finally, how can we as practitioners help others change? And how can we know whether what we do is effective? First, I want to emphasize that intensive study and considerable supervision are essential components of a complete answer to the first question. What can be achieved in a single lecture is analogous to opening a crack in the doorway and pointing a direction.

The concept of performance enhancement involves change, and intervention implies action by another. I believe the essence of what we can do to help others change can be identified by four words: clarify, inform, explore and support. By clarify, I mean help others become more aware of reasons to change and reasons not to; more aware of exactly what they want to change, what they anticipate about changing and about its outcome and consequences; more aware of options, alternatives and choices; and more aware of goals and intentions and the apparent obstacles or barriers to their accomplishment.

In our efforts to help others, we also can inform. The information may be about the importance of tolerating frustration and experiencing discomfort during change and after. We may describe new skills and proceed to teach them. We can explain negative thinking patterns and provide new techniques to deal with them. And we can emphasize the necessity of practicing new skills and making a commitment to continue doing so.

Exploration is another significant and fertile area in our work. Specifically, we can assist in examining the content of resistance by identifying difficulties or barriers. We can explore whether behavior still represents an old "survival" issue, as mentioned earlier. We can investigate the extent of unpleasant feelings, such as fear, guilt, resentment and sadness, or of conflicting desires that interfere with change. We can also review whether the original goal is attainable.

Finally, we can provide support and offer encouragement to keep going. We can listen without judgment. We can help protect against self-criticism. We can highlight beginning change, acknowledge frustration and inspire courage to face and tolerate anticipated fears. We can give feedback about progress made as part of encouraging persistence in efforts to reach desired goals.

Prochaska and colleagues emphasize the importance of matching the appropriateness and timing of interventions to the stage of readiness of the participant. They caution against overlooking or minimizing this matching, the consequence of which might be decreased motivation. In addition to the individual's readiness, I would add that appropriateness and timing of interventions also depends on the practitioner's readiness, the relationship between the two levels of readiness, and the content of the intervention. A practitioner's readiness would be related to his/her work experience and familiarity with the sport.

How can we know whether what we do is effective? Can we evaluate this effectiveness in any way other than the traditional research design of observation before and after intervention, with appropriate controls? Anything else is often described pejoratively as "anecdotal," and therefore unfortunately discounted. Relying on an individual's own report may be seen as too "subjective." Yet subjective change can be evaluated in the same way a clinician does an initial evaluation, without psychological testing, i.e. by observation, inquiry, intuition, and experience. We can do this by exploring several areas of function, including work, recreation, personal and social relationships, self-awareness, patterns of thinking, how feelings are handled, and the level of self-worth and self-esteem. With athletes, performance improvement is only one way of evaluating effectiveness of interventions. Satisfaction or enjoyment or even less involvement in sport can also be indications of their effectiveness.

For many clinicians, ongoing evaluation is an inherent part of the work. It is frequently not addressed as a discrete entity or separate subject. It includes such questions as: How is this person experiencing and describing their situation today? And how are they viewing themselves? How do these answers compare to the previous visit or to last month or last year? Evaluation need not be limited to outcome, such as symptom relief or behavior change. It can also include the process of changing; that is whether the individual is developing the inner resources to deal with future difficulties. This last point bears on the question of how long benefits last. Even if the original gains begin to slip away, newly developed inner resources can initiate a sequence to bring about change again.

As part of my discussion of how we can help others, I'm going to describe two sessions with an athlete in some detail. My purpose is to illustrate some possible interventions and my rationale for selecting the ones I chose.

A young adult tennis player began having difficulty concentrating and staying focused during matches in the year since college graduation. The problem was intensifying as games became more competitive, and he said, "I got more interested in looking good than in playing good." His audience had become more important to him than his playing, and his concern was that he would be judged critically. There were several possibilities for my beginning intervention. I'll mention a few, with a brief comment about each, and describe the one I chose and the reasons for my choice.

A direct approach would be to teach concentration skills, methods to increase focus and decrease distraction. For those practitioners who do this well, and for athletes who are able to use it, this is an excellent choice. Another approach would be to help him strengthen a positive view of himself by emphasizing his personal assets. This might counteract the anticipated disapproval and critical judgment of others, but it usually requires an established, solid relationship with the athlete, and one in which he or she is open to self-affirmation. An advantage of this approach is that it sometimes works fairly quickly. A disadvantage is that it doesn't usually last very long. A third approach would be to deal with the internal critic, perhaps by trying to shut it off, explore its origins or challenge its objectivity or reliability. The purpose would be to loosen the grip it has on the athlete's self-image. This can also be very effective, but occasionally quite time-consuming.

The approach I chose was a modification of the second, that is, using a positive judgment by others to help him feel better about himself. Let me explain this more fully. It's always important to start where the athlete is. In this case, he was starting with a strong, negative external image that judges him inadequate. My idea was to help him change that view of himself to a strong, positive internal one. I believed that to try to do that in one step, however, would be quite difficult for him, so I decided to divide it into two steps. Instead of attempting to help him change an external negative view directly to an internal positive one, I began by helping him change the external negative to an external positive. Since he was placing the power to evaluate him outside himself, I believed this to be a more promising first step. Subsequent work, if desired, would be to help him accept the external positive view as his own.

Using guided imagery, he returned to the recent match in which he played poorly because of the problem. I suggested that he imagine that the three best friends he had mentioned earlier were in the stands. These were three he had selected when I asked him which people in his life were most accepting of him, and genuinely appreciated him for himself, not just for what he accomplished. I encouraged him during the imagery to allow their feeling and attitude toward him to be with him as he replayed the match. He was quite able and willing to do that. Instead of the heaviness he had felt in his legs during the real match, he described a lightness during the imagery, and noticed that he was faster on his feet. With no further prompting from me, he began to make points he hadn't made in the actual match. When the imagery ended, he reported having played very well, and felt warm, positive and confident. The session ended and off he went to compete in a tournament.

In the next session, he reported that he had not done too well: "I lost both matches." He realized in the discussion that followed, however, that he had not been as concerned with how he looked to others as he had before. Nevertheless, he played with a lack of intensity. With the game again more in focus than the audience, he came to see that playing itself was less significant to him than it had been. This led to his describing how important his application to medical school was. Playing in this last tournament had come from an earlier desire, which had since lessened in strength. He had originally hoped to do well in it before giving full attention to his future career, but the timing of his wish didn't correspond to his experience.

It was my hypothesis that his concern about how he looked when he played was already evidence of the loss of commitment which later emerged. I believe this illustrates that what presents on the surface as a problem is sometimes an indication of other conflict beneath. In his situation, he described feeling some guilt and embarrassment about his changing interest, and expected disapproval from others because of it. After discussing this, he felt more accepting of the changes taking place within, less critical of himself, and had less anticipation of judgment from others. He did not, however, wish to continue working on the second step; that is, to internalize a positive view of himself.

The change of interest he experienced is not uncommon among athletes. It may also be an important issue for us as practitioners. There may be times when our work is less stimulating and we are less creative. Any solution we think of may seem inadequate. We may feel stuck. Hopefully, some of the ways we have available to help athletes may also be useful for us to help ourselves. An eloquent and poignant passage describing such an experience, and illustrating resistance and breakthrough was written by a psychologist named Clark Moustakas in a workshop I attended some 20 years ago. I've kept it because of its personal meaning to me, and I would like to conclude my presentation by reading it.

"Sometimes I know that the best possible thing for me to do would be to let go -- to allow myself to fully experience my feelings of loneliness, pain and grief. Yet even as I know this, I hold back. I try to maintain my life as it has been. I try to respond to others as if I were not in pain. I even try to hide it from myself. I don't want to feel. I don't want to experience the agony. I've done it before; why must I go through it all again? Is there no rest, no peace, no guaranteed end? Yet, I feel the deadness that comes with hiding from myself. I feel angry at the lies I'm living, of smiling when there's no smile within me. I desperately search for some cure that will take away the loneliness, the pain, the deadness. And when there is none, I feel more lonely, more pain and more deadness.

And then it comes. It is no longer possible for me to hold back the feelings. I am flooded, consumed, and engulfed with all that I've hidden. I mourn the deadness inside me. I grieve for the anguishing spirits within. And with that mourning and grieving there is beginning life. Slowly, like the sun rising through the trees, life flows into my soul. I begin to feel cleansed and whole. Everything around me seems cleaner and brighter. And I rejoice for I am alive!"

References

Cooper, A., & Cooper, J. (1991) How People Change With and Without Therapy. In R.C. Curtis & G. Stricker (Eds.). *How People Change, Inside and Outside Therapy.* (pp. 173-189). New York: Plenum.

Curtis, R.C. (1991). Toward an Integrative Theory of Psychological Change: A Cognitive –Affective Regulation Model. In R.C. Curtis & G. Stricker (Eds.). *How People Change, Inside and Outside Therapy.* (pp. 191-210). New York: Plenum

Hoffer, E. (1952). *The Ordeal of Change.* New York: Harper & Row.

Land, G. (1973). *Grow or Die.* New York: Random House.

Lippitt., R., Watson, J., & Westley, B. (1958). *The Dynamics of Planned Change.* New York: Harcourt Brace.

Moustakas, C. (1975). Personal Growth Workshop. Unpublished.

Prochaska, J.O., DiClemente, C.C., & Norcross, J.C. (1992). In Search of How People Change. *American Psychologist.* 47(9), pp. 1102-1114.

Ravizza, K. (1986). Increasing Awareness for Sport Performance. In J. M. Williams, (Ed.), *Applied Sport Psychology.* (pp. 149-161). Mountain View, CA: Mayfield.

Seligman, M.P. (1994). *What You Can Change and What You Can't.* New York: Alfred A. Knopf.

Wachtel, P. (1991). The Role of "Accomplices" in Preventing and Facilitating Change. In R.C. Curtis & G. Stricker (Eds.). *How People Change, Inside and Outside Therapy.* (pp.21-37). New York: Plenum.

Wheelis, A. !973). *How People Change.* New York: Harper & Row.

Psychological Issues in Sport Performance

In recent years, there has been a growing interest and awareness in sport psychology. The exact nature of what is involved, however, is not widely understood. In this presentation, some of the more important psychological issues in sport performance will be discussed. Other aspects of sport psychology that will not be addressed here include: study of exercise and its benefits, youth sport, coaching education, sport injury, transitions in the life of athletes, gender, racial, and sexual bias, the college athlete, disabled athletes, the problems of violence and drug abuse in sport, eating disorders in athletes, team cohesion, parent involvement, the Olympics, and others.

Self-Confidence and Self-Esteem

Given the demands that sport competition places on the athlete, it is essential that he/she have the self-confidence necessary to meet these requirements. Primarily, this involves trusting one's ability to perform the necessary physical and mental tasks. Developing this trust begins with a realistic appraisal of one's competence, and an awareness of what can and cannot be controlled. It also involves recognition of personal responsibility for making choices and decisions, and for clarifying one's values and goals. All of this is based on a foundation of self-worth and self-esteem, even before one attains the achievement and accomplishment that is so widely emphasized. The most significant obstacle to developing or maintaining this foundation is self-criticism and self-condemnation.

Positive and Negative Thinking

In striving for excellence, many athletes believe it is necessary to criticize, reprimand, or condemn themselves for mistakes, difficulties, or performance that is below expectations. Unfortunately, this approach has undesirable consequences, leading to a decrease in self-confidence and self-esteem, which contributes to impairment in optimal performance. This kind of negative thinking can also lead to predictions of poor performance, descriptions of oneself as inadequate and unfavorable comparison of self to others. In contrast, athletes can focus on their areas of competence, on excellence of preparation for the task at hand, or on current and past satisfactions. In addition, positive thinking need not be limited to sport performance. In fact, appreciation of oneself outside of sport will improve one's perspective, and help prepare for situations that may arise in the future, such as injury or retirement.

Motivation and Commitment

Athletes participate in sport for many different reasons, among them being: enjoyment, stimulation, excitement, satisfaction, accomplishment, external rewards, recognition, belonging, and others. During the course of a career in sport, however, there may be times when the original reasons for participating begin to diminish. At such times, a sense of commitment, i.e., a determination to pursue one's original goals is essential to get through the difficult times. This may require refocusing on the original motivations, examining current ones, and re-evaluating whether that determination is still present. If it is not, it may be worthwhile to explore what accounts for the difference. It may be: interest in other pursuits, stress from outside sources dissatisfaction with current participation, or even a satisfied readiness to move on.

Goal Setting

An important element in achieving optimal performance is goal setting. While the idea of goal setting is generally accepted, certain considerations improve its effectiveness beyond what can be attained by the more general instruction: "Do your best." Goals are most useful when expressed as what to do, rather than what not to do. In addition, it is advisable to set specific, realistic, and somewhat difficult goals; to set short-term intermediate and long-term goals; and to set performance and process goals, rather than outcome goals. An outcome goal, which is not controllable, represents the results of a competition, i.e., the order of finishing. A performance goal would be the particular time one was aiming to attain; and a process goal might be how best to achieve it. Examples of process goals might be the lap times run in practice, splits during a race, the amount of running done in a day or week, or any behavior addressed to how to attain a given performance goal. This might also include adequate rest, proper nutrition, and cross training.

Attention and Focus

As much as an athlete might practice a certain routine, the results may not be satisfactory, if he/she is unprepared to deal with distractions. The ability to focus one's attention on the required task is an essential component of performance excellence. Attentional focus can be external or internal. External focus can be broad (viewing the whole track), or narrow (seeing how close the next runner is). Internal focus can be on one's physical sensations, thoughts, or emotions. At different times during competition, each of these may be relevant, and sometimes rapid shifting from one to the other is required. Focusing involves concentration, as well as eliminating distractions in order to direct one's energies to the task at hand. This requires alertness, involvement, and presence, i.e., being right here, right now.

Stress and Anxiety

It is difficult to imagine participating in competition, completely free of stress and anxiety. While in some sports increased arousal is desirable, for the most part the opposite is true. Most athletes perform better when not overloaded by stress, tension, and anxiety. Stress occurs when the demands of a situation exceed athletes' perception of their resources. The result may be tension and anxiety. These can lead to decreased ability to focus and concentrate, impaired coordination and judgment, and diminished self-confidence. Fortunately, methods are available to lessen anxiety before and during performance. The most common of these are the many ways to promote relaxation, i.e., breathing exercises, biofeedback, the use of cue words, and contraction/relaxation exercises.

Coping Skills

Part of preparation for competitive performance consists of developing skills to deal with stress, in order to reduce anxiety to manageable levels. The use of imagery for mental rehearsal is a favorite among elite athletes. It can help improve performance by enabling the athlete to anticipate a favorable sequence of action, as well as to prepare for circumstances that interfere with optimal conditions. Other coping strategies include time-management, control of negative emotions, confidence building, positive self-talk, retraining of negative thinking patterns, and focusing attention in the presence of distractions. Which among these are most useful depends on the experience and personality of the individual athlete, the nature of the stressor, the sport, the time of season, and other factors.

Over-training and Burnout

Some athletes are so driven in their striving for excellence that they train too much and go too far in their preparation. This could consist of going well beyond recommended levels of training, i.e., too frequently, too intensely, or for too long a duration. Other examples of overtraining include persistence despite important injury, decreased consideration of general health, giving little importance to other interests, or neglecting other people in their lives. This becomes evident in their loss of effectiveness, loss of interest, and dissatisfaction; and may eventually lead to "burnout." At this point there may be mental exhaustion, withdrawal, irritability, anxiety, depression, and a host of physical symptoms, including loss of appetite, impaired sleeping, lethargy, gastrointestinal symptoms, and a susceptibility to illness or injury. Prevention of these consequences involves early intervention, careful examination of the behavior and its results, as well as thorough review of goals, values, beliefs, and priorities.

Summary

Several important psychological aspects of sport performance have been identified. For each of these, sport psychology can offer methods to enhance an athlete's performance. Some of these have been mentioned in the topics discussed. The possible interventions have by no means been completely covered. It is also worth repeating that performance enhancement, although the most widely known aspect of sport psychology is only one area of the field. Some of the others were listed in the introductory paragraph.

Psychological Assessment without Psychological Tests

How can a clinician do assessment without formal psychological testing? What "instruments" does a psychodynamically trained practitioner have? How can we know whether what we do is effective?

Can we evaluate this effectiveness in any way other than the traditional research design of observation before and after intervention, with appropriate controls? Anything else is often described pejoratively as "anecdotal," and therefore unfortunately discounted. Relying on an individual's own report may be seen as too "subjective." Yet subjective change can be evaluated in the same way a clinician does an initial evaluation, without psychological testing, i.e. by observation, inquiry, intuition, and experience. We can do this by exploring several areas of function, including work, recreation, personal and social relationships, self-awareness, patterns of thinking, how feelings are handled, and the level of self-worth and self-esteem. With athletes, performance improvement is only one way of evaluating effectiveness of interventions. Satisfaction or enjoyment or even less involvement in sport can also be indications of their effectiveness.

For many clinicians, ongoing evaluation is an inherent part of the work. It is frequently not addressed as a discrete entity or separate subject. It includes such questions as: How is this person experiencing and describing their situation today? And how are they viewing themselves? How do these answers compare to the previous visit or to last month or last year? Evaluation need not be limited to outcome, such as symptom relief or behavior change. It can also include the process of changing; that is whether the individual is developing the inner resources to deal with future difficulties. This last point bears on the question of how long benefits last. Even if the original gains begin to slip away, newly developed inner resources can initiate a sequence to bring about change again.

Let's look for some answers in Who? What? When? Where? Why? and How?

Who? The clinician uses the self as the main instrument of assessment. To do this requires a significant amount of self-awareness – What do I know about myself that will help me see, hear, feel, and do? What do I want? What do I need? What is important to me? What are my expectations? How do I react when I don't get what I want or need? What gives my good feelings about myself? What does the opposite? What upsets me and how do I react when I get upset? What would I like to change? What's in the way of changing?

What? Observation provides us with important information about the challenges facing the particular athlete, coach, team, administrator, referee, or parent we are working with. We observe what's present, and consider what's absent. We look, listen, think, and feel. What we see includes the person's appearance and movement– eye contact, facial expression, hair, body, clothing, posture, position, gestures. What we hear includes the words, tone, volume, pauses, trailing off, and rate of speech. We listen to their language for clues to blaming or fault finding, to all or nothing thinking, to self-doubt, self-criticism, and also how questions are answered. This last point can provide good information about the relationship between you and the other person. Finally, what we think and feel can offer clues to our own inner experience, or to what the other person might be thinking or feeling. When others describe their thoughts, consider asking about their feelings. When feelings are expressed, inquire about the thoughts that are connected. And in both instances, ponder the unexpressed wants.

When? This question highlights the importance of timing. At what point in a person's life is a particular behavior initiated or intensified. Is it at a beginning or an ending? Is it about relationship, communication, or some other activity? The concept of readiness is useful here. Consider what they are not ready for - this can be helpful in determining what they might be ready for.

Where? Our attention needs to include the setting and context of the meeting place, and the impact of these on ourselves and the person we are working with. Our focus will shift from one to the other and back again, as we try to understand the process.

Why? To understand and interpret another's experience requires an appreciation of what that experience actually is for that person. We must be able to separate our perception of what's happening from what is actually happening for them. (i.e., intuition vs. projection). The meaning we give to a behavior is not necessarily its real meaning.

How? Gestalt therapy emphasizes the process of how something is done, in contrast to the more traditional question of why something is done. As a result, it is sometimes possible to bring about change even without knowing the reasons for the original pattern of behavior. Using these "instruments," there are some general questions that a practitioner can keep in mind (without necessarily asking them) to enrich the assessment process.

1. How does the person perceive themselves in their environment, relationships, communication?
2. How do they experience the present problem? What are they feeling? thinking? doing? wanting?
3. Is this situation similar to their usual experience or different from it? What is the difference?
4. How much self-awareness do they have?

5. What do they believe about their self-worth?
6. What seems possible for them now? (Their view and ours).

Early training - In the traditional model, a "history" is taken first (including past, family, social, physical, sexual, health and medical, education, work, relationships, and interests). Then a diagnostic formulation is developed. Then treatment is begun. This approach is essential at the beginning of one's training. One must have a foundation on which to build a personal style.

Current practice – In my work now, assessment is done concurrently with "treatment" and continued throughout the contact. From the beginning, the process consists of alternating following with leading. I often begin a session by asking the athlete "Where would you like to start?" Then I follow the athlete, focusing on their present in-the-moment experience, occasionally asking for clarification or elaboration, until I hear or see something that represents what I call an "entry point." This is something that suggests it might be useful to explore in more depth. At this point, I will lead, by bringing the athlete's attention to something that might not have been considered. Then I follow again, observing the response, or lack thereof, until another entry point arises, and so on. Following and leading is the method of concurrent assessment and intervention.

Coaches Have Their Own Needs

Sport psychology offers many suggestions for providing psychological services for athletes who need assistance with problems in performance, communication, time management, transitions, relationships, and health issues. Unfortunately, the same volume of interest has not been shown in attending to similar problems and needs of coaches. Although sport psychology does offer programs and techniques for coaches to deal with athletes' problems, there is relatively little about how coaches themselves can be helped to cope with the stresses of coaching and still meet their own needs. Other than the many articles about coaches' stress and burnout, the needs of coaches before burnout occurs have not received the attention they deserve.

Psychological Needs

Coaches are performers, educators, administrators, leaders, planners, motivators, negotiators, managers, and listeners, but they are also people. As such, they bring to their roles and tasks fundamentally the same psychological needs as other people. These needs include security, self worth, identity, autonomy, mastery, intimacy, belonging, and a sense of meaning or purpose. In working with coaches, we have been impressed by how significantly these basic human needs influence coaches' performance.

When a team does well, most coaches feel good about themselves, and may experience a significant increase in their self-esteem. Some coaches also find satisfaction in how they go about coaching, not just in winning. When challenged by planning for a difficult competition, coaches have an opportunity to experience their sense of mastery. Their need to belong may be satisfied by being part of a closely-knit organization, although some coaches would not have this need high on their list of priorities. In addition, teaching athletes new skills, tactics, strategies, and values can be highly satisfying and beneficial to a coach's sense of self-worth.

Psychological needs are just as fundamental to growth as are physical needs. Unless both are adequately met, growth may be impaired. One approach that can be used to improve the experience of coaches is to increase their self-awareness.

Self-Awareness

Self-awareness involves knowledge of one's own behavior, thoughts, feelings, needs, and wants. It can lead to a fuller knowledge of oneself, and a greater appreciation of one's complexity and wholeness. A major advantage of such knowledge is an increased ability to be in charge of oneself, enabling individuals to be less distracted by their own feelings, wants, and values, and better able to respond to others effectively. It is important that self-awareness be non-judgmental. Within each of us is the capacity to observe what we do, what we think, what we feel, and what we want. This observer part of us neither approves nor disapproves. It does what I've called "neutral noticing:" no criticism, no reprimand, no disapproval, and no judgment.

Self-awareness can lead to improvement in coaching performance. Without it, feelings can surface in unexpected or undesired ways. For example, unawareness of fear can lead to controlling or dominating behavior. Unawareness of guilt or shame can result in defensiveness or blaming others. Consider coaches who might realize that their plan did not work, but to avoid feeling guilty about selecting a poor strategy, they blame their athletes for not trying hard enough. In this example, if the coaches were aware of their guilt feeling, they might choose to deal with the situation differently. Awareness of guilt might be difficult, however, for coaches who are unable to accept responsibility for their mistakes. In addition, if a coach is not aware of her or his wants, a feeling of powerlessness, or a self-perception as a victim can result. When coaches forget why they coach and what they want from coaching, they may feel trapped when they face difficult situations, and be unable to see alternative choices.

Self-awareness also provides an opportunity for change. Most often, we become aware of a problem behavior after it occurs. When this happens, we may say "I see that I did that." With a commitment to change and repeated awareness of the behavior, awareness begins to occur earlier. When it is present during the behavior, we may say "I see that I am doing that right now." With additional time and practice, awareness moves earlier in time, until it is present before the undesired behavior occurs. At this point, we can say "I see that I am about to do that." When awareness precedes the behavior, a choice can be made to behave differently. This is an opportunity for change and is represented by the statement "I can do it differently."

Unfortunately, the self-awareness that is necessary to identify and manage personal concerns is often not emphasized in traditional coach education programs. Occasionally, coaches in training are introduced to the importance of self-awareness, and understanding their coping patterns. Some coach education programs even provide participants opportunities for self-examination. Self-awareness, however, is more than a onetime activity or exercise. True awareness of oneself, including the advantages and disadvantages of one's personal style, is an ongoing process that requires work and effort over time.

Because of the impact coaches have on their athletes, it is important for coaches to know their own feelings, needs, and wants, in order to be able to give priority to their athletes' needs. Gaining information about oneself needs to be a continuous goal, but coaches, because of the position of power that they hold, often do not get much direct feedback from players or their assistant coaches.

Psychological Barriers

In a growth and development model, a basic assumption is that we all have an inherent capacity for optimal functioning, and would be able to do so if nothing interfered. Optimal coaching is more likely to occur in the absence of obstacles. More specifically, whether a coach's task is preparing practice routines, planning game strategies, or becoming more self-aware, distractions diminish effectiveness. Just as physical barriers (i.e., fatigue, illness, or injury) can interfere with performance, so too can psychological barriers. When psychological barriers impair self-awareness, they can result in energy-draining distractions that interfere with focusing on important tasks.

Barriers can arise from problems with family, administrators, colleagues, or athletes. In addition, barriers to self-awareness can develop from personal issues; that is, from the coach's own thoughts, feelings, behavior, or wants. For example, thinking barriers include self-doubt, self-criticism, low self-confidence, or perfectionism. Feeling barriers could be anxiety, guilt, anger, shame, sadness, or emotional hurt. Behavioral barriers are overworking, impulsiveness, poor communication, or giving up. Psychological barriers related to what we want include poor motivation, loss of desire or commitment, or conflicting interests. When barriers block self-awareness, removing them can restore that awareness. Sport psychology can be helpful in accomplishing this goal.

Giges, B., Petitpas, A. J., Vernacchia, R. A. (2004). Helping coaches meet their own needs: Challenges for the sport psychology consultant. *The Sport Psychologist*, 18, 430-444.

Beyond Psychopathology: An Alternative to the Medical Model s in Sport

Abstract: The purpose of this presentation is to offer an alternative perspective to the medical model, which traditionally involves diagnostic categories, psychopathology, and treatment of disorders. The advantages and disadvantages of diagnostic labeling will be described, and another approach to understanding problems will be offered. The overlapping boundaries of treatment and education will be discussed, along with the implications for the therapist and the educator. After some general introductory comments, specific illustrations from my own sport consulting practice will be presented, with discussion about the interventions used and possible alternative choices. Questions will be raised about the issues discussed, and answers will be sought from the participants, in addition to those presented.

Basic Principles

1. The presence of a particular skill in a practitioner does not determine how or when to use it. Knowing how to do something doesn't mean that's what's indicated.

2. The presence of a diagnosis in an athlete also does not determine the appropriate interventions. As clinicians, we are accustomed to making a diagnosis and prescribing treatment. In sport performance work, it may be possible to address the problem directly without treating the diagnosis.

Diagnostic labels

Advantages: to help us decide treatments, communicate with other professionals, be alert to issues beneath the surface, protect ourselves legally, and obtain insurance payments.

Disadvantages: shifts the focus from the person to the pathology. Diagnostic label comes to define the person – "He/she is a (diagnostic label,)" - rather than seeing the person separate from the label. It also shifts the emphasis from the person's strengths to the person's weaknesses. Imagine a DSM of "Psychological Health, Growth and Well-Being."

Brief Contact Interventions in Sport Psychology: Theory and Practice

Sport psychology consultants are often called upon to provide consultation without an opportunity for extended interviewing. These situations may occur on the field, during practice, at competitions, or during travel with a team. The unique challenge in offering such service is to address the athlete's need with only limited time and background information. Care must be exercised to remain focused on performance issues rather than psychopathology. In this colloquium, practical and theoretical considerations in brief interventions will be presented and discussed. The theory behind such interventions derives from both traditional and strategic therapeutic approaches. The strategies are action-oriented, present-centered, solution-focused, and limited to the issue identified by the athlete.

Principles from counseling psychology, gestalt therapy, and cognitive therapy provide significant contributions to the theoretical basis for these strategies. From counseling comes emphasis on client's strength; from gestalt is the importance of present functioning; and from cognitive therapy is the significance of thinking as the major determinant of feelings. Each of these will be discussed more specifically in the presentation. In practical terms, the consultant follows the athlete's lead, staying focused on his or her abilities and options in the present, and assists in creating a shift in the athlete's perception of the situation. Examples of these principles and strategies will be drawn from the consultants' experiences in sport psychology consultation. The audience will then have the opportunity for questions, comments and discussion.

Giges, B. and Petitpas, A. J. (2000). Brief contact interventions in sport psychology. *The Sport Psychologist*, 14, 176-187.

At the Finish Line: Sport Psychology Consultation in a Central Park Tent

Immediately after running a marathon, runners may experience a number of physical and emotional reactions. At the New York City marathon finish line area, tents are set up to treat any reactions that require significant medical care. In addition, some tents are available for runners, who do not need "treatment" but who may want or need time to rest and recover before they are ready to be with their families and friends. These recovery tents, which are called "family tents," contain many cots, and are equipped to treat minor medical conditions. The professional staff includes volunteers who are nurses, podiatrists, athletic trainers, massage therapists, chiropodists, or medical students.

In such a setting, sport psychology practitioners can provide important services by offering consultation to the staff and brief contact interventions to the runners. These services can include small group meetings with the staff to describe what to listen and look for regarding runners' thoughts and emotions that might warrant a consultation with the sport psychologist. In addition, the consultant may assist other professionals in their direct services to runners, by providing psychological support to both the runners and the practitioners. This support includes a solution-focused mindset, is limited to here-and-now functioning, and often consists of cognitive restructuring.

Direct intervention with a runner starts with the athlete's definition of the problem, builds on what is presented, stays focused on present options, and attempts to create a shift in the athlete's perception of the situation. Some examples of the consultation experience will be presented. These include working with staff members who felt insecure and uneasy, and with runners who were frightened, discouraged, angry, or depressed.

Part IV

Workshops

Self-Awareness for Sport Psychology Practitioners

Abstract: It is important for sport psychology practitioners to know their own feelings, wants, and needs well enough to assure that the work they do addresses the needs and goals of their clients rather than their own. This workshop is based on an assumption common to most therapeutic approaches: that some of the practitioner's inner experience is not in their awareness, and that lack of such awareness might be to the detriment of the client. The purpose of this workshop is to provide opportunities for practitioners to increase their self-awareness and avoid this problem. The workshop will include didactic material drawn from concepts in Gestalt Therapy, Transactional Analysis, and Cognitive Therapy. This will include 1) the benefits of self-awareness; 2) barriers to self-awareness; 3) self-awareness without self-criticism; 4) the language of feelings; and 5) the significance of wants as part of our experience. Experiential exercises will be offered to enhance participants' access to their feelings, needs, wants, and thoughts. These will include visualization, journal writing, dialogue in pairs, and demonstration in the large group. There will also be an exploration of a work or family problem using self-awareness to increase understanding.

INTRODUCTION - "The journey of learning the art of helping others is a personal one, requiring you to know yourself as you learn to help others."

Mark Young (1998), "Learning the art of helping."

Purpose - performance enhancement for practitioners
Method - didactic and experiential

GO-ROUND - What are you aware of right now?

DEMONSTRATION

1. Awareness Continuum – Now I'm aware…(repeating)
2. Focus on: thoughts, feelings, wants - in the moment

FOCUS OF AWARENESS

Outer world - Senses - see, hear, smell, touch, temperature, taste, balance;
Behavior- action in contact with outer world
Inner world - Physical- pain, tightness, tingling, vibration, palpitation
- Psychological- thoughts, feelings, wants, needs, and values

PAIRS - "I think or I feel or I want" -Awareness of self as subject/listener
Which one was most frequent? Is that usual or unusual?
Which one was least frequent or most difficult?
Repeat exercise with only that one.
Purpose - To increase awareness of inner psychological experience

BENEFITS OF SELF-AWARENESS

1. Fuller knowledge of self - complexity or "wholeness"
- opportunity for increased self-acceptance

2. More in charge of self – if unaware of feelings, they can surface in unexpected or unknown ways - fear can lead to controlling behavior
- anger can lead to criticizing others
- guilt can lead to defensiveness
- shame can lead to blaming others
- if unaware of wants - one can feel powerless, like a victim

3. Opportunity for change- "Alphabet of Change"
Awareness before
Behavior gives
Choice for a
Decision to apply
Effort and
Focus on a
Goal"

4. Better able to be responsive to others - to be fully "Present"- (here, now)
- less distracted by own inner experience - alive, open, ready
- more understanding of others' experience (insight vs. projection)

BARRIERS TO SELF-AWARENESS

A. External - problems at work, school, home, relationships
- energy-draining distractions

B. Internal
1. Discomfort - "negative" feelings - can lead to avoidance
2. Discounting - "not important" -can lead to unfamiliarity
3. Disapproval - reprimand, criticism, judgment
- can criticize content - what you're doing or process - how, when, or why you're doing it
- Examples: "early, on time, late"; "Wizard of Oz" - critic is seen as expert

- Importance of "Neutral Noticing" - blind man at intersection – motives for helping
4. Automatic Compliance/Defiance - dependence or counter-dependence
5. Blaming - "4 B's of Responsibility" - burden, blame, business, being

GUIDED FANTASY –"Wise person on Mountain"- important question about yourself or something in your life.

VOLUNTEERS – Question, Answer, Reaction to answer.

PAIRS - Describe experience - Listen for changes, difficulty, or omissions. Purpose—to access your inner wisdom

THOUGHTS - ideas, beliefs, opinions, reasons, judgments, speculations, decisions, expectations, attitudes, and memories

- awareness of our thoughts includes how attached we are to those thoughts

1. thoughts are the basis for most feelings - the meaning we give to situations – if seen as challenge, may feel excitement; if seen as threat, may feel anxiety

2. thoughts are the link between others' behavior and our feelings - e.g., relay

3. thoughts are the link between others' behavior and our behavior - "Burt's Bus." Others' behavior may be the stimulus, but is not the explanation of our behavior.

4. negative thinking - can be about task, person, situation; past, present, future
a. present to permanent - now to always - negative in time - baseball

b. particular to pervasive--here to everywhere - negative in space
c. possible to probable - maybe to likely - pessimism - baton, fumble
- an exaggeration - an error, mistake, mishap - becomes a calamity

"I don't have time" - had time for everything you did – priorities and choices

FEELINGS - (psychological not physical – emotion - not sensation or intuition)

Types

Basic - early in life, physical sensation, range of language for joy, sadness, anger, fear, (disgust?)

Learned - almost basic, not as early, some sensation, no range of language, guilt (wrongdoing), shame ("bad"), embarrassment (exposure), hurt (worth)

Complex - basic plus - envy, jealous, helpless, confused, alienated, inadequate, bored

General - upset, uncomfortable, strange, funny, peculiar - unclear

The word "feel" or "feeling" can be used with other meanings than emotion:
"I feel that" - means think, believe, suspect, imagine, predict
"It is my feeling" - impression, judgment, understanding, belief, suspicion

GUIDED FANTASY - "Meeting child on the road" - exchange questions about feelings, what's important to you - do activity together that both would enjoy - pick up child, (if that's ok), ask if child will return with you. If yes, allow to merge inside you as you return. If no, say goodbye and ask if they would like to meet again.

VOLUNTEERS – describe fantasy or difficulties

PAIRS or TRIOS - Listen for changes, difficulty or omissions
Purpose - to be aware of the past you inside the present you

NEEDS - inner psychological experience - basic elements in growth - long range, broad, enduring - Not usually in everyday awareness - therefore, were not specifically in the earlier awareness exercise.

Another group of so-called "needs" ("acquired needs" - Giges 1996) represent attempts to cope with unmet needs, and become problems in themselves. Here are some examples of what may happen if basic psychological needs are not met.

Basic Needs (Maslow)	**"Acquired Needs"** – (attempts to cope with unmet needs)
Safety and Security	Control/ Dominate (*or the opposite)*
Self-worth/self-esteem	Please/placate/seek approval
Self-acceptance	Criticize/judge/disapprove (self or other)
Autonomy/Mastery	Dependency/defiance/ rebellion
Relationship/Intimacy	Workaholic/womanizer/ prostitute

Belonging(Group/Purpose) Withdraw/join cult

Meaning/Purpose (Frankl) Addiction/hedonism

Self-Awareness - not a need - knowledge of our experience - helps us meet our needs
Competitiveness - not a need - meets basic needs (self-esteem, mastery, purpose)

WHISPERING EXERCISE - (Close your eyes. Go back in time--5 years at a time). As a child, what short statement would have been good for you to hear about yourself from your mom or dad? - A few words that would give you good feelings about yourself. Whisper that statement in the ear of everyone whose eyes are closed (half of the group). Now (other half) - open your eyes and do the same thing. Come back 5 years at a time - say it to yourself at each age, and ask for something that you want at that age. Do you believe it today?

Purpose - an affirmation for the present, to the child in you

WANTS - specifics to meet underlying needs or what's important to us.

Purpose
A. to achieve enjoyment, satisfaction, or comfort
B. to avoid discomfort - not seen as want - "I can't," or "I have to."

Eric Hoffer – "We can never get enough of what we don't really want."
BG - "We often forget that what we want is not only what we don't have."
- "If we don't get what we need, we may "want" (lack) a lot."

"Priority of Wants"- everything we do is connected to a want.

"Have to" – if want is not in awareness - e.g., going to a party vs. studying

Want vs. Should – Should is not experienced as a want – the hidden want is to avoid discomfort or to present a good image.

"Me First" (Wayne Dyer) vertical (hierarchy) - I'm more important
Alternative - horizontal (sequence) – I'll consider me and you

KNOWING/ NOT KNOWING - "I don't know what I want" – May start with what the other person wants – to clarify what I want or trigger complying/defying
1) may have given up first choice
2) conflicting wants - almost equal
3) discount importance - eventually lose awareness
4) haven't found new interest/excitement - gave up familiar
5) don't "deserve" it - "selfish" - leads to justification

"I don't know if I want to..."- reluctance to acknowledge or express a want directly - behavior is clue to the stronger want, e.g., stay or leave

ASKING/NOT ASKING – Indirect asking – Would *you* like…?
- complaint - what you don't want – contains implicit want.
- May avoid asking if you think you're won't get it, or if unpleasant consequences are imagined.
- If not entitled to ask, may seek to be justified.
- "I shouldn't have to ask" implies "If you cared about me you would know" - may hide difficulty asking.

GETTING/NOT GETTING
How do you react when you don't get what you want? Varying levels of intensity – disappointment, hurt, fear, anger – if want is seen as need.

Hurt – "If you love me, you will do what I want" – starts in childhood – child tries it, it doesn't work, feels unloved, unlovable, less worthy.

Fear – If I don't get it now, I may never get it - loss, survival.

FEELING METER EXERCISE- (Groups of 3 or 4)
Imagine a meter with scale of feeling 0-100
Get reading for yourself - then group average. The challenge is to raise group average. After 10-15 minutes, take new reading - take new group score. Have each group report **how** they went about it - i.e., did each person raised their own? did the group had fun? was the group focused on nurturing the person with the lowest score? did the members discover things in common? Purpose - To increase group awareness of what was done and how.

In this workshop:
1. what was important?
2. what was uncomfortable? difficult?
3. what was enjoyable? satisfying?
4. what, if anything, did you learn about yourself

Personal Assessment of Inner Experience at Work or School (Pairs)

1. What is your main source of enjoyment or satisfaction?
2. What gives you good feelings about yourself?
3. What do you want most from your work?
4. What upsets you? How do you usually react when upset?
5. What might give you bad feelings about yourself?
6. What would lead to your feeling guilty? hurt?
7. What might lead to your feeling embarrassed? ashamed?
8. What do you fear?
9. What do you pretend?
10. Which questions were more difficult or uncomfortable to answer?

Description of Present Satisfactions at Work or School (Pairs)

What are your current satisfactions?
Who is the primary source for each of these satisfactions - something you
do or something someone else does?
If it's something you do, what is that?
Can you identify how that behavior led to your satisfaction?
If it's a result of someone else's behavior, how did that lead to your satisfaction?
Which of these sources is the predominant one?
How do you react when this satisfaction is not available?
What are your thoughts?
What are your feelings?
What is your behavior?

Review of Past Problem at Work or School (Pairs)

Think of something you did at work and would do differently if you had a chance to do over - something you might have regrets about, or be bothered by.

1. What was the behavior?
2. What was your reaction afterwards? (thinking, feeling, wanting)
3. What was your major concern? a. impact on your job
    b. effect on athlete or team
    c. effect on others
    d. other
4. What were the actual consequences?
5. How did that compare with your concern?
6. How would you do it differently now?
7. What different consequences do you imagine?
8. How do you view it now, as you look back on it?

Observation of Current Problem at Work or School (Pairs)

Think of a current problem, i.e., what type of situation or person causes you difficulty or upset?
Identify the external and internal components - separate the problem into the situation and your inner experience. (P=S+I). You may need a colleague to assist you in making the separation.

What do you know about yourself that made the situation a problem for you?

VOLUNTEER
Note: The above outline will be expanded to become part of a chapter on "Awareness, self-awareness, and mindfulness: The application of theory to practice" in the forthcoming book "The Cambridge Companion to Mindfulness and Performance," Amy L. Baltzell, Ed., to be published by Cambridge University Press (www.Cambridge.org).

A Counseling Approach to Performance Enhancement

Abstract: In sport psychology, performance enhancement consultation usually involves mental skills training, i. e., goal setting, visualization, concentration, relaxation, self-talk, etc. This presentation will discuss and demonstrate an alternative, namely, a counseling approach to performance enhancement.

This is an experientially based (rather than skill based) approach that focuses on performance issues and present experience. It is grounded in counseling theory, and utilizes a growth and development model, in which problems are seen as the result of patterns of thinking, feeling, and behaving learned in the past. This approach aims to change those patterns with new learning in the present, and thereby, diminish the impact of the problems. In addition, performance is viewed as a process ("performing") rather than an outcome, allowing the dialogue to include not only what was done, but also how it was done.

The methods include following the athlete's lead as he or she describes the situation, and remaining focused on the athlete's abilities and options in the present. Following an introductory discussion, an interview will be conducted with a volunteer from among the participants in the workshop. The volunteer will be selected on the basis of a willingness to present a real life situation, preferably involving a sport performance issue. The objective of the interview is to illustrate the counseling approach to performance enhancement. An opportunity will be provided for discussion, comments, and questions after the interview.

Theoretical Basis

Psychoanalytic Theory- Basic Principles- all behavior has meaning; internal processes influence present functioning; the relationship between the practitioner and the client occupies a central role in the effectiveness of the consultative work.

Gestalt Therapy- "organismic self-regulation"- an inner process in which a need emerges into the foreground, is satisfied, and recedes into the background of our experience. This allows another need to emerge and be satisfied; and a continuing flow of needs and satisfaction occurs. This process may be interrupted by our thoughts, feelings, conflicting desires, or by external influences. When this occurs, the unsatisfied need remains and interferes with the flow. In this approach, the focus is on present functioning, aimed at removing the interruptions to satisfaction. It starts with what is known, and explores what is not in awareness.

Growth and Development Model- people have the inherent capacity for optimal functioning, and could do so if nothing interfered. Psychological problems, which are obstacles to this growth, are mostly the result of what we have learned, rather than sickness or disease. What we learned in the past can be changed by what we learn in the present.

Methods

Although originally trained as a clinician, with a background in medical research, I've come to see myself more as an educator. The focus of my work with athletes and others is to help them change the learned thinking patterns that contribute to distressed feelings or troublesome behavior, and to remove the barriers to their optimal functioning. This focus is primarily on present experience based on the hypothesis that past negative experience might recede unless present patterns of thinking and feeling keep it in the foreground. The language used by the athlete is followed closely, because it not only expresses the present thoughts and feelings, but also contributes to them.

Describe entry points and leading/following in consultation. Explore behavior, thinking, feeling, and wanting.

Definitions (Dictionary)- "performance"- the execution of an action (an event). "excellence"- eminently good (an outcome).

In this presentation, think of "performance" and "excellence" as processes, as "performing" and "excelling"- focus on how it is done rather than the result.

Performing and excelling as processes- internal experiences rather than external evaluations.
- fully present- Here, Now, "Present."
- fully focused- whole self- (Zen-"when you sit, sit" "when you practice, practice").
- requires awareness, commitment, and energy.
- can be applied to any task or situation.

"Golden-Haired Lion"- (Sufi story- modified)

Disciple- "Master, when lions seize upon an opponent, be it elephant or rabbit, they make exhaustive use of their power. Where does this power come from?

Master- "It comes from the spirit of excellence- putting forth one's whole being, in which nothing is kept in reserve, nothing goes to waste. When you can perform in this way, you too can be a golden-haired lion."

George Bernard Shaw- "By the time I die, I want to be all used up."

Audience Participation

- Think of a recent performance of yours- in sport, work.

- Did you perform with excellence?
- If yes, how did you measure it?
- If not, what was in the way? What seemed to interfere?
- What is your concept of excellence when you perform?
- What would it take for you to perform with excellence?

"In learning to live with greater self-awareness, we enhance our possibilities for freedom, creativity, and caring which are based on that awareness." Edward Cell - (1984), "Learning to Learn from Experience" (SUNY Press, Albany).

Psychological Barriers to Excellence in Sport Performance

"The quality of a person's life is in direct proportion to their commitment to excellence." Vince Lombardi

Abstract: Most interventions in performance enhancement in sport involve mental skills training. Techniques such as goal setting, relaxation, visualization, and self-talk are among those usually described. This presentation will discuss an alternative approach, namely, the identification and removal of psychological barriers to performance excellence. These barriers may be cognitive, affective, behavioral, or conative. The process of removing psychological barriers is experientially based, and consists first of identifying it with specificity and clarity; then examining the meaning given to it; and finally creating a shift in this meaning. In examining the meaning given to the barrier, its content, origin, impact, or background can be explored. In creating a shift in the meaning, the focus of the work can be on options, anticipations, or fantasies. The method focuses on present experience and the language used by the athlete to express it. Examples of this process will be presented from my work with athletes, and indications for its use will be discussed.

Barriers- aspects of experience that interfere with excelling in performing.

External- weather, time, place, problems with work, school, others.

Internal- Physical- injury, illness, fatigue, poor nutrition, substance abuse.
Psychological- cognitive, affective, behavioral, conative.

Characteristics of Psychological Barriers

- they are going to happen to all athletes at some point –
- they don't mean something is wrong with them.
- they represent something getting in the way of what's important to the athlete.
- they don't always require help from others to remove or get through.
- they are not as obvious as a cinder in the eye, but just as important to remove.
- they are often present in combination with other psychological barriers

.

Types of Psychological Barriers (with examples)

Cognitive- (thoughts, beliefs, opinions, judgments, expectations, attitudes) - self-doubt, self-criticism, low self-confidence, low self-esteem, perfectionism, blaming

Affective- (emotions, feelings) - anxiety, guilt, sadness, anger, shame, embarrassment, disappointment, emotional hurt

Behavioral- (action or inaction) - overtraining, impulsiveness, giving up, pushing too hard, getting into fights, poor communicating

Conative- (pertaining to issues of striving or desire) - conflicting wants (personal vs. others, sport vs. other interests), low motivation, excessive desire

Removing Psychological Barriers (Present focused; depends on consultant and athlete).

Identifying and Clarifying- "feeling uncomfortable" may need more specificity.

"I can't" may require helping athlete to take responsibility- e. g., "I won't."

Selecting- determining which of several barriers are in the foreground: work with either the most important or the most available for change. What did athlete come for?

Examining meaning and importance- impact on the athlete; part of a larger, deeper issue; if necessary, describing its origin- when and where.

Initiating change- creating a shift in the athlete's perception of the situation, by exploring options; comparing actual experience with fantasy; identifying all-or-nothing and either/or thinking; evaluating anticipatory thinking ("what if" vs. "what is"). The goal in each interview is to start the change process (vs. "end results"). Discuss "Readiness"- look for what one is ready for, and start with that.

Audience Participation
- Think of a recent performance of yours- in sport, work, relationship.
- What in your performance needed improvement?
- What seemed to be in the way of accomplishing that improvement?
- What might be a first step toward removing the barrier?

Giges, B. (2000). Removing psychological barriers: Clearing the way. Chapter in *Doing Sport Psychology* (pp.17-31), M. B. Andersen, Ed. Champaign, IL: Human Kinetics.

Non-Verbal Approaches to Increase Team Self-Awareness: When words are not enough

Abstract: Sport psychology consultants working with teams are often presented with problems in relationships and communication among the athletes or with the coaches. Sometimes, words are not enough to clarify the nature of the difficulties that team members are experiencing.

There are several possible reasons that this may occur. For example, it may be due to the athletes' reluctance to expose their feelings, a hesitancy to discuss their ideas, or an uneasiness to reveal what they want. Fear of disapproval by coaches or teammates, as well as embarrassment about speaking out can also be factors. In addition, some athletes may not know how to describe the problem in words.

This experiential workshop is intended to help consultants increase athletes' and coaches' awareness and understanding of such problems. To assist in achieving this goal, non-verbal approaches will be described and demonstrated. The underlying purpose of all these exercises is to increase awareness for both the group and the individual. They involve elements of risk-taking, feeling, and doing.

These exercises will involve the workshop participants in roles as athletes and coaches of the same team. They include: group sociogram, sub-group identification, influence lines, pairings, inclusion structures, approach-avoidance steps, and decision-making tasks. Participants will then have the opportunity to discuss their experience with the exercises, and how they might be applied to different situations with teams.

1. Inclusion exercise:

Instruct group members to place themselves as close to, or as far from a designated spot on the floor that represents the center of the group (i.e., how much they feel they really are part of this group). When they are all placed, tell them to look around and notice where others are. Then ask them to move to a place that they would like to be, or to remain where they are. Ask those who moved, is there something that prevents them from making that change in real life. For those who didn't move, ask whether the reason they remained stationary was that they were 1. satisfied where they are; 2. reluctant to reveal what they wanted; or 3. some other reason they are aware of.

2. Group Sociogram:

Have the group stand in a random arrangement, then ask them to move, and place their right hand on the left shoulder of the person: that they know best; after that, then the person they know least; after that, then the one they want to know better; and last, the person they feel uncertain about or tension with. Every person moves to their choice, even if there are several hands on their shoulder (take them all with you). Allow time between each instruction for people to look around and see where others are, and to pay attention to how they feel.

3. Influence line:

Ask the group to form a single straight line, and place themselves along the line in accordance with the amount of influence they exert in this group. No doubling up or stepping to the side is allowed. It must be single file. When they are in a single line, suggest that they look up and down the line to see who is where, and be aware of what they are thinking, feeling and wanting. After that has been done, tell them that they can now move themselves or anyone else to a different position according to their own opinion of who belongs where.

4. Approach/Avoidance:

Ask for two people who are uncertain about or feel tension in their relationship with each other to come forward. (Use the last exercise in 2. if they are part of a group. If no one volunteers, use your intuition and "pick two volunteers"). Tell the others (if there are others) to observe carefully what occurs. Remind the two people doing the exercise of the importance of not speaking at any point. Have them face each other about 15 feet apart. Tell them that are to alternate taking one step at a time in any direction, forward, backward, sideways, or diagonally. The step is to be an expression of how they are feeling toward the other person or what they want right before they take a step. Tell them you will let them know when the exercise is over. When there has been some closure, ask each of the participants what their experience was during the exercise. If necessary, help them to be more specific. After that, ask the observers what they noticed.

5. Non-Verbal Expression:

After reminding the group about not speaking during the exercise, have them arrange themselves in a circle, and look around at each of the other members. When they are ready, they may go over to any other member, non-verbally express their feelings toward them, and return to their position in the circle. Instruct them to be respectful of the other person's space in expressing their feelings. Each person must take at least one turn.

6. Decision-making:

Remind them of the non-verbal requirement. Instruct the group to divide into two groups, and give no further instructions. Observe how they go about doing it for later discussion. When they are two groups, instruct them to chose a leader, and give no further instructions. Observe how they do it, with particular attention to who made the decision or exerted the most influence (the covert leader).

7. Sub-groups:

Depending on the make-up of the group, you can select any of the following ways to divide them into sub-groups. The closer you get to what's really going on in the group, the more relevant it will be for the group's functioning. Ask them to divide up according to: their age, gender, birth order (oldest, middle, or youngest), cultural (language, birthplace, time in this country), region of US they were born in, or color. (I think sexual identity would potentially have undesirable consequences). With every division into sub-groups, give them each a task about the thoughts, feelings, desires, and consequences of being a member of their sub-group.

The Process and Content of Change

Think of an important change that you have made in your life.
What motivated you to make that change?
Were you seeking enjoyment or satisfaction?
Were you ending something that was uncomfortable?
Was it some of both (as is often the case)?
What helped you make the change?
What made it difficult?
How did you finally get yourself to do it?

Now, shift to thinking of an important change you are currently considering. If there is none, imagine one you would like to make.
What seem to be the reasons to do so?
What are your reasons not to?
If you were to guess right now what decision you'll make, which would it be?
What do you think about the choice you made?
How do you feel having made it?

Think of a decision that you are currently facing and having difficulty making.
What are the alternatives?
Imagine that you already decided on one. It doesn't matter which one you do first.
For the next few moments, that is what you are going to do.
Pay attention to whatever feelings, thoughts, and wants come into awareness.
Now switch to the other choice, and stay with that one for the same amount of time. Now compare the two experiences - see if you can recognize which one is stronger.

"Decision by sound"

Imagine you decide to change - create a sound that represents that decision. Now imagine you decide not to change – create a sound that matches this one. Compare the two sounds and observe their meaning. What do you conclude?

Aspects of Change
1. Content - What can be changed?
2. Timing - When does it occur? Are there prerequisites?
3. Process - How does it occur?
4. Resistance – What are the barriers or obstacles?

Content of Change
Awareness – often a first step in changing – alternatives, opportunities for choice
Behavior – habits, patterns of acting
Thoughts - opinions, judgments, beliefs, values, goals, viewpoints, attitudes
Feelings - anger, fear, sadness, guilt, shame, embarrassment
Wants - desires, choices, expectations, commitment
Situations - job, career, residence
Relationships – beginning, continuing, or ending
Communication – how we listen and how we speak
Meaning given to others' comments or behavior
Importance given to any of the above – focus on only one can miss other change

Timing of Change
Balance between motivation and hesitation – question about "ability" to change
Readiness - desire to change stronger than desire to stay the same
- discomfort of not changing greater than discomfort of changing

Process of Change

As a process, changing is fundamentally similar to staying the same. Any pattern of behavior requires continued reinforcement, including the pattern of staying the same. It is an active, on-going practice. Therefore, it is not too different from changing, which is also an active, on-going practice. What is different is the content of the practice. Staying the same means continuing to respond in the same way as before. Changing implies responding in a different way than before. Therefore, since people know how to stay the same, they already know how to change. The question is whether the right conditions exist to respond with a different content than before.

Importance of beginning change – small step in the direction of change may be possible; comparing present situation with complete change may seem difficult.

Resistance to Change - adherence to same pattern – protecting against loss or anticipated threat.

Thoughts –

"I'll never be able to change" (behavior or feeling, not awareness).
"Change is not important"
"It won't solve the problem"
"It won't even help"
"If it does work, it won't last"
"It won't prevent the problem from recurring"
"It will be a mistake"
"I'll regret it - the consequences will be worse than the original problem."

Feelings –

Fear - failure; criticism, disapproval or judgment; inadequacy
Anger - defiance or retaliation – if change is someone else's agenda.
Guilt – if someone will be hurt.

Shame – if a hidden undesirable trait will be exposed.
Sadness – if the loss involved is too painful.

Wants – conflicting want may be stronger than wish to change.
- want to avoid discomfort greater than want to seek satisfaction.

How Can I Win If I Don't Come In First?

Abstract: For most competitive athletes, striving to win is a significant factor in their participation in sport, and winning, therefore, is a highly valued goal. This possibility is often a driving force in training, practice, and competition. Most often, it involves beating another athlete or team, or coming in first in individual events. This experiential workshop is intended to provide participants with an opportunity to explore their beliefs, attitudes, and emotions about winning, not winning, and failure. The question of whether athletes can win when they don't come in first will be approached using guided imagery, memory about winning and not winning, and related observations, feelings, and attitudes toward self and others. Discussion and questions about failure, perfectionism and winning as a process will also be included.

Imagine that this workshop is an individual session with a consultant in sport psychology. What are some possible answers to the question in the title? (Write them on blackboard.)

"I can't"
"There is no such thing."
"I don't know"
"I don't understand"
"What do you mean"
"Tell me."
"I have an idea"
"I think I know"
"Let me think about it"
"I know, but I don't want to say."

Think of a time when you won. (Preferably a sport experience.)
What was the situation?
What did you do?
What did you feel?

What did you think?
What did you want?

Now, think of a time when you didn't win. (Preferably a sport experience.)
What was the situation?
What did you do?
What did you feel?
What did you think?
What did you want?
What do you get when you win?
What do you get when you don't win?
What are the differences?
What is the essence of the difference?
Can this essence be obtained in other ways?

What gives you good feelings about yourself? (Write them on blackboard.)
-accomplish a task -apply something I've learned
-give my all -see others benefit
-create something new -bring clarity to confusion
-solve a problem -get praise from others

Return to title question.
Redefine "winning" as a process, not just an outcome (beating others).
-an inner experience- a "win-win" situation
-being in the present- Here, Now, "Present"
-fully focused- whole self- (Zen- "sit," "eat," "practice")

"Golden-Haired Lion" (modified Sufi story).

Disciple- "Master, when lions seize upon an opponent, be it elephant or rabbit, they make exhaustive use of their power. Where does this power come from?"

Master- "It comes from the spirit of being- putting forth one's whole self, in which nothing is kept in reserve, nothing goes to waste. When you can perform in this way, you too can be a golden-haired lion."

Return to example of "didn't win" situation.
Are there of the sources of "good feelings about yourself?"
What's in the way?
What's interfering with feeling good about yourself?
Can it be changed?
Can this barrier be removed?

Failure- Failure is not a description. It's a judgment.
Description- "I didn't accomplish my goals.
Judgment- "I'm not good enough."

"Perfectionism"- High standards are not the problem. They give us something to strive for, something we can feel good about ourselves for having. The problem occurs when there is self-criticism for not reaching them.

An Eclectic Approach to Sport Psychology Consultation

Abstract: Our education and training in graduate school become the foundation upon which we build our professional experience. As practitioners, what we do derives from multi-dimensional considerations. It is at least a blend of what we have learned – from teachers, colleagues, clients, books, and journals, and what we created from our own experience. What we do depends too on our own thoughts, feelings, needs, and wants. Hopefully, it also derives from the people we are trying to help, the situations we deal with, the focus of the work, and the techniques we use.

This workshop will provide an opportunity to observe and participate in a presentation of an eclectic approach to sport psychology consultation. The presenter will describe an approach that incorporates four different theoretical foundations, and demonstrate a synthesis of these theories, blended together by a philosophical perspective of interviewing. With volunteer participants from members of the workshop, the consultant will illustrate this approach in real life interviews. After each interview, there will be ample opportunity for discussion and questions.

Theoretical Foundations

From medical research background - the importance of careful observation and evaluation--to inquire how something worked, what happened that made a difference.

From psychoanalytic theory - all behavior has meaning, past events and unconscious processes influence present functioning; the relationship between practitioner and client is critical.

From gestalt therapy - the significance of awareness and of present experience--how the athlete is functioning in the "here and now."

From transactional analysis - the child within, and its influence on communication/relationships.

From cognitive therapy - thinking is the major determinant of feelings and behavior (and I regard feelings as the important mediator between thinking and behavior).

Philosophical Perspective

Although originally trained as a clinician, with a background in medical research, I've come to see myself more as an educator. This change involved a shift from the medical model of illness and disease to a growth and development model, in which problems are seen as the result of learned thinking patterns. The focus of my work with athletes and others is to help them change those patterns that contribute to distressed feelings or troublesome behavior, and to remove the barriers to their optimal functioning. This focus is primarily on present experience, based on the hypothesis that past negative experiences might recede into the background, were it not for the fact that present patterns of thinking and feeling keep them in the foreground. I believe that what we learned in the past can be changed by what we learn in the present.

Principles of Technique – process-oriented, experientially based – rather than skill-based.

My Agenda- understand experience; identify barriers; initiate beginnings.

Follow, lead, follow - Entry points - I listen very carefully as the athlete (coach, parent, etc.) describes thoughts, feelings, wants, or problems. In describing their experience, athletes will often say something that is an opportunity for more in-depth exploration. At this point, I call it an "entry point," I shift from following what's being said to leading, i.e. offering some comment or question that encourages the person to consider an alternative perspective, or a deeper exploration of the issue. I then shift back to following by listening to the reaction to what I introduced. This cycle of following, leading, following, continues throughout the whole session.

Importance of language - The language used by a person is followed very closely, because it not only expresses present thoughts and feelings, but also contributes to their development.

Transitions: Endings and Beginnings in Sport and Life

Abstract: Participants in this experiential workshop will have the opportunity to explore past, present, and future transitions in their experience as an athlete, or in their lives outside of sport. After an introduction in which the transition process is discussed, workshop members will have the chance to reflect on life changes they have previously experienced, are currently involved with, or anticipate in the future, and to examine the significant endings and beginnings involved in those transitions.

The presenter will facilitate this exploration using guided imagery, recollections, and observations, feelings, and attitudes about these experiences. Participants will be invited to describe their transitions in terms of the challenges presented, the outcomes, and thoughts and feelings before, during, and after the changes. Discussion and questions will be encouraged throughout the workshop.

Transitions in Sport and Life – traditional view
-Ending" - ask for personal examples (retirement, injury, graduation, divorce, etc.)
-Implied "loss"- of something valued and important.
-Often not by one's own choice.
-Usually refers to an external situation.

This workshop takes a broader view of transitions- change with endings and beginnings.
-Every ending is also a beginning; and every beginning is also an ending-
(graduation = "commencement")
-Either can precede the other; experience can be positive as well as negative.
-Both are anticipated, experienced and reflected upon to varying degrees.
-Transitions may occur internally as well as externally- examples (wants/feelings)

Start with endings- leaving, finishing, completing, closing, letting go.
-T. S. Eliot - "At the end of all our exploring, we will arrive where we began, and know this place for the first time."
-Endings present their own challenges/opportunities.
-Because endings are also beginnings, they create other beginnings.

Continue with beginnings- starting, entering, initiating, opening, originating.
-H. Hesse- "In all beginnings dwells a magic force for guarding us and teaching us to live."
-Beginnings present their own challenges/opportunities.

Experiential
Think of a transition you had in the past-
Was it primarily an ending or a beginning?
Was it your choice?
If so, what motivated you?
If not, what was your reaction?
What helped you make the transition?
What made it difficult for you?
Think of a transition you will be facing in the future- (If there are none, imagine one).
What do you anticipate?
Is it primarily an ending or a beginning?
Are you looking forward to it?
Are you uneasy about it?
What will help you make it?
What will make it difficult for you?
Conclude with a present transition-
What transition are you currently in?
What change is occurring in your present situation?
What endings and beginnings already exist?
If no external situation applies, look internally, and ask the questions.

Self-Reflection and Change: At Home, At Work, and in Transition

Throughout our lives we are confronted with many situations that challenge our inner resources. Whether such occasions become problems depends in large part on the extent to which we know ourselves. This workshop will offer participants an opportunity to increase self-knowledge through the changing process of self-reflection. The elements of self-reflection, including self-awareness, self-exploration, self-understanding, and self-acceptance, will be discussed and explored through didactic teaching and experiential learning.

The benefits of and barriers to self-awareness will be presented, with particular attention to thoughts, feelings, and behavior, and with emphasis on the less frequently discussed areas of wants and needs. Self-exploration and self-understanding will be facilitated through exercises using guided imagery, focused attention, and directed recall. Participants will also have the opportunity to appreciate aspects of their wholeness, and examine patterns of functioning in difficult relationships, work situations, and life transitions, with the added perspective of self-reflection.

Self-acceptance will be encouraged and supported in dialogue and discussion. The workshop will also contain a detailed examination of the process of change, including the importance of beginning change, how change actually occurs, what readiness involves, what the consequences are, what constitutes resistance, what makes change difficult, and what makes it easier. An especially interesting idea about change is that as a process, changing is fundamentally similar to staying the same.

Self-Reflection in Presenting a Workshop and Conducting an Interview

Reflection has been called the fourth "R" of basis education by Daniel Siegel, a psychiatrist at UCLA. In his book *"The Mindful Brain: Reflection and Attunement in the Cultivation of Well- Being"* (2007), he writes, "Reflection is at the heart of both social and emotional intelligence, offering us the ability to be aware of our own internal states and those of others, so we can engage in life in a more flexible and compassionate way."

Self-Reflection
1. Self-Awareness – neutral noticing – thoughts, feelings, wants, behavior
2. Self-Exploration – search for motives, attitudes, priorities, values
3. Self-Understanding – reasons, meaning
4. Self-Acceptance – non-judgmental perspective

Importance of Self-Reflection in:
1. Developing professional philosophy - What is yours?
2. Presenting Workshops – style, goals, satisfactions, difficulties
3. Conducting Interviews – interpersonal sensitivities, internal issues

Experiential
A. Professional Philosophy (beliefs about problems, personal growth, and change)
1. What is personally important to you that contributes to your philosophy?
2. Where might you have "blind spots?" (Johari Window)

B. Conducting an Interview
1. Initial – "Intake" – history, assessment – scope (sport, life), emphasis.

2. Ongoing - Style – questioning, paraphrasing, confronting; follow/lead.
3. Ending – Who initiates it? What criteria do you use?
4. What difficulties have you had or do you anticipate?
5. What reactions have you had to prior interviews (internal and external)?

C. Presenting a Workshop
1. Origin – invitation, assignment, self-initiated (purpose?).
2. What difficulties have you had or do you anticipate?
3. What reactions have you had to prior workshops (internal and external)?
4. How are you affected by 1) the setting? (local, regional, national, int'l); 2) the participants (other professionals, students, coaches, athletes, admin.).

Artistic and Creative Aspects of Sport Psychology Consulting

Creativity - "It is the source of our intuition, the flexibility that leads to innovative models, and the energy that drives our most inspired inventions. Creativity is the essence of what makes each one of us unique, and helps us maintain freshness and stay energized."

Jeffrey Kottler, *On Being a Therapist*, 1993, Jossey Bass.

Dictionary Definitions:
Artistic - skillful, discriminating, sensitive
Creative - inventive, original, imaginative
Both – originality of thought and expression

Participant Exercise

Do you see yourself as artistic/creative in your work?
If yes, can you describe some examples?
If no, are you lacking these traits, or having difficulty expressing them?
If you lacking them, do you believe they can be acquired?
If they can be acquired, are you interested in acquiring them?
If you are interested, how will you go about doing so?
If you're having difficulty expressing them, what's in the way?
If you know, are you interested in removing the difficulty?
If you are interested, how will you go about doing so?
If you don't know, are you interested in finding out?
If you are interested, how will you go about doing so?

Skills and Qualities in Being Artistic and Creative
1. Open – eyes, ears, mind – perceptive and sensitive to self and others
2. Present – here/now – experience in the moment - gift of aliveness
3. Innovative – able to modify or refine knowledge or methods

4. Spontaneous – able to express new thoughts, ideas, desires, or behavior
5. Flexible – able to see alternatives and options
6. Curious – interested in knowing more – searching beneath the obvious
7. Courageous – willingness to risk being innovative

Paths to Develop Artistic and Creative Qualities
1. Self-exploration and increased self-awareness
2. Self-acceptance and appreciation of one's wholeness
3. Seek new opportunities for new experiences
4. Re-visit past problems and practice different solutions
5. Blend external stimuli with internal experiences for new synthesis

Consultant's Self-Awareness in Sport Psychology Consultation

Although consultant's self-awareness was considered important for sport psychologists more than twenty-five years ago (Nideffer, 1981), it has received little attention in the sport psychology literature or in the training of graduate students in sport psychology (Giges, 1999).

In recent AASP Conferences, considerable interest has been expressed in workshops that demonstrate how experienced sport psychology consultants interview athletes. These presentations usually consist of role-playing situations, in which the interviews are completed before any comments are made.

The present workshop will differ in several ways. First, a brief presentation will be made on the importance of self-awareness for sport psychology practitioners, as well as on psychological barriers to self-awareness. Second, the volunteer athlete interviewed will be dealing with a real life situation rather than role-playing. This will allow the consultant to observe the athlete's actual experience in the interview, and be guided by this experience in his interventions.

Finally, the consultant will utilize his own self-awareness during the interview by occasionally commenting before some interventions are made. Specifically, at unscheduled times during the interview, and with the prior agreement of the athlete, the consultant will interrupt the interview, turn to the audience, and describe his own immediate experience. This may include telling his thoughts or feelings, explaining the reason for his next intervention, or describing any difficulty he may have in knowing how best to proceed. This technique will provide an opportunity for members of the audience to observe what goes on in the mind of the consultant just before he makes some interventions. As a result, workshop participants will be able to understand more clearly the connections between the athlete's remarks and the consultant's responses. After the interview, there will be an opportunity for the participants to discuss the consultation.

Consultation with an Athlete: Options in the Moment

In previous AASP Conferences, much interest has been shown in presentations that demonstrate different approaches in consulting with athletes. Some have been workshops in which consultants of diverse backgrounds have interviewed individual athletes. Others have been discussions of a single case report by several consultants. There have also been theoretical symposiums in which consultants described the philosophical considerations underlying their consultations. One workshop focused on the consultant's self-awareness, and another, on contrasting styles in working with athletes' emotions. Videotapes have also been produced, in which different consultants interview the same athlete in sequential order, or several consultants conduct brief interviews with various athletes.

The purpose of the present workshop is to allow participants to observe how consultants might differ in their immediate response to an athlete's comments. The format will be unique in allowing two consultants to propose alternative suggestions, ideas, or questions to a third consultant who is conducting an interview with an athlete. These interruptions will occur immediately after the athlete speaks, before the consultant doing the interview has responded. All comments from the two consultants will be made directly to the interviewer, not to the athlete. After considering the suggestion or question, the interviewing consultant will explain to the audience the choice and reason for whatever response he decides to make. This procedure will be described in detail before the interview, so that the volunteer athlete will know exactly what to expect. Discussion and questions will follow.

The Meaning of Trust in Mentoring, Sport, and Life

Abstract: Trust means different things to different people. The purpose of this workshop is to identify and clarify these differences in different relationships, situations, and settings. Specifically, trust in mentoring, in sport, and in life will be examined. After a few introductory exercises to illustrate trusting and not trusting, trust and mentor will be defined. Workshop participants will be asked to give examples of trusting and not trusting in their relationships with mentors. Discussion will include characteristics of a good mentor, and barriers to developing trust in some mentoring relationships. The workshop will describe the implications of trusting in sport, including trusting oneself, teammates, coaches, and officials. Participants will be asked to describe experiences they had involving trust. The focus of the workshop will then be broadened to explore the meanings of trust in our everyday lives. Questions will be raised about what it means to trust ourselves, to trust other people, and to trust an intimate, a person we live with and love.

Exercises - 1 - Blind walk; 2 - Fall back; 3 - Group lift

Definitions - Trust - reliance on a person's integrity, strength, and ability.

- Mentor - a wise and trusted counselor.

Trusting a Mentor - relying on a wise counselor's integrity, strength, and ability. (To be trusted carries the responsibility to be trustworthy).

Trusting the process - allowing an activity to continue without knowing the outcome

- examples of trusting and not trusting a mentor – from participants
- characteristics of a good mentor; barriers to trusting

Trusting in sport - myself - releasing conscious control of movement
- teammates - relying on their support, cooperation, and competence
- coaches – relying on them to communicate, teach, and be available
- officials - relying on them to be competent and unbiased

Trusting in life - myself - relying on my own integrity, strength, and ability
- others - relying on them to:
- be competent keep their promise
- be reliable do what they say they will do
- be truthful act in my best interest
- take my side stay interested in me
- examples from workshop participants' own experiences
- an intimate – in addition, relying on an intimate partner to **not:** hurt me - reject me - lie to me - betray me - leave me - judge me - ridicule me - criticize me - attack me - abuse me - threaten me -undermine me - embarrass me - contradict me - discount me - ignore me - take advantage of me - control me - disappoint me - think less of me - upset me tell my secrets - turn against me

Working with Athletes' Emotions

Abstract: During participation in sport, athletes often experience intense emotions, such as frustration, anxiety, anger, and depression. Sport psychology practitioners can help athletes identify and clarify what they are feeling, explore and understand the basis for these feelings, and learn new options for managing them. This workshop will provide an opportunity for the participants to increase their self-awareness, as they examine their own experience with strong emotions. This increased self-awareness can then be used to assist athletes in a similar process.

Audience Participation- Think of a recent event in which you had strong feelings. If you don't recall one, think of the last time you got upset about anything.
What was the emotion?
What was your reaction to that emotion?
What was the situation that triggered your emotion?
What did you think was the cause of your emotion?
Was this a familiar experience?
How did you deal with it?
Is there something you would do differently next time?
Is there something in the way of your making that change?

Language- Clarify meaning of "feelings" (intuition, sensation)
"I feel that..."– means think, believe, imagine, suspect, predict
"It is my feeling..."– means opinion, impression, belief, understanding
"I feel like..."– may mean "I want"

Types of feelings

Basic- early in life, physical sensation, range of language – sadness- loss; fear- anticipation; anger- not getting what you want; joy- pleasure

<u>Learned</u>- not as early, physical, less range of language, with implied meaning: guilt (wrongdoing), shame (badness), hurt (worth), embarrassment (exposure)

<u>Complex</u>- Basic plus- helpless, bored, jealousy, envy, confusion, inadequate.

<u>General</u>- uncomfortable, strange, funny, peculiar- ambiguous

Identifying and Clarifying- "I don't know what I feel"- can result from discounting, disapproval, or avoidance of feelings in past

Exploring and Understanding-
a) "trigger/stimulus"- external situation or incident
b) "meaning"- how interpreted- the "explanation"
c) importance- how much impact; part of deeper issue

Behavioral options
1. Expressing- Directly- words, actions- venting
   - Indirectly- joking, bravado
2. Talking about it- with other or a counselor
3. Suppressing- holding it in; tightening
4. Withdrawing- by choice or as victim
5. Blaming- the other or self
6. Retaliating- "getting even"- sabotage,

Cognitive options
1. Shift in perception- i.e., meaning given
2. "Letting go"- acceptance without action
3. Broader perspective- "larger picture"

Lingering Emotions- a) continuing "cause" (stimulus)
b) unexpressed, not talked about, not let go, unchanged
c) "holding on"- for strength or punishing (self or other)

Part V

Book Chapters

Reprinted with permission from Mindfulness and Performance (2016), edited by Amy L. Baltzell (New York, NY: © Cambridge University Press), 488-512.

Awareness, Self-Awareness, and Mindfulness: The application of theory to practice
Burt Giges, Gerald Reid

Learning the art of helping others is a personal journey, requiring a commitment to knowing and understanding yourself.

Mark Young (1998, p. 2)

The purpose of this chapter is to provide educational, didactic, and experiential material to help practitioners increase their awareness of their own thoughts, feelings, wants, and behaviors, to assure that they are effectively meeting the needs of the client with whom they work. Specifically, the chapter will identify the ways in which mindfulness can benefit sport psychology consultants' (SPCs') practice by increasing self-awareness. This can enhance the counseling relationship and working alliance, key parts of effective sport psychology consultation (Andersen & William-Rice, 1996; Petitpas, Giges, & Danish, 1999). Mindfulness can help with the flexibility and tact required to maintain the give-and-take between themselves and the client. While there is currently a paucity of literature on this topic in the field of sport psychology, research from other fields and supplemental exercises will inform how mindful and self-aware SPCs can be more effective in their practice.

Theoretical Background

Self-awareness can be viewed through a number of theoretical orientations. From psychoanalytic theory (Munroe, 1955), we learn that all behavior has meaning, past events and unconscious processes influence present functioning; and the relationship between practitioner and client is critical. Transactional analysis (Berne, 1961) describes the child within, and its influence on communication and relationships. Gestalt therapy (Perls, 1969) emphasizes the significance of awareness and of present experience, i.e., how the client is functioning in the "here and now." Cognitive therapy (Beck, 1967) adopts the principle that thinking is the major determinant of feelings and behavior. Cognitive-Behavioral therapies teach that our thoughts (e.g., core beliefs, automatic thoughts, and appraisals), feelings (i.e., emotions and somatic sensations), and behaviors (e.g., adaptive or maladaptive) interact with one another, leading to conditioned patterns (Barlow et al., 2011). No matter how one conceptualizes the origins of thoughts, feelings, and behaviors, perhaps the most important skill an SPC can develop to best serve their clients is *self-awareness.* A recent article by Ridley, Mollen, and Kelly (2011) in the *Counseling Psychologist* explains why this is so. While competencies (e.g., assessment and intervention) and microskills (e.g., paraphrasing and summarizing) are fundamental to counseling, it is through metacognitive thought (i.e., mindful self-awareness) that counselors develop the good judgment and critical thinking: the *know-how* for effectively navigating the complexity of counseling. Similarly, mindful self-awareness can allow SPCs to practice "flexibility within fidelity," meaning they follow guidelines of evidence-based practices, while also being client-centered (Kendall, Gosch, Furr, & Sood, 2008). As an analogy, competencies and micro-skills are the tools and mindful self-awareness guides SPC's to "use the right tool for the job."

"*Awareness* is the conscious registration of stimuli, including the five physical senses, the kinesthetic senses, and the activities of the mind" (Brown, Ryan, & Creswell, 2007, p. 212). Awareness of the external world includes the use of our senses of sight, hearing, smell, touch, taste, and temperature. Awareness of our internal world, *self-awareness*, which this chapter will focus on, consists of our physical sensations (such as pain, tingling, tightness, vibration, palpitation, itching, or burning), and our psychological experience, including our thoughts, feelings, wants, and needs (although needs are not usually in our everyday awareness). It also includes awareness of our behavior, which is the bridge between our inner and outer worlds, allowing us to observe our actions in response to our thoughts, feelings or wants.

It is important to describe a primary rationale for practicing mindful self-awareness before introducing the first self-awareness exercise. The practice of mindfulness is defined as "self-regulation of attention so that it is maintained on immediate experience, thereby allowing for increased recognition of mental events in the present moment...with curiosity, openness, and acceptance" (Bishop et al., 2004, p. 232). Mindful self-awareness is important because habitual reactions, feelings, and biases in perception, thoughts, or behavior can become learned and automatically activated outside one's awareness – i.e., reacting on "auto-pilot" (see Vago, 2014 for a review). There can be a wide range of automatic reactions elicited in SPCs while working with clients. For instance, in the scenario of a client expressing an intense anxiety about an upcoming event, one SPC may have the natural disposition to tolerate their client's strong emotion, while another may instantly feel the very anxiety of their client and become uncomfortable themselves. Neither reaction is right or wrong; rather, it is whether or not the SPC is aware of their reaction and what they do with it that may determine the success of their work with their client.

The first step of mindful self-awareness is to recognize the reaction itself, instead of letting it unfold into a habit outside of one's intentional volition or choice. Brown and colleagues (2007) describe:

> People need to be attentive to their inner states and behavior to pursue reflectively considered goals. Failing to bring sufficient attention to oneself tends to foster habitual, overlearned, or automatized reactions, rather than responses that are self-endorsed and situationally appropriate. Directing attention to subjective mental, emotional, and physical experience is key to healthy self-regulation. Indeed, the willingness to 'look inside' is foundational to the development of self-knowledge from which regulated action proceeds (p. 216).

Let's start by practicing this willingness to 'look inside.' The first exercise will introduce the focus of awareness. Self-awareness is a long-term process, and requires continued practice.

Exercise I: Focus of awareness to increase awareness of inner psychological experience

For this exercise, limit your awareness to your thoughts, feelings, or wants (modified from the gestalt therapy "continuum of awareness"). It is important to note that a willingness to reflect on one's inner psychological experience takes some courage because it requires facing whatever arises. You may want to start with a mental note: 'looking inside' or 'checking in' is part of the journey to become your best as an SPC. Therefore, viewing it as a challenge instead of a threat may help you feel proud for taking this courageous step. Also, by looking within with a non-judgmental perspective, we may realize that thoughts and feelings, on their own, are not actually harmful.

Part 1.Mindful self-awareness

Find a partner. Each of you will have two minutes to report to your partner what you are aware of, narrowing your focus to your thoughts, feelings, or wants in any order or frequency. Repeat the question "What am I aware of right now?" after each answer. Suspend all judgment about the arising thoughts, feelings, or wants. Instead, non-judgmentally notice ("neutrally notice") them with acceptance, curiosity, and an openness to their manifestation in your consciousness; this is mindful self-awareness (Hölzel, Lazar, Gard, Schuman-Olivier, Vago, & Ott, 2011).

Part 2. Notice

Notice which of the three categories (thoughts, feelings, or wants) was most frequent, and which was least frequent. Choose the one that was least frequent, and take another two minutes to report only that one to your partner. Then your partner will do the same. Discuss with each other your understanding of your least frequent awareness. If none of the three categories emerge, reflect on your experience with the exercise, and consider which is least comfortable to express to others.

Benefits of Self-Awareness

"Cultivating awareness of mental states, such as thoughts and feelings in self and others, is the most common fundamental factor in the conduct of psychotherapy."

Jon G. Allen & Peter Fonagy (2008), *Mentalizing in Clinical Practice*

What benefits do we derive from increasing our self-awareness through such exercises? Self-acceptance, intentional action, and the opportunity for change are three benefits of mindful self-awareness, all of which have important implications for consultation. The rationale is outlined below.

Self-Acceptance

First, increased self-awareness allows us to gain a fuller knowledge of ourselves, of our complexity and wholeness, and offers the opportunity for increased self-acceptance. Mindful self-awareness is not just about being more aware of our inner experience; it is doing so with non-judgment, non-reaction, and a sense of self-compassion. Consider the example of an SPC struggling in a session with an athlete who is expressing anger about the season. The SPC is trying to help the athlete develop a positive re-frame of the situation; but the athlete is becoming more irritated and adamant about how frustrated he/she is. A mindful SPC would be aware that their approach is not going as planned. By mindfully noticing their internal frustration and self-critical thoughts (e.g., "This is terrible), the SPC could come to terms with the ineffective intervention with a sense of acceptance, self-compassion, and adaptability. For example, the SPC may understand the client's negative reaction as information to learn from (e.g., right now the client needs validation or time to process their frustration), which informs next steps, instead of viewing it as a failure.

An important construct that has been linked to resiliency in the face of failure and uncomfortable reality is self-compassion (Neff, Kirkpatrick, & Rude, 2007), which is closely tied to mindfulness. Self-compassion can come in the form of objectively acknowledging mistakes as part of the process without over-identifying with the frustration and mistake itself; and to bring attention back to what you can do in the present moment to move forward (Neff, 2003). This can be especially beneficial for SPCs, since work with athletes is not always quick and straightforward. It is often a process that requires the SPC to mindfully accept the inevitable barriers to change. In one study, a therapist in training reported that mindfulness practice helped them to "shift from automatic negative self-evaluation to a stance of compassionate witnessing" (Christopher & Maris, 2010, p. 123).

Furthermore, mindful self-awareness may help SPCs acknowledge their limits and prevent them from burnout fatigue. For instance, therapists with mindfulness training reported a greater awareness and "more sensitivity to their body's need for rest, hydration, and movement, noticing what their bodies needed before they became ill, exhausted, parched or stiff" (Christopher & Maris, 2010, p. 117).

Intentional Action

Second, self-awareness provides the opportunity to be more in charge of ourselves and better able to make decisions consistent with our values and plan of action. If we are not aware of our feelings, they can surface and interfere in unexpected or unknown ways. Goleman (1995) wrote, "Emotions that simmer beneath the threshold of awareness can have a powerful impact on how we perceive and react, even though we have no idea they are at work" (p. 55). For example, an SPC may feel anxiety about an inability to help a high profile athlete in the consulting sessions and without self-awareness may become over-controlling (e.g., try too hard to prove a point and force an intervention). Barlow and colleagues (2011) would describe this as an emotion-driven behavior because the attempts to control others or the environment are really attempts to avoid one's own uncomfortable feeling. This is analogous to trying to find an external solution to an internal problem, which often leads to reactive ways of thinking and acting that are ultimately less intentional and counterproductive.

Similarly, unrecognized guilt may lead to defensiveness, and hidden shame may trigger blaming others. For instance, an SPC working with a player referred for causing a lot of team turmoil may realize that this player needs a lot of support to feel better about him/herself and develop coping skills before their troublesome actions change. This leaves the team in turmoil for a period of time, for which the SPC may feel guilty. Without being aware of this guilt, and feeling responsible for the team's functioning, the SPC may end up blaming the athlete and losing patience with his/her progress. This reaction serves to protect the SPC from feeling responsible for the team's struggle. SPCs can benefit from becoming mindfully aware of uncomfortable emotion, and act intentionally toward the goal of helping the client.

Opportunity for Change

Third, awareness also creates the opportunity for change. How such change occurs with mindful self-awareness was first described in an earlier workshop (Giges, 1996), then published (Giges, Petitpas, & Vernacchia, 2004). Here is an excerpt from that article:

Most often, we become aware of a problem behavior after it occurs. When this happens, we may say "I see that I *did that.*" With a commitment to change and repeated awareness of the behavior, awareness begins to occur earlier. When it is present during the behavior, we may say "I see that I *am doing* that right now." With additional time and practice, awareness moves earlier in time, until it is present before the undesired behavior occurs. At this point, we can say "I see that I am *about to* do that." When awareness precedes the behavior, a choice can be made to behave differently. This is an opportunity for change, and is represented by the statement "I can do it differently"(p. 433). The process has been called "the Alphabet of Change" (Giges, 2011).

When **A**wareness precedes
Behavior, we have a

Choice, can make a
Decision, and apply
Effort toward a
Focus to reach a
Goal.

Furthermore, mindful SPCs can seize opportunities to promote clients' hope by making connections and noticing strengths. For example, and SPC may say, "I remember you mentioned how much you love to strategize and figure things out on the field. In our work together, we're going to do just that – learn how your mind works best and develop a few strategies that can help in particular situations." Mindful SPCs can also be more cognizant of subtle opportunities to build a positive connection when working with teams by being aware of and offering specific praise for small things that may have gone unnoticed. For example, in passing an SPC may say, "By the way, I noticed how you took the lead and spoke up the other day." Also, mindful SPCs may notice when follow-up questions are needed to get to the heart of an issue, or when referral is needed to address an issue outside their competence.

The Gift of Presence

Fourth, being more self-aware can enhance our ability to be more fully "present", meaning less distracted by our own experience, more responsive to others, and more understanding of their experience. Goleman (1998) stated "Self-awareness serves as an inner barometer, gauging whether what we are doing (or are about to do) is, indeed, worthwhile" (pp. 57-58). Often, if we know what we are experiencing, we can sense what others are experiencing. If it turns out we are right, we call that "insight" (meaning we have a relatively accurate sense of what the client is experiencing and how the interaction is unfolding). Of course, if we are wrong, then it may be "projection" (attributing our own experience to others). For example, an SPC may assume a client is anxious to discuss something, which may be based upon the SPC's own discomfort.

The three meanings of the word "present" contain the essence of awareness – to be here, to be in the now, and receive a gift - of aliveness - open and ready. A genuine understanding of clients' perspective, experiences, strengths/weaknesses, stage of motivation, and points of entry for effective intervention and support requires SPCs to pay attention to what their clients say, what they don't say, and how they say it. Qualitative research on therapists in training showed that mindfulness practice led them to become less "preoccupied with themselves" and more "present and sensitive to the client's experience and non-verbal communication" (Christopher & Maris, 2010, p. 122).

Mindfully being attentive to the unfolding of experience (as opposed to entering interactions with a rigid pre-determined agenda) is related to greater empathy (Dekeyser, Raes, Leijssen, Leysen, & Dewulf, 2008), an essential skill for building a relationship with a client in sport psychology consultation (Sharp & Hodge, 2011); and is inversely related to treatment dropout in clinical practice (Norcross & Wampold, 2011).

Barriers to Self-Awareness

What considerations or circumstances might interfere with self-awareness? There are four barriers germane to SPCs, including external distractions, motivation to avoid unpleasant internal experiences, disregard for the value of self-awareness, and fear of judgment. Each is outlined below.

First, there are external distractions that may detract one from self-awareness. It takes cognitive effort to look inward and maintain self-awareness. Problems with work, school, home, or relationships can be energy draining distractions that might draw our attention away from our inner experience. Being overly-busy has become the norm (even considered a status symbol) and can detract from self-awareness, a major theme of Edward Hallowell's (2006) book *Crazy Busy*. For example, in a qualitative study of recently graduated SPC's it was stated, "As my caseload got bigger and I got busier, I sometimes notice that I move towards being solution-focused... I have to consciously not do that" (Tod, Andersen, & Marchant, 2011, p. 100). This is a clear example of how we SPCs can easily get caught up in our own mental clutter, instead of being fully present in the room with the client.

Second, internal experiences may also distract SPCs from self-awareness. If awareness leads to negative feelings such as guilt, fear, anger, sadness, or shame, this might result in not wanting to be aware, in order to avoid the discomfort. Without developing *distress tolerance,* the capacity for tolerating uncomfortable or unpleasant internal states (i.e., thoughts, feelings, physical sensations) (Feldman, Dunn, Stemke, Bell, & Greeson, 2014), one may attempt to avoid uncomfortable feelings and therefore become less self-aware. Mindfulness can improve distress tolerance (Robins, Keng, Ekblad, & Brantley, 2012) while in pursuit of a goal (Feldman et al., 2014). Therapists have reported that mindfulness training helped them attend to manifestations of stress, anxiety, irritation, and confusion by noticing such experience non-judgmentally. Their awareness helped ease the tension, instead of viewing the feelings as "bad" with self-judgment that would have intensified the tension. This in turn helped their clients do the same (Christopher & Maris, 2010), perhaps by providing a helpful model for their clients.

Third, dismissing the importance of one's internal experience can also be a barrier to self-awareness. If we have been taught that our inner experience is not important, we can eventually become less familiar with our feelings and wants, and lose awareness of them. Fourth, if there is an expectation of disapproval, reprimand, criticism, or judgment, awareness might be avoided because of its anticipated unpleasant consequences. It is, therefore, essential that awareness be without criticism, a non-judgmental observing without reprimand or disapproval ("neutral noticing") (Giges, 2004).

Exercise II: To Increase Your Awareness of Your Inner Critic.

You may be well acquainted with your inner critic, whether it comes in the form of ruminating over conflict, chastising yourself, "Why did I say that?!" after an interaction, or other typical frustrations. And yet, through the following exercise you may be surprised to notice how the inner critic can seep into almost all circumstances. Consider a situation in which you are meeting an athlete for the first time.

- Imagine you have come to the appointment early. Think of a self-criticism for doing that.
- Imagine you have come to the appointment late. Think of a self-criticism for doing that.
- Imagine you have come to the appointment on time. Think of a self-criticism for doing that.

Now, repeat the exercise about coming early, late, or on time, and for each, think of a self-statement that is complimentary or self-supporting. Which came easier: the criticism or the compliment? Are critical or self-supporting thoughts more frequent for you? Self-criticism is not uncommon; especially for SPCs who not only provide a service to athletes and teams, but also have the added pressure of needing to convince others that their work has utility.

Whenever we have a strong internal critic, there can be disapproval of what we are doing, how we are doing it, when we are doing it, or why we are doing it. Any thought, feeling, want, or behavior can be the subject of the criticism. Imagine an old man standing at a busy intersection waiting for help to cross the road. You decide to help him, and he expresses his appreciation. As you're walking away, the critic in you says, "You only did that to make yourself feel better!" While helping others is a source of good feelings about ourselves, we can also have a genuine desire to help other people. The critic in us ignores the latter consideration.

When people say, "I'm so stupid," they are not only expressing disapproval of themselves, they are also contributing to feeling worse about themselves. And the internal critic is seen as an expert. To loosen the grip the critic has on us, the question can be asked, "Is all of you stupid? Is the part of you that's calling you stupid also stupid?" This question usually attracts some attention. *The Wizard of Oz* may serve as a useful metaphor. What appears to be wisdom from an expert is nothing more than someone playing a recording. And that is how the internal critic can be understood – an old recording that keeps repeating. The loudest, most critical voice is not always the wisest voice; but rather a habit of the mind. Positive Psychology teaches the value of noticing the good (Seligman & Csikszentmihalyi, 2000) and of self-compassion (Gilbert, 2009; Neff et al., 2007), which can be antidotes to such habitual self-criticism.

Critiquing one's evolving practice as an SPC is part of growing as a practitioner. Research suggests that healthy perfectionism, which is conceptualized as one who has high personal standards that are self-oriented (not socially-referenced), and low levels of judgment for mistakes, fear of failure to live up to expectations, and self-criticism, is actually adaptive. It is associated with greater success, less distress, and relatively good adjustment, and better performance, compared to unhealthy perfectionism, defined by the opposite characteristics of healthy perfectionism (for a review see Stoeber & Otto, 2006). Healthy perfectionism is in line with Carol Dweck's research on the value of a "growth-mindset", where one seeks out useful feedback and challenges and strives for self-referenced improvement (Dweck, 2006). This is important for SPCs, as they can embrace a healthy process of growth with humility by learning and making adjustments along the way instead of getting derailed by an unhealthy self-critic. In summary, a balanced approach of mindfully noticing and toning down the distracting and unhealthy self-critic, while also being attuned to healthy and constructive feedback for growth, fosters self-awareness and more effective SPC consultation.

Fifth, another barrier to self-awareness is an automatic compliance or defiance, with no time to reflect about your inner experience. If you are thirsty and going for a glass of water, and a parent harshly said, "You're not drinking enough! I told you to drink more!" you might be distracted by an automatic defiance and walk-away thinking, "Nobody's going to tell me what to do," a thought driven by rebellious feelings. The problem is that, in the absence of self-awareness, one can very quickly become overwhelmed and react so quickly that the initial thoughts and feelings that drove the behavior in the first place (e.g., "I feel less in control and weak when I'm told what to do") may go unnoticed. Similarly, the Mindfulness, Acceptance, and Commitment (MAC) approach (Gardner & Moore, 2007) teaches us that habitual, automatic reactions easily manifest when we don't access clarified personal values that provide wise perspective (e.g., "They are trying to help me, not control me").

Internal Psychological Experiences

Thoughts

Included in the category of thoughts are: ideas, beliefs, opinions, reasons, judgments, appraisals, speculations, decisions, expectations, attitudes, and memories. Awareness of our thoughts also includes how attached to them we are, how much they influence us. From cognitive therapy, we accept the principle that our thoughts are the basis for most of our feelings and behavior. The meaning that we give to situations and appraisals of them influences our experience. For example, if a situation is seen as a threat, we may feel anxiety; if seen as a challenge, we may feel excitement (Jones, Meijen, McCarthy, & Sheffield, 2009).

Thoughts are the link between others' behavior and our feelings. An example would be of a relay runner who felt hurt and disappointed when the coach asked him to change from running anchor leg (last) to running second. The anchor leg is usually the fastest runner on the relay team. In this example, the relay runner might have thought that the change meant that his coach lost confidence in him. However, when the coach explained that another team was running their fastest runner in the second position in an attempt to get far ahead of the other teams, the runner's thoughts changed: He became pleased that he was chosen to prevent that from happening.

Thoughts are also the link between others' behavior and our behavior. Consider a crowded team bus, with standing room only. The bus suddenly lurches and one athlete steps on another's foot. Think of a dozen different behaviors the person stepped on might do. When you see that there are numerous possibilities for action, it shows that another person's behavior is the stimulus, but not the explanation for what we do. Our inner experience determines what we decide to do. Cognitive flexibility (i.e., the ability to adapt one's thinking approach to understand a new condition) is a significant skill for SPCs because an important task is to understand where their client is coming from and find ways to tailor interventions to fit their client's personality and context. Mindfulness can help with this; mindfulness has been shown to be related to cognitive flexibility (Moore & Malinowski, 2009). Furthermore, Ellen Langer's definition of mindfulness is one's ability to be mindfully open to the unfolding present experience as opposed to mindlessly viewing one's current experience through rigid cognitive biases of the past (Langer & Moldoveanu, 2000). In conceptualizing a case, it is important for SPCs to not only consider the accumulated data gathered through assessment, but to also consider the question, "*How* am I thinking about this client?" in order to avoid an over-reliance on preconceived notions or biases that interfere with progress.

Negative thinking

Negative thinking is an interpretation or prediction of undesirable consequences. It can involve a task, person, situation, and can be applied to the past, present, or future. While thoughts focused on the negative can be accurate and adaptive (e.g., problem-solving), maladaptive negative thinking can be inflexible, inaccurate, and consist of an exaggeration or overgeneralization, where an error or mistake becomes a calamity.

a. **Present to permanent** – now to always - if something bad happens once, it will continue to happen. For example, when a batter strikes out, the negative thought is that striking out will keep happening.
b. **Particular to pervasive** – here to everywhere – if a problem is here, it will be everywhere. Consider a student who does poorly in one subject, and therefore believes that poor performance will affect all subjects.
c. **Possible to probable** – maybe to likely – if it might go wrong, it will go wrong. For example, if a relay team drops a baton in an important race, the members think they will probably drop the baton in other races. In his book, *Learned Optimism*, Martin Seligman (2006) describes the "possible to probable" style as pessimism (p.76).

Uncertainty is part of the human experience and so most importantly is one's reaction to uncertainty, which is often a source of worry and anxiety. When adaptive, worried uncertainty prompts us to work harder and become more prepared, which allows us to pursue excellence. Conversely, at its extreme, an inability to tolerate uncertainty can turn into Generalized Anxiety Disorder or Panic Disorder (Boswell, Thompson, Hollands, Farchione, & Barlow, 2013). At any level, uncertainty can have a significant impact on how we cope with situations and make decisions. It is important for SPCs to be aware of their uncertainties (e.g., how a session will go), and to develop strategies to cope with them. To remain effective in their practice, consultants need to avoid maladaptive rumination or misguided and distracting attempts to control the uncontrollable or excessively seek out reassurance (e.g., trying too hard, over-preparing, or constantly seeking approval). To do so may reduce the discomfort of uncertainty in the short-term, but undermine one's trust in themselves and in their ability to cope effectively with whatever comes their way. It may also interfere with SPCs ability to come across as natural, personable, and self-assured.

Exercise III: To Increase Your Awareness of Your Uncertainties.

Get in a comfortable position and close your eyes. Observe your breathing. Increase the rate and volume of breathing by inhaling and exhaling deeply and rapidly for three or four breaths. Now return to normal breathing.

Imagine that you are out in a field at the foot of a mountain. The sun is shining and there is a gentle breeze. You decide to begin ascending the mountain, being careful to avoid any logs or stones. Step over a small brook, and continue to climb. There is a path you can follow without too much obstruction. As you climb, you notice there is a plateau just ahead. As you reach the plateau and look around, you see a small shack. As you approach the shack, you see a wise old person sitting outside. When you reach the shack, the old person greets you, and asks what your question is. Choose a question that involves uncertainty and is of some importance to you in your life. Wait for the answer. Then express your thanks and slowly make your way back down the mountain, and back to your starting point.

Find a partner. Describe the experience, including the question, the answer and particularly your reaction to the answer. Are you left with other questions? Will you seek any answers?

Feelings

In this section, feelings pertain to psychological emotions, not sensations or intuition. The word "feel" or "feeling" can be used with other meanings than emotion: "I feel that" can mean I think, believe, suspect, imagine, or predict. "It is my feeling" can mean my impression, judgment, understanding, belief, or suspicion. In this section, the word feeling is limited to meaning emotion.

Awareness of emotions can be increased by having clarity and understanding of the different types of emotion, and appreciating the meaning and intensity of them. The types of emotion describe below are: basic, learned, complex, and general. With each category, the specific emotions are listed, along with the range or meaning of each emotion.

Basic Emotions

There are four basic emotions: joy, sadness, fear, anger. They occur early in life, and have a range of language to describe them. They are usually accompanied by strong physical sensations, and vary in intensity from mild to moderate to severe. Here are some examples of the four basic emotions.

Joy: pleased, content, satisfied, happy, delighted, or ecstatic
Sadness: disappointed, discouraged, unhappy, dejected, or despair
Fear: uneasy, insecure, apprehensive, worried, panic, or terrified

Anger: irritated, annoyed, resentful, angry, mad, enraged or fury

Learned Emotions

Learned emotions are almost basic, have physical sensations, but do not occur as early in life, and have little range of language. Some authors consider shame a basic emotion. The meaning of each is described below.

Guilt. "I did something wrong"
Shame. "I am a bad person"
Embarrassment. "I've been exposed"
Hurt. "I'm not as worthwhile or important"

Complex Emotions

Complex emotions contain one or more basic emotions plus one or more thoughts. They are called complex because they contain more than emotions. They each have some thought or thoughts associated with the emotions.

Envious. resentment + "I wish I had or did that."
Jealous. fear, resentment + "Someone else is loved more than I"
Helpless. fear, sadness, anger + "I can't do anything."
Confused. fear, anger + "I don't know what's going on."
Inadequate. fear, sadness, anger + "I'm not good enough."
Bored. uneasiness, anger, disappointed + "I'm not interested."

General Emotions

General emotions can be understood as those that are not specific enough to understand the individual's actual experience. The words *upset, uncomfortable, strange, funny,* and *peculiar* can represent several thoughts and feelings. They need to be clarified. Questions to help clarify general emotions can be followed up with asking questions such as, "What type of upset?" or "Strange in what way?" Such follow up prompts by the SPC may help to identify the specific thoughts and feelings contained in the general emotions category. Usually, there are several thoughts and feelings associated with each general emotion.

For practicing SPCs, interactions in sessions may spark strong emotions within the SPC themselves. For instance, a client may initially express resistance to receiving help, which may lead the consultant to feel discouraged, frustrated, or angry, and result in unproductive behavior (e.g., giving up or arguing). Dialectical Behavior Therapy, which is rooted in mindfulness, teaches that one may perceive interpersonal struggle as unacceptable (e.g., "This is not fair!"), push one's own agenda (e.g., "They're just not listening!"), or give up (e.g., "This is not going to be effective!") instead of "doing what works" by taking steps to work with what we are presented with instead of fighting against it (Brodsky & Stanley, 2013, p. 203). An effective motivational interviewing strategy is to respond to client resistance by becoming aware of the client's feelings and current stage of change (e.g., contemplative), "rolling with their resistance" to the idea of change, and working with the client's viewpoint. To argue with the client about their stance would increase resistance (Miller & Rollnick, 2002). Mindful awareness of positive emotions may also be helpful for SPCs who are searching for a creative solution in their work. Positive emotion has been linked to a broadening of attention and creativity (Fredrickson, 2001), which may help SPCs and their clients discover effective and innovative approaches for intervention. For instance, a SPC may mindfully be aware of how grateful (a positive emotion) they feel for being able to work in their profession, which may help them find ways to connect with a more challenging client. They may also laugh with their client or notice a positive quality in them, which could open the possibility of having new insights.

Exercise IV: To Increase Awareness of the Past You Inside the Present You

Get in a comfortable position and close your eyes. Observe your breathing. Increase the rate and volume of breathing by inhaling and exhaling deeply and rapidly for three or four breaths. Then return to normal breathing.

Imagine you are out on a grassy plain, with nothing to see all around except a path in front of you. As you are walking on this path, off in the distance, you can see a small child coming toward you. At first, you cannot determine who it is, and then you realize it is yourself as a small child, about 4-5 years old. When you meet, ask the child what they would like. After the child answers, imagine they ask you what you would like. Then ask what they are feeling right now. After the answer, have the child ask you the same question. Finally, you ask the child what's important to them. After the answer, the child asks you the same question. Then you do an activity together that both of you would enjoy. After playing, you ask the child if you can pick them up in your arms; then ask if the child will return with you. If yes, allow the child to merge inside you as you return. If no, say goodbye and ask if they would like to meet again.

Find a partner. Describe the experience, including the questions, the answers, and your reaction to the child's answers. Increased awareness of the child within can heighten one's self-understanding and perhaps self-acceptance.

Wants

Wants are the specifics to help us meet our underlying needs. According to Regulatory Focus Theory, people have two different regulatory systems related to motivation (Higgins, 1997): Promotion-focus to pursue an opportunity or a gain, which leads to pleasure and cheerful emotions (e.g., happiness, joy, excitement) and Prevention-Focus to avoid a loss and maintain security and safety, which leads to the avoidance of negative feeling (guilt, fear, embarrassment, shame) and low-energy positive emotions (e.g., calmness, contentment, relief) (Halvorson & Higgins, 2013). Both motivations for pursuing a gain and avoiding a loss are *wants*.

Everything we do is connected to something we want. Many times what we want is expressed as a complaint. For example, "It's too hot in here" contains the want to be cooler or to avoid the discomfort of the heat. Other times, a want is expressed as a "have to" or a "can't." Consider the student who has the choice of going to a party or studying for an exam. He or she may say, "I want to party, but I *have to* study." What is the want contained in "I have to study?" Although partying may be a stronger want than studying, doing well on an exam is more important than partying; hence the choice to study. This is called a "priority of wants." Sometimes, thinking "I should do this" conceals the want to avoid the discomfort of not doing it. Also, "I can't" avoids taking responsibility for the decision expressed by "I won't." An important component of self-awareness is to notice the different ways of indirectly expressing wants, and understanding why one is chosen over the other.

If we don't get what we need, we may "want" (lack) a lot. Eric Hoffer (1952) wrote that we can never get enough of what we don't really want. In other words, substitute gratification will never fully satisfy an unmet need (outlined in next section). Take for instance the issue of professional relationship boundaries while traveling with a team, not an uncommon scenario (Stapleton, Hankes, Hays, Parham, & Roberts, 2010). An SPC may feel socially disconnected in his/her own personal life, and subsequently be tempted to accept the offer of their client to hang out informally one of the evenings. The "want" for building the informal relationship may in fact function to fulfill their need for feeling socially connected, as opposed to the SPC thinking critically about the context of the relationship. Mindful self-awareness of "wants" can help SPCs make prudent and wise ethical decisions.

Understanding "wants" can also be helpful for SPCs to understand why they make the decisions they make, which may come in the form of pursuing a gain/opportunity or preventing a loss/pain. For instance, an SPC working with a client may cautiously avoid an issue when in fact their client would benefit from discussing it more directly. The SPC's decision to avoid may be driven by their "wanting" to prevent some discomfort (e.g., addressing potential issues for which they lack competence). Conversely, a SPC may be over-bearing in their interactions with clients due to their "wanting" to be perceived as helpful. It is important for SPCs to look inward to recognize how their behaviors and choices are driven by underlying "wants" and whether or not these behaviors are serving their clients.

Exercise V: To Increase Awareness of Your Past Experience of Wanting

Close your eyes. Think of a recent decision you've made; perhaps a decision you made while working with a client. Think about the implications and consequences of that decision. What did you get out of the decision, how did the decision affect the client, and what was required of you by the decision?

Now think back to the decision-making process. What were the "wants" that led you to make the decision? Explore the "wants" in detail. What made the "wants" important to you? Were the "wants" facilitative to making a wise decision for the long-term or more of a distraction for short-term gratification? Were the "wants" masking underlying unmet needs? Mindfulness is an especially helpful way to objectively notice emerging "wants" and consider whether or not they are facilitative or distracting.

Needs

Needs consist of the basic elements of psychological growth. They are long range, broad, and enduring, and are not usually in our everyday awareness (Frankl, 2006; Maslow, 1962). Mindful self-awareness is not a need. It is, rather, a skill to help people get what they need. Carol Ryff endorses the following psychological needs for well-being: autonomy, environmental mastery, personal growth, positive relations with others, purpose in life, and self-acceptance (Ryff, 2014). Additionally, Abraham Maslow has described physiological needs (e.g., food, water, sleep) and safety needs (e.g., security, shelter), love/belonging needs (e.g., friendship), esteem needs (e.g., self-esteem, achievement), and self-actualization needs (e.g., creativity, personal growth, problem-solving) (Maslow, 1943). Two additional needs theorized by Martin Seligman are positive emotion and engagement/absorption in one's activities while frequently using one's personal strengths (Seligman, 2011).

In addition to basic needs, there is another group of "needs" that we have called "acquired needs" (Giges, 1996). Although the word "needs" is used, they are not actually necessary for growth. Rather they represent attempts to cope with unmet needs, and become problems in themselves (Watzlawick, Weakland, & Fisch, 1974). Here are some examples of what may happen if basic psychological needs are not met.

If the needs for security and safety are not satisfied, individuals may develop the "need" to control their environment or dominate other people, in their attempt to provide some sense of safety or security. These are not real needs; they are attempts to achieve external solutions to internal problems. Some individuals may seek an opposite solution, and develop the "need" to depend on others to provide the sense of safety or security. Either of these "acquired needs" can be problematic for SPCs; such as becoming overly-controlling in the consultant-client relationship or the SPC depending too much on others (e.g., supervisor/consultation) to make simple decisions.

For those who lack a sense of self-worth (a basic need), their attempt to compensate for this deficiency might lead to the "need" to please (an acquired "need") or constantly seek approval. Similarly, when individuals have a strong internal critic, the need for self-acceptance may not be satisfied. Attempts to ineffectively cope with this un-met need might lead to the "need" to criticize, judge, or disapprove of oneself and/or others.

Another important basic need is the need for autonomy, with its associated sense of mastery. If not met, the acquired "need" to be dependent might develop, leading one to follow someone else's lead (e.g., being overly client-centered and not directive enough). An opposite coping mechanism would be the "need" to be defiant or rebellious, acting as if you are making an independent decision by doing the opposite of what is expected in a given situation.

When the basic need for relationship and intimacy is not met, an individual may avoid involvement with others, and become completely absorbed in work, the so-called "workaholic." Alternatively, some may become involved with others as "objects," attempting to compensate for the deficiency with repetitive superficial relationships. Issues of counter-transference may manifest in the counselor/client relationship if relationship needs are being met through their professional counseling relationships.

Related to the need for relationships is the need to belong. Usually, the need to belong can be satisfied by becoming part of a group, small or large. For those who are unable to make these connections, they may have a "need" to withdraw. For SPCs working with a team who welcomes them as "part of the team," an inability to fulfill the need to belong may interfere with their ability to build connections with the team. On the other extreme, an SPC may over-identify with the team to fulfill a need to belong, such as becoming pre-occupied with the outward success of the team, which can distract them from knowing their place and role on the team.

Finally, the need for meaning and purpose, eloquently described in Frankl's (2006) book, *Man's Search for Meaning,* has more recently come into prominence, as changes in family and social roles become more frequent. Without a sense of meaning and purpose in life, individuals have a "need" to escape, and may drift into some form of addiction. Alternatively, they may develop a hedonistic lifestyle, in which nothing has meaning unless it's pleasurable. A foundational meaning or purpose in life can be energizing, and provide balance that can allow SPCs to do their best work.

Exercise VI: Part 1

The following questions are intended to stimulate self-reflection, and to heighten awareness of thoughts, feelings, and wants in everyday experience. Each question should be followed by a moment's pause to allow for some response other than the first thing that comes to mind. For each question, write down something that will help you reflect on your response at a later time.

What is your main source of enjoyment or satisfaction?
What gives you good feelings about yourself?

What do you want most that you don't have?
What do you have that you don't want?
What type of situation upsets you? What type of upset is most common?
How do you usually react when you get upset?
What might give you bad feelings about yourself?
What would lead to your feeling guilty? Hurt?
What might lead to your feeling embarrassed? Ashamed?
What do you fear?
What do you pretend?
Which questions were more difficult or uncomfortable to answer?

Exercise VI: Part 2

The purpose of this two-part exercise is to reflect on a past problem and on a present one. The exercise helps us to learn about an identified problem and also our relationship to the problem itself, which is important for developing awareness of how we react to problems. As we teach our clients to learn from experience, we can do the same.

Review of a Past Problem

Think of something you did and would do differently if you had a chance to do over. Please select a past problem you might have regrets about, or be bothered by when you think about it.

1. What was the behavior?
2. What was your reaction afterwards? (thinking, feeling, wanting)
3. What was your major concern?
Impact on your job, your relationships?
Effect on others?
How you would be judged?

4. What were the actual consequences?
5. How did that compare with your concern?
6. How would you do it differently now?
7. What different consequences do you imagine?
8. How do you view it now, as you look back on it?

Observation of a Current Problem

Think of a current problem (i.e., a situation or person presently causing you difficulty or upset). Attempt to identify the external and internal components (i.e., separate the problem into the situation and your inner experience). The problem can be conceptualized by the following formula: *Problem = External Situation + Internal Experience*. You may need assistance in making the separation.

An illustration of this process would be an athlete who has a problem with his/her coach who demands on-time adherence to a schedule. The external situation is a coach who is very strict about time. The internal experience for the athlete is that when being told what to do, a feeling of being controlled emerges, and a strong urge to resist complying interferes with accepting the rules. Hence, the situation becomes a problem. Awareness of the internal experience may help the athlete accept the external situation, and cope with it more effectively. And knowing about your own internal experience may help you see what makes a situation a problem for you.

Reflection

In this workshop:
What was important for you?
What was uncomfortable?
What was difficult?

What was enjoyable?
What was satisfying?
What, if anything, did you learn about yourself?

These questions are intended to increase your knowledge of your inner psychological experience. In addition, the discussion and exercises about thoughts, feelings, wants, and needs highlight the particular areas involved in heightening your awareness and understanding of your motivation and behavior. With this knowledge, more effective functioning as a consultant can occur.

Conclusion: Learn from Experience

"In learning to live with less self-awareness, we also diminish those distinctively human possibilities for freedom, creativity, caring and ethical insight which are based on that awareness."

Edward Cell (1984, p. 9)

In summary, mindful self-awareness has myriad benefits for applied sport psychology consultants. Mindful self-awareness allows SPC's to foster self-acceptance instead of criticism, act with intention instead of habit, and embrace the gift of full presence in working with clients. There are many barriers to self-awareness, including external distractions, such as being overly busy; and internal distractions, such as an inability to tolerate uncomfortable thoughts and feelings, dismissing one's internal experience, self-criticism, and failing to acknowledge one's thoughts, feelings, wants, and needs. Mindful strategies to foster self-awareness include developing a more extensive vocabulary of emotions, practicing distress tolerance, non-judgmental noticing of internal states, acting with awareness to "do what works" and make wise decisions, and making sure basic psychology needs are met in order ensure they do not lead to compensating "acquired needs."

REFERENCES

Andersen, M. B., & Williams-Rice, B. T. (1996). Supervision in the education and training of sport psychology service providers. *The Sport Psychologist, 10*, 278–290.

Barlow, D. H., Ellard, K. K., Fairholme, C. P., Farchione, T. J., Boisseau, C. L., Allen, L. B., & Ehrenreich-May, J. T. (2011). *The Unified Protocol for Transdiagnostic Treatment of Emotional Disorders.* New York, NY: Oxford University Press.

Beck, A. (1967). *Depression: Clinical, experimental, and theoretical aspects.* New York, NY: Hoeber.

Berne, E. (1961). *Transactional analysis in psychotherapy.* New York, NY: Grove Press.

Bishop, S. R., Lau, M., Shapiro, S., Carlson, L., Anderson, N. D., Carmody, J., . . . Devins, G. (2004). Mindfulness: A proposed operational definition. *Clinical Psychology: Science and Practice, 11*(3), 230-241. doi: 10.1093/clipsy.bph077

Boswell, J. F., Thompson-Hollands, J., Farchione, T. J., & Barlow, D. H. (2013). Intolerance of uncertainty: A common factor in the treatment of emotional disorders. *Journal of Clinical Psychology, 69*(6), 630-645. doi: 10.1002/jclp.21965

Brodsky, B., & Stanley, B. (2013). *The Dialectical Behavior Therapy Primer: How DBT can inform clinical practice.* Somerset, NJ: John Wiley & Sons.

Brown, K. W., Ryan, R. M., & Creswell, J. D. (2007). Mindfulness: Theoretical foundations and evidence for its salutary effects. *Psychological Inquiry, 18*(4), 211–237. doi: 10.1080/10478400701598298

Christopher, J. C., & Maris, J. A. (2010). Integrating mindfulness as self-care into counselling and psychotherapy training. *Counselling and Psychotherapy Research, 10*(2), 114-125. doi: 10.1080/14733141003750285

Dekeyser, M., Raes, F., Leijssen, M., Leysen, S., & Dewulf, D. (2008). Mindfulness skills and interpersonal behaviour. *Personality and Individual Differences, 44*(5), 1235-1245. doi: 10.1016/j.paid.2007.11.018

Dweck, C. (2006). *Mindset: The new psychology of success.* New York, NY: Ballantine Books.

Feldman, G., Dunn, E., Stemke, C., Bell, K., & Greeson, J. (2014). Mindfulness and rumination as predictors of persistence with a distress tolerance task. *Personality and Individual Differences, 56*, 154-158. doi: 10.1016/j.paid.2013.08.040

Frankl, V. E. (2006). *Man's search for meaning: An introduction to logotherapy.* Boston, MA: Beacon Press.

Fredrickson, B. L. (2001). The role of positive emotions in positive psychology: The broaden-and-build theory of positive emotions. *American Psychologist, 56*(3), 218-226. doi:10.1037/003-066X.56.3.218

Gardner, F., & Moore, Z. (2007). *The Psychology of Enhancing Human Performance: The Mindfulness-Acceptance-Commitment (MAC) Approach.* New York, NY: Springer Publishing Company.

Giges, B. (1996). Self-awareness for sport psychologists. *Thirteenth*

Annual Conference on Counseling Athletes. Springfield, MA: Virtual Brands.

Giges, B. (2011). *Self-awareness in sport psychology consulting.* DVD. Available from Virtual Brands, Wilbraham, MA: Virtual Brands.

Giges, B., Petitpas, A. J., & Vernacchia, R. A. (2004). Helping coaches meet their own needs: Challenges for the sport psychology consultant. *The Sport Psychologist, 18*(4), 430-444.

Gilbert, P. (2009). Introducing compassion-focused therapy. *Advances in Psychiatric Treatment, 15*, 199-208. doi: 10.1192/apt/bp.107.005264

Goleman, D. (1995). *Emotional intelligence.* New York, NY: Bantam Books.

Goleman, D. (1998). *Working with emotional intelligence.* New York, NY: Bantam Books.

Hölzel, B. K., Lazar, S. W., Gard, T., Schuman-Olivier, Z., Vago, D. R., & Ott, U. (2011). How does mindfulness meditation work? Proposing mechanisms of action from a conceptual and neural perspective. *Perspectives on Psychological Science, 6*(6), 537-559. doi:10.1177/1745691611419671

Hallowell, E. M. (2006). *Crazy busy: Overstretched, overbooked, and about to snap.* New York, NY: Ballantine Books.

Halvorson, H. G., & Higgins, E. T. (2013). *Focus: Use different ways of seeing the world for success and influence.* New York, NY: Penguin Group.

Higgins, E. T. (1997). Beyond pleasure and pain. *American Psychologist, 52*(12), 1280-1300. doi: http://dx.doi.org.ezproxy.bu.edu/10.1037/0003-066X.52.12.1280

Hoffer, E. (1952). *The ordeal of change.* New York, NY: Harper & Row.

Jones, M., Meijen, C., McCarthy, P., & Sheffield, D. (2009). A theory of challenge and threat states in athletes. *International Review of Sport and Exercise Psychology*, 2(2), 161-180. doi: 10.1080/17509840902829331

Kendall, P.C., Gosch, E., Furr, J.M., & Sood, E. (2008). Flexibility within fidelity. *Journal of the American Academy of Child & Adolescent Psychiatry*, 47(9), p.987. doi: 10.1097/CHI.ObO13e31817eed2f

Langer, E. J., & Moldoveanu, M. (2000). The construct of mindfulness. *Journal of Social Issues, 56*(1), 1-9. doi: 10.1111/0022-4537.00148

Maslow, A. H. (1943). A theory of human motivation. *Psychological Review, 50*(4), 370-396. doi: 10.1037/h0054346

Maslow, A. H. (1962). *Toward a psychology of being.* Princeton, NJ: Van Nostrand.

McCann, S. C. (2000). Doing sport psychology in the really big show. In M. B. Andersen (Ed.), *Doing Sport Psychology* (pp. 209-222). Champaign, IL: Human Kinetics.

Miller, W. R., & Rollnick, S. (2002). *Motivational interviewing: Preparing people for change* (2nd ed.). New York, NY: The Guilford Press.

Moore, A., & Malinowski, P. (2009). Meditation, mindfulness and cognitive flexibility. *Consciousness and Cognition, 18*(1), 176–186. doi: 10.1016/j.concog.2008.12.008

Munroe, R. L. (1955). *Schools of psychoanalytic thought.* New York, NY: Dryden Press.

Neff, K. D. (2003). The development and validation of a scale to measure self-compassion. *Self & Identity, 2*(3), 223-250. doi: 10.1080/15298860309027

Neff, K. D., Kirkpatrick, K. L., & Rude, S. S. (2007). Self-compassion and adaptive psychological functioning. *Journal of Research in Personality, 41*(1), 139-154. doi: 10.1016/jrp.2006.03.004

Norcross, J. C., & Wampold, B. E. (2011). Evidence-based therapy relationships: Research conclusions and clinical practices. *Psychotherapy, 48*(1), 98-102. doi: 10.1037/a0022161

Perls, F. S. (1969). *Gestalt therapy verbatim.* Lafayette, CA: Real People Press.

Petitpas, A. J., Giges, B., & Danish, S. J. (1999). The sport psychologist-athlete relationship: Implications for training. *The Sport Psychologist, 13*(3), 344–357.

Ridely, C.R., Mollen, D., & Kelly, S.M. (2011). Beyond microskills: Toward a model of counseling competence. *Counseling Psychologist.* 39(6), 825-864. doi: 10.1177/0011000010378440.

Robins, C. J., Keng, S.-L., Ekblad, A. G., & Brantley, J. G. (2012). Effects of mindfulness-based stress reduction on emotional experience and expression: A randomized controlled trial. *Journal of Clinical Psychology, 68*(1), 117-131. doi: 10.1002/jclp.20857

Ryff, C. D. (2014). Psychological well-being revisited: Advances in the science and practice of eudaimonia. *Psychotherapy and Psychosomatics, 83*(1), 10-28.

Seligman, M. E. P. (2011). *Flourish: A visionary new understanding of happiness and well-being.* New York, NY: Free Press.

Seligman, M. E. P., & Csikszentmihalyi, M. (2000). Positive psychology: An introduction. *American Psychologist, 55*(1), 5-14. doi: 10.1037/0003-066X.55.1.5

Sharp, L.-A., & Hodge, K. (2011). Sport psychology consulting effectiveness: The sport psychology consultant's perspective. *Journal of Applied Sport Psychology, 23*(3), 360-376. doi: 10.1080/10413200.2011.583619

Stapleton, A. B., Hankes, D. M., Hays, K. F., & Parham, W. D. (2010). Ethical dilemmas in sport psychology: A dialogue on the unique aspects impacting practice. *Professional Psychology: Research and Practice, 41*(2), 143-152. doi: 10.1037/a0017976

Stoeber, J., & Otto, K. (2006). Positive conceptions of perfectionism: Approaches, evidence, challenges. *Personality and Social Psychology Review, 10*(4), 295-319. doi: 10.1207/s15327957pspr1004_2

Tod, D., Andersen, M. B., & Marchant, D. B. (2011). Six years up: Applied sport psychologists surviving (and thriving) after graduation. *Journal of Applied Sport Psychology, 23*(1), 93-109. doi: 10.1080/10413200.2010.534543

Vago, D. R. `(2014). Mapping modalities of self-awareness in mindfulness practice: A potential mechanism for clarifying habits of mind. *Annals of the New York Academy of Scienecs, 1307*(1), 28-42. doi: 10.1111/nyas.12270

Watzlawick, P., Weakland, J. H., & Fisch, R. (1974). *Change: Principles of problem formation and problem resolution.* New York, NY: W. W. Norton.

Reprinted with permission from Becoming a Sport Psychologist (2014), edited by Paul McCarthy and Marc Jones. (Oxon, UK: © Routledge), 9-18.

ON BECOMING A SPORTPSYCH PRACTITIONER

Burt Giges

Beginning in Sport

I like beginnings. So this time, I'm going back 75 years to the beginning of my involvement in sport. In my early years, "street games" were my chance to play, compete, and sometimes win. The games were literally played in the street, and included roller skate hockey, stick ball and box ball (the last two patterned on baseball). Because we played in the "gutter," we frequently had to stop to let the cars go by. Then I added neighborhood football, played not in the street, but on the nearby park grass. I was grateful for that grass when I injured my knee trying to tackle a ball carrier who kept running. I was a chubby kid, and I played fullback, with a fierce determination to get that extra yard. What I did not know then, but observed repeatedly over the ensuing years, was that in both sport and my professional life, I was intensely competitive. I not only had an inner drive for excellence, to be the best that I could be, but also a hidden desire to be "first" – better than anyone else.

During high school, I was manager of the high school track team, and assisted the coach with timing the runners' laps. I also helped by carrying the medical box, and when athletes were injured, I was right there to help the trainer or the coach tend to the athlete. Back then, I had no idea I would eventually become a physician. In college, I continued my participation in sport as a member of the fencing team, a foil fencer. I once made the mistake of substituting for a teammate who was not able to compete in a sabre match. In foil, the head is off-target; not so in sabre. My opponent's first point was all he needed. It came from a slap (read "slam!") on the side of my head, hard enough for me to see stars. I gracefully withdrew from the rest of the match (lesson learned). My involvement in sport changed many years later, when I was a resident in psychiatry. A friend of mine, who was the coach of a high school football team, appointed me their team doctor. That's where I first learned about coach stress (he told me first-hand), parental involvement (I heard the father screaming at his son), and the connection between an athlete's emotions and injury (they got hurt when they were starting to lose). Again, I had no idea I would later get involved in sport psychology.

I expanded my own participation in "sport" by adding exercise as a parent of two young girls. In those days, "working out" was not generally considered part of sport. I was drawn into serious exercising because I had virtually no stamina in trying to teach my older daughter to ride a bicycle. At first, the exercises were from the Royal Canadian Air Force group, and then I settled down to indoor bicycling and strength training. Today, at 86, I'm still at it, adding the treadmill two days a week.

Beginning in Psychology

My involvement with psychology came first as a patient in psychoanalysis and then as a resident in psychiatry. I was in analytic treatment twice, once before entering psychiatric residency and once after completing my training. I went into analysis the first time because of feelings of anxiety, loneliness, and isolation as a researcher at the Rockefeller Institute for Medical Research, NY. The second time resulted from an unsatisfying ending to the first, and the fact that I had decided to become a psychiatrist, knowing that more personal work was needed. There was a significant difference in the style of my two analysts and in my own readiness to change. I think both factors contributed to the very satisfying outcome of treatment. One unexpected result was that after the completion of my analysis, I was able to water ski for the first time in my life - free of anxiety and feeling exhilarated. I loved it!

During residency, we studied psychodynamics, psychopathology, group and family dynamics, child development, and social factors. I found myself much more interested in the psychological issues than in the medical model of diagnosis and treatment of psychopathology. Years later, as a practicing psychiatrist, I came to realize that I had actually become much more of a psychologist than a medical doctor. I had drifted away from prescribing medication and had started referring those who needed drugs or hospitalization to other psychiatrists. Long after sport psychology became my main interest, a colleague, Dan Begel, who was the first president of the International Society of Sport Psychiatry, came to a conference of the Association for Applied Sport Psychology (AASP). We spent some time together, and he invited me to speak at his society's conference. In describing the program for that conference in their Newsletter (Begel, 1996), he wrote, "Burt Giges, my favorite anti-psychiatry sport psychiatrist, will be presenting some provocative ideas regarding our methods and role, based not upon his prejudices but upon quite a few years' work in sport psychology." That was a reassuring confirmation for me that my views and practice were in fact different from those of sport psychiatrists. Here's what I wrote about my own perspective on my website last year (Giges 2010).

Although originally trained as a clinician, with a background in medical research, I've come to see myself more as an educator. This change involved a shift from the medical model of illness and disease to a growth and development model, in which problems are seen as the result of learned thinking patterns. The focus of my work with athletes and others is to help them change those patterns that contribute to distressed feelings or troublesome behavior, and to remove the barriers to their optimal functioning. This focus is primarily on present experience, based on the hypothesis that past negative experiences might recede into the background, were it not for the fact that present patterns of thinking and feeling keep them in the foreground. The language used by the person is followed very closely, because it not only expresses present thoughts and feelings, but also contributes to their development. I believe that what we learned in the past can be changed by what we learn in the present.

Merger of Sport and Psychology

As I reflected back over my professional life, I noticed that it changed direction about every 10 to 12 years. I realized later these career changes were attempts at external solutions to internal problems. Whatever the change, it was a great comfort to me that my wife and two daughters were always supportive. The first cycle included the time I spent in medical research and practice. The research was in liver disease at the Army Medical Research and Graduate School at Walter Reed Army Hospital in Washington, D.C. and at the Rockefeller Institute for Medical Research in New York. This was followed by several years of practice in medicine. As an outgrowth of my first psychoanalytic treatment, I changed direction and switched my specialty from internal medicine to psychiatry. At the time, I never imagined that the three years I had spent in medical research would serve me well later on. My years in psychiatric practice were in an office doing psychodynamic psychotherapy. Recognizing a growing restlessness, staleness, and diminished aliveness, I changed again and became involved in the Human Potential Movement, participating in encounter groups, group therapy, gestalt therapy, and transactional analysis. During this time, I became more active in the therapeutic process, and eventually led group sessions for many years.

The final change came 21 years ago, at the age of 65, when my connection to sport psychology officially began. The suggestion that I explore sport psychology came from my older daughter who is a psychologist and knew of my interest in track and field. The idea seemed to fit my desire for something new; and combining my interest in sport and psychology sounded just right. It must have been right because I'm still involved well after the 10-12 year cycle. Many years before this last change, I had seen several patients who were avid sport participants (in golf, tennis, swimming, and running). I had used techniques that are an intrinsic part of sport psychology, but had not yet studied or practiced the psychology of sport. An example was my work with a serious runner who was approaching his first marathon, anxious about whether he would be able to finish. During his sessions, we worked on his maintaining his focus, visualizing his completing the run, and thinking positively about his commitment. He did finish and was very happy, and I was pleased that I was able to help him achieve his goal.

Once I decided to pursue this new career direction in the field of sport psychology, I went at it fiercely. I went to every conference and workshop I could find, including a Continuing Education workshop at an APA Division 47 Conference. I subscribed to sport psychology journals and joined organizations devoted to sport psychology. I began reading avidly and over the years eventually read more than 60 books about sport psychology or running.

In this new endeavor, I was uncertain about what to call myself. I am not a psychologist, so that term was out. I did not want to be called a sport psychiatrist, with its emphasis on diagnosis, psychopathology, and treatment of illness. Yet I did want to make known my interest in merging sport and psychology. The term that appealed to me was a combination of sport and part of psychology. And so I became a "*sportpsych practitioner.*" That allowed me to teach graduate students, mentor colleagues, consult with athletes, coaches, teams, and parents, and write about my experiences.

Early Experiences as a SportPsych Practitioner

My first official step in the direction of applying my new knowledge as a sportpsych practitioner was to call a local track coach, who was the coach of an international elite track team. I told him I was a psychiatrist with a lifelong interest in track and field, and that I would like to talk with him about the possibility of consulting with the team. I also said I would not charge a fee for my services. I had decided that because I wanted this to be my hobby rather than my business, and that was a freeing experience. In addition, I had a strong urge to give back to others and to feel good about doing that. The coach was agreeable to my coming to practice sessions. I became helpful immediately, but not in the way I had anticipated. He suggested I join him in timing the runners' laps (still timing laps 50 years later). Some of the runners thought I was an assistant coach, because I was not formally introduced as a psychiatrist (I was glad for that, but not for the fact that I was not introduced as anything else). For one year that was my contribution.

After that year, the coach asked if I would see one of the runners who had trouble finishing her races. This first referral was a most significant experience for me because it served as a turning point in my thinking about how I might consult with athletes. I saw that after only two sessions, the shame that she felt when being passed in a race was no longer present during a four year follow-up (Giges, 2000). As I mentioned in my keynote address on How People Change (Giges, 1995), "For a psychiatrist, particularly one trained in psychoanalytic psychotherapy, this was an astounding experience. How can important things happen so quickly? Doesn't it take years to get profound change? It was difficult to let go of a long-standing belief I had, that depth of work correlated with length of time."

Another early and important experience was the opportunity to serve on the Psyching Team of the New York City Marathon, which I did for several years. In looking for something special to do, I approached the director of what was called the Family Tent – a large tent that served as a recovery tent for those who did not need serious medical attention. It contained about 50 cots and was staffed by physical therapists, nurses, podiatrists, athletic trainers, massage therapists, and medical students. I offered to talk with the staff about what they might expect to see, and what they might do for the runners who may have psychological symptoms, whether or not they finished the race. I would be available to provide back-up support if they needed it, either as a consultant to them or for direct contact with the runners. This consisted of a solution-focused mind set, limited to here and now functioning. It was an exciting and fascinating time.

An unexpected consulting experience I had at the beginning of my new career was that the sport I knew best turned out to be my least effective consultation. Having been on the fencing team at college, I was looking forward to a session with an elite college fencer. As I began to ask questions, I became more occupied with his fencing technique and less with his fencing experience. I was drifting somewhere between a coach and an admiring fan about his technique. I lost the connection that's necessary to be effective as a consultant. There was no real rapport, no beginning relationship. After that first session, he did not return or call. When I called him, he merely said he was not interested in continuing. Another lesson learned.

At the first conference I attended, I was excited and eager to learn, and also anxious about starting something new and wanting to show my competence. I did feel confident, however, that I would eventually find a place for myself and be able to make a contribution. That happened sooner than I expected. When I asked one of the speakers whether his satisfaction depended entirely on the athlete's improved performance, his answer was "Of course it does." That reply told me there was already something worthwhile I could contribute. Drawing from the concept of counter-transference in psychoanalytic theory, I developed the idea of a workshop on "Self-Awareness for Sport Psychology Practitioners." Its purpose was to assure that the athlete's needs, rather than the consultant's, were primarily served. I knew from my earlier experience with the marathon runner that the practitioner would also derive benefit, but that was not the primary consideration. I have since given that workshop at more than a dozen universities around the country and as a Continuing Education workshop at an AASP Conference. In addition, Virtual Brands made a video (2011) in which I interviewed two athletes and two coaches and discussed some of the principles and techniques involving self-awareness in sport psychology consulting.

I met Ken Ravizza at that first conference. He became my friend and mentor in the years that followed. It was Ken who told me not to expect too much in my first year of consultation, making it much easier to tolerate timing laps and moving hurdles. Among my other important early contacts were the Athletic Counseling faculty at Springfield College (Al Petitpas, Judy Van Raalte, and Britt Brewer), who also became good friends and mentors. This connection led to my being asked to give workshops to the graduate students at Springfield. After a few years of these workshops, the following important conversation took place with Al at one of the AASP Conferences:

<u>Al</u>: You're like one of the Springfield family, Burt.
<u>Burt</u>: Would you be willing to make that official?
<u>Al</u>: What do you want?
<u>Burt</u>: How about an appointment as Clinical Professor?
<u>Al</u>: I'll see what I can do.

A few weeks later I received a letter appointing me to the staff of the Athletic Counseling Program in the Department of Psychology. And so began a long and fruitful affiliation with Springfield College. A bonus to working with Judy and Britt came when they formed their video company and invited me to participate in the videos they were creating (Giges et al. 2002, 2000). I met Mark Andersen through them, and that led to my writing a chapter in Mark's book *Doing Sport Psychology* (Giges, 2000). The Springfield connection was also a springboard to other valuable experiences; the most important to me was my invitation to be a keynote speaker at an annual AASP Conference (Giges, 1995).

The Intervening Years

Each conference I attended gave me new ideas about presentations I could give. The first workshop I gave at AASP (Giges, B., Ravizza, K., Gordin, R., & Gould, D., 1992) was on "Examining the Process of Sport Psychology Consulting." Three of us interviewed different athletes to demonstrate the differences and similarities in the consultant's approach, and Dan Gould led the discussion. It seemed that the differences were more in our behavior, and the similarities were more in the philosophical principles underlying that behavior. I also developed workshops about consultant self-awareness, psychological barriers, non-verbal approaches, winning, transitions, trust, and working with athletes' emotions. As the years passed, the number of workshops and lectures increased, and I recently did some counting. Somewhat to my surprise, I've given over 75 presentations over the 20 years. They probably had something to do with being invited to run for election as AASP President.

Among the many other presentations, I've selected three for special mention.

<u>The most challenging:</u> In 2002, I was invited by Professor Jose Maria Buceta to give a workshop at his university (U.N.E.D.) in Madrid, Spain. The idea was for me to give a lecture, and then conduct a live interview with an athlete. The lecture I gave was on "Psychological Barriers to Performance Excellence in Sport: A Counseling Approach to Performance Enhancement." For the

lecture, the audience and I were wired for simultaneous translation. (I spoke in English; they listened in Spanish). No problem. It got more challenging when the Spanish athlete I interviewed did speak "English." So without a translator, I had to translate her "English" into my English. I felt anxious about how effective I would be with this language difficulty. Fortunately, the interview went very well. In the 30 minutes allotted, she was able to see that she was holding herself back, and this awareness helped her to decide to change that behavior.

The most satisfying: As President-Elect of AASP in February 2007, it was my privilege to represent AASP at the Annual Meeting of the Joint Commission on Sports Medicine and Science. I was scheduled to talk on what I had titled "Common Ground: Where Sport Psychology and Sports Medicine Meet" with two other speakers, both from the field of Sports Medicine. Because of last minute emergencies, neither was able to attend the meeting. As alternatives were discussed, I suggested that if someone from among those attending would volunteer, I would be willing (in fact, eager) to demonstrate a consultation in sport psychology. Someone did volunteer, and after the interview one of the participants in the audience said, "Now I understand what my wife meant about how to listen."

The most fun: For a profession that values and depends a lot on talking, perhaps it is not too surprising that my most enjoyable workshop was one I gave at the AASP Conference in 2006, "When Words are Not Enough: Non-Verbal Approaches to Team Self-Awareness". All of the exercises were completed with no talking allowed, and they varied from interesting to fascinating, and from serious to hilarious. The participants left wanting more.

Another significant activity during these years was my involvement with Springfield College. Being a teacher and mentor to the graduate students and consultant to the Women's

Track and Field team were quite enjoyable and very satisfying. I became the women's track team consultant after the coach had an unsatisfactory experience with one of the graduate students, and we hoped that my serving temporarily in that capacity might bring him back into the fold. What followed, however, was much more than a transition. My work with the coach and the team lasted eight years, unexpected but indeed worthwhile. A few years after I began, the graduate students joined me in working with the team, and took over after I left.

Guiding Principles as a SportPsych Practitioner

The work I do as a sportpsych practitioner is based on a foundation of guiding principles. In addition, I use the research tools I learned years ago to ask how and why something happened, as well as what possible conclusions follow from the information obtained.

Follow, lead, follow. In every interview, my focus is on here and now functioning. I listen very carefully as the athlete (coach, parent, etc.) describes thoughts, feelings, wants, or problems, until I hear something that may be an opening to further exploration. At this point, an "entry point," I shift from following what's being said to leading, i.e. offering some comment or question that encourages the person to consider an alternative perspective, or a deeper exploration of the issue. I then shift back to following by listening to the reaction to what I introduced. This cycle of following, leading, following, continues throughout the whole session.

The importance of beginnings. When people think of change, they often compare where they are now with where they want to be, and that may involve many steps and much time. If they can see themselves taking a small step, a beginning, they will see that they know how to change, and may feel an early confidence that they can continue. I think that's one of the essential elements of change...the realization that you can begin a change process. A small shift in behavior, if continued, can make a significant difference after time has passed. If one is too focused on a change in behavior or feelings, however, another important beginning change (in awareness or perspective) may go unnoticed.

Consultation in sport and therapy. It is important to make a distinction between a consultation about sport performance and therapy about some underlying issue. In an AASP newsletter in 1996, I wrote the following Commentary.

An important distinction must be made between therapy in a clinical context and intervention in sport performance. In the world of sport, sometimes the symptom *is* the problem. Whatever underlying issues there may be, they are not necessarily the focus of the work. Even the presence of some diagnostic entity does not determine the appropriate intervention. It may not be why the athlete came for help; and sometimes, relieving the symptom removes the problem. I have seen this happen with runners whose performance was impaired by anxiety, anger, self-doubt, or loss of confidence, motivation, or concentration. In such instances, when the symptoms were dealt with directly, no further exploration (of deeper issues) was required... Sometimes a careful follow-up of an intervention may reveal unexpected lasting benefit from what seemed initially to be "first aid." In other situations, where no such benefit is obtained, or when recurrences continue to interfere with performance, underlying difficulties might then be addressed.

Experiences outside of sport. For each problem athletes might have in their sport participation, they may be able to draw on inner resources that were helpful in their lives outside of sport. For example, a runner was having difficulty with his performance and was not feeling successful. He was, however, doing well with a book that he was writing. He felt strong, clear, and competent in his writing ability. In his work in the sessions, he was able to transfer that strength and competent feeling to his running, using his legs to do the "writing" on the track. And a golfer I worked with was able to use his love of learning to change his attitude toward himself from a "lousy golfer" to a great "student of golf."

The Present

Currently, I am mostly involved in activities other than consultation with athletes. I continue to do some part-time teaching of graduate students at Springfield College. I have recently created a website that describes my work in sport psychology over the past 20 years. I have also started mentoring at a distance for sport psychology practitioners and graduate students. With the benefit of current technology, I am able to view the work of the person I am mentoring directly using videotape, DVD, or Skype. In addition, I have been asked to serve as a co-editor for a special journal issue of *The Sport Psychologist*, containing case studies in sport psychology.

Thoughts for Students

At the beginning of a new career, there is often a mixture of excitement and anxiety: the excitement of venturing into something unknown and the fear that comes with not knowing enough. Most students are concerned about whether they will learn fast enough to be seen as competent. Here is what I wrote in the AASP Newsletter in 2006:

To borrow from Zen teaching, when being a student, just be a student. Be as fully a student as you can be. Soak up new information, whether it matches your prior ideas or not. Be open to differences as an expansion of your knowledge, rather than a threat to your beliefs. Learn from teachers, coaches, books, journals, fellow students, athletes, and especially from your own experience. Being an excellent student is different from being an excellent consultant, teacher, or researcher. As a student, your excellence is in your dedication and commitment to learning, and in your acceptance of what you have not yet learned or cannot yet do. Be mindful of your long-term development as a professional, and consider that every step of the way is preparation for the next step.

In essence, my advice is "Be present. Be Open. Be curious."

References

Begel, D. (1996, April). The president's view. *International Society for Sport Psychiatry Newsletter.*

Giges, B. (2011). *Self-awareness in sport psychology consulting.* Wilbraham, MA: Virtual Brands.

Giges, B. (2010). *My work in sport psychology: Home page.* Retrieved from www.burtgiges.com

Giges, B. (2006). Ten burning questions with Burt Giges M.D. *Association for the Advancement of Applied Sport Psychology Newsletter, 21*(1), 5-6.

Giges, B., Ravizza, K., & Murphy, S. (2000). *Three approaches to sport psychology consulting.* Wilbraham, MA: Virtual Brands

Giges, B., Ravizza, K., Van Raalte, J., & Zaichkowsky, L. (2002). *Brief contact interventions in sport psychology,* Wilbraham MA: Virtual Brands

Giges, B. (2000). Removing psychological barriers: Clearing the way. In M. B. Andersen (Ed.), *Doing sport psychology* (pp.17-32). Champaign, IL: Human Kinetics.

Giges, B. (1996). Commentary. *Association for the Advancement of Applied Sport Psychology Newsletter,* 11(3), 24.

Giges, B. (1995, September). *How People Change.* Keynote address delivered at the annual meeting of the Association for the Advancement of Applied Sport Psychology, New Orleans, LA. Retreived from http://www.burtgiges.com/Lectures_Workshops.html

Giges, B., Ravizza, K., Gordin, R., & Gould, D. (1992). *Examining the process of sport psychology consulting.* Workshop given at the annual conference of the Association for the Advancement of Applied Sport Psychology, Colorado Springs, CO.

Reprinted with permission from Routledge Companion to Sport and Exercise Psychology: Global perspectives and fundamental concepts (2014), edited by Athanasios G. Papaioannou and Dieter Hackfort. (Oxon, UK: © Routledge), 908-921.

Understanding Athletes' Psychological Needs

Burt Giges and Paul McCarthy

SUMMARY

Psychological needs are fundamental requirements of personal growth, health, and well-being, for athletes and the wider population, alike. They are long-range, broad, and enduring. At any stage of development and in any type of activity, these elements exist and influence our functioning (Deci, 2002; Erikson, 1950). Among the more common ones are the need for security, autonomy, identity, self-worth, mastery, intimacy, belonging, and a sense of meaning or purpose in life (Erikson, 1950; Frankl, 1992; Maslow, 1987). Although needs appear frequently in our daily language, they are not usually part of our everyday awareness. Therefore, it is important to understand how needs are satisfied, what happens when they are not, and how they influence individuals' wants, feelings, and behaviors. This chapter will discuss how sport psychology practitioners can identify and understand athletes' psychological needs, and help them with needs that have not been fulfilled.

INTRODUCTION

Psychological needs are as important to growth as physical needs, and this is arguably more evident in sport and exercise contexts than in most others. Unless both are satisfied, growth may be impaired (Deci, 2002; Maslow 1987). Deci pointed out that innate psychological needs are necessary conditions for psychological growth, integrity, and well-being; and that satisfaction of these basic needs facilitates autonomous motivation. It is therefore important to be able to recognize when a particular need is not being met. For example, when an athlete does not have a sense of security, anxiety may result and interfere with performance and relationships. If athletes do not view themselves as independent and in charge of themselves (need for autonomy), they may experience a sense of powerlessness and feel like victims who lack adequate resources when faced with difficult challenges. When athletes do not have self-worth or a sense of meaning or purpose in their lives, they may be vulnerable to depression.

In contrast to those whose needs are not met, athletes who feel secure tend to have: an appreciation of their ability to cope with challenges (mastery); a sense of their own value (self-worth); an awareness of their independence and ability to make meaningful choices (autonomy); a capability for close relationships (intimacy) and integration within a group (belonging); and, a sense of purpose in their lives. Such individuals can function without being distracted by their own unmet needs, and they are better equipped to function effectively and respond more openly to others.

OBJECTIVES

After reading this chapter you should be able to:

1. Identify and describe basic psychological needs of athletes;
2. Recognize how athletes' basic psychological needs are satisfied;
3. Understand the relationship between athletes' needs and wants;
4. Describe the consequences of athletes' unmet needs;
5. Understand the concept of acquired needs for athletes; and
6. Recognize the importance of self-awareness.

UNDERSTSANDING BASIC CONCEPTS

Understanding athletes' basic psychological needs begins with identifying them and defining what they mean. A brief description of the key needs that this chapter will focus on is as follows: (a) *security*: the importance of feeling safe and not preoccupied with imminent danger; (b) *identity*: a clear sense of yourself and who you are; (c) *autonomy*: being in charge of yourself, independent, and able to make choices; (d) *self-worth*: recognition of your own value and importance; (e) *self-acceptance*: ability to acknowledge your shortcomings without self-criticism; (f) *mastery*: a sense of your competence and ability to successfully meet challenges; (g) *intimacy*: a longing to have relationships with closeness, trust, and mutual acceptance; (h) *belonging*: being an integral part of a group and connected to others; and (i) *meaning/purpose*: being aware and dedicated to something worthwhile beyond yourself.

THE CONCEPT OF BASIC AND ACQUIRED NEEDS

When basic psychological needs are not met, and direct satisfaction is blocked or not available, people might depend on dysfunctional solutions to satisfy these deficits. Basic needs may then change into 'acquired needs', or attempts to compensate for unmet basic needs, which can sometimes create their own set of problems. The following table illustrates what may happen when these attempts are themselves the source of problems. The ideas underlying this perspective derive from the strategic, interactional approaches from family systems research centers (Watzlawick, Weakland, & Fisch, 1974).

These basic and acquired needs are expanded on in the paragraphs just below. Importantly, they should be distinguished from the place in which they are often seen (or achieved) in a sporting context – i.e., competitive arenas. Particularly in sport, *competitiveness* may be deemed a basic need by some individuals. Thus, it is mentioned in this chapter to clarify and highlight that competitiveness is not a basic need, but instead it should be recognized as an opportunity for athletes to get their basic needs met, such as autonomy, mastery, and belonging.

Table 1. *Basic needs and their (potential) corresponding acquired needs.*

Basic needs (modified from Maslow)	**Acquired needs** (solution is problem)
Safety and security	Control/dominate (*or the opposite*)
Self-worth	Placate/seek approval (*or the opposite*)
Self-acceptance	Criticize/judge/disapprove (self or others)
Autonomy	Dependency/defiance/rebellion
Mastery	Avoidance/pessimism
Relationship/intimacy	Objectification of others/partners
Belonging (group/cause)	Withdraw/join faction
Meaning/purpose	Addiction/hedonism

When the need for safety and security has not been met during psychological development, an uncertainty clouds all areas of functioning, including work, play, and relationships. This can lead to a persistent undercurrent of anxiety, with an internal turmoil that seeks an external solution, and may result in attempts to control other athletes, situations, or events. This pattern of behavior may be called a 'need to control', but – like competitiveness – is not actually a true need. Rather, it is behavior that has an urgency driven by the unmet need for security. An alternative coping mechanism might be for an individual to manipulate others to assume responsibility for what is the individual's own behavior. For athletes, both approaches would cause problems, resulting in either conflict with team members, or lack of confidence about their own decisions and performance.

Similarly, a lack of self-worth and self-esteem might lead to placating behavior and a constant 'need' to seek the coach's approval; or the opposite might occur, such as inflating oneself by boasting or putting others down. The absence of self-acceptance can lead to being self-critical and judgmental about one's skill, effort, or performance. The damage done by self-criticism includes lack of self-confidence, diminished self-worth, and self-punitive behavior. These feelings and actions can lead to overtraining and burnout in athletes. Alternatively, a lack of self-acceptance can manifest itself as repeated disapproval of others' behavior, which can create conflict within a team and/or with coaches.

Athletes who do not have a sense of their own independence or their ability to make choices (autonomy) may also become too dependent on coaches or teammates. And those who believe they cannot cope with difficult challenges (mastery) might avoid them by not exerting sufficient effort and not practicing conscientiously. For those who have difficulty developing and maintaining intimate relationships, the result might be abuse of partners or treating many partners as objects. This sort of behavior may spill over into athletes' training and competition arenas (e.g., with training partners or other competitors).

Although many athletes are members of teams, some do not have a real sense of belonging or connection to others. As a result, they may withdraw from full participation and feel isolated. Their withdrawal is an attempt to cope with the feelings of not belonging, but unfortunately this contributes to the very isolation the athlete is trying to avoid.

Somewhat related to the feeling of belonging is the importance of having a sense of meaning and purpose in life - something that is larger than oneself and goes beyond personal issues. Athletes whose lives have meaning only in sport, whose whole identity is about being an athlete, and whose main purpose in life is sport participation, may experience an emptiness inside themselves even when involved in sport. In seeking to avoid or fill this emptiness, they may turn to alcohol, drugs, or a hedonistic way of life. For these athletes, when they are faced with the ending of their sport experience, the transition to other careers or activities may be quite difficult (Pearson & Petitpas, 1990).

NEEDS AND WANTS

Needs are essential elements of psychological well-being. Wants are the main channel for fulfillment of needs. Therefore, a thorough discussion of wants is included in this chapter as they apply to the athletic domain. If we consistently don't get what we want, our needs may not be satisfied. And if we don't get what we need, we may *want* (lack) a lot. Eric Hoffer (1952), a philosopher and writer, believed that you can never get enough of what you don't really want; i.e., substitute gratification does not satisfy our needs. For example, if an athlete needs to feel a sense of mastery in their sport, then no amount of food or drink will satisfy their actual need.

The sporting environment provides several opportunities for athletes to be reminded that what they want (personal best or an Olympic medal) can often be what they don't have. For successful athletes, most of what they have achieved is the result of their wanting something and being able to get it (often through hard work and years of training). But sometimes when individuals achieve their wants or goals, they frequently lose touch with wanting the very things that they spent years focused on obtaining. When they no longer want the same things, athletes can usually discard the respective want or goal and move on to another, as some other want will usually present itself (e.g., from initially just 'making the team', to 'being the highest goal-scorer').

In sport and other domains, the word 'need' is often used to exert more influence on others to give us what we want. Everything we do is connected to something we want. That does not necessarily mean we will enjoy the activity we choose; but if an important result is sought, we may choose the less pleasant behavior. For example, if an athlete is invited to a party the night before an important game, he or she may prefer to party rather than to stay at home to rest. However, the athlete may choose to stay at home because being ready for the big game is more important than the party. This has been called a 'priority of wants' (Giges, 1996).

This principle also leads to understanding that there are no 'have to' behaviors. Our decisions about what we do comes from whatever wants are most important to us. If athletes lose sight of this, their decisions and actions will seem like things they *have to* do. For example, the following dialogue represents a discussion between an athlete and a sport psychologist regarding the athlete's perceived 'have to' dilemma.

Athlete: I 'have to' go to practice.

Sport psychologist: No, you don't.

Athlete: What do you mean, "No, I don't"? If I don't go to practice, then I won't know the plays.

Sport psychologist: So, you won't know the plays...

Athlete: Right. If I don't know the plays, then I'll be benched.

Sport psychologist: OK, so, you'll be benched...

Athlete: Again, "So"? If I'm benched, then I won't get to play.

Sport psychologist: OK...

Athlete: I don't want to be benched. I want to play!

Sport psychologist: Oh, now I understand. You want to play, and a way to do that and not be benched is to know the plays, and a great way to do that is to go to practice. So you don't "have to" go to practice, but going to practice is a great way to help you get what you want.

The point is slightly overstated here to highlight this perspective is not just a difference in semantics. It actually affects the quality of peoples' lives because it reflects their approach to tasks as well as their perceptions about them. Individuals are ultimately able to decide what they do (autonomy); i.e., they are in charge of themselves, rather than being the victim of outside pressure. Even when someone is strongly influenced by 'shoulds', there are underlying wants, such as avoiding guilt, criticism, disapproval, reprimand, or rejection. Everything that individuals do is indeed connected to something they want.

In the context of sport, it is important to recognize that there may be several possible reasons for athletes being unclear about what they want. The more that sport psychology consultants understand about the reasons why athletes lack clarity about what is wanted, the better the support that can be provided to that individual. Some reasons for lack of clarity include that athletes may have:

- given up their first choice (e.g., if they can't achieve the gold medal that they really want, they don't want anything else);
- conflicting wants (e.g., two opposite wants – such as *performing well in the next-day's competition* and *partying with friends the night before* – which are so close to being equal, that athletes may not know which they want more). In these instances, what they choose to do indicates their preference in the moment, even if they are not aware of what they want.

- discounted the importance of what they want (e.g., if their coach made them feel that their wants don't matter, they may lose touch with what they want).
- feared criticism or judgment for being 'selfish' if they say what they want, and so in time they learn not to say it directly (e.g., a runner may not want to tell the coach that they would prefer to focus on their individual event rather than that plus a team relay event, and so instead tells the coach they don't get on with members of the relay team in order to avoid running the relay).
- thought they didn't deserve what they wanted, hence were reluctant to ask for it. This may (un-/consciously) lead to attempts to justify getting what they want without asking for it. For example, if a married athlete wants a night out with friends instead of staying at home, an argument may be provoked that leads to, "That's it, I'm going out!" This feeling of being justified avoids feeling guilty.
- uncertainty about what to do next. For instance, after a change in sporting status (such as career transition or termination), there may be a period where athletes struggle to find new interests or excitement.

Some athletes are clear about what they want to achieve, but for a variety of reasons they may not succeed. When that happens, the emotional experience will depend on the meaning the individual has attached to that performance or outcome. If the intended want was not deemed very important by the athlete, then it may only cause minor disappointment. But if it was considered highly important, then not getting it may trigger hurt, anger, or fear. For example, athletes may feel hurt if they interpret that they are not valued by their coach; anger if they judge the opponent as selfish or cruel; or fear if they think they might never achieve the level of performance that they want.

NEEDS AND EMOTIONS

When needs are satisfied, positive emotions will most likely be present. We can be more fully present, peaceful and relaxed, interested in and more responsive to others, curious about our environment, ready to take on new challenges, and able to enjoy our activities and relationships. When needs are not met, we are likely to feel unhappy, anxious, discouraged, depressed, and chronically angry. If the latter is true, there are three choices that individuals can make: (1) do nothing; (2) get involved in a dysfunction solution; or (3) pursue satisfaction in a healthy way. If athletes choose to do nothing, it may lead to increased feelings of restlessness, uneasiness, frustration, and dissatisfaction – with themselves and others, and their personal and sporting lives. The consequences of dysfunctional solutions were discussed in the section above on acquired needs (e.g., dependency, withdrawal, avoidance). The third option is likely to yield the best overall outcome – including the presence of positive emotions – but pursuing satisfaction of needs requires self-awareness, openness to change, and new behavior, and can be quite a challenging road for many athletes/individuals to follow.

POSITIVE EMOTIONS

Sport psychology consultants and researchers are often concerned with the role of emotions in sport. Knowing about emotions and the unique influence they have on thoughts and behavior provides practitioners and researchers with valuable insights to help athletes perform better in sport settings, as well as enjoy the processes and outcomes of this involvement. In this section, the way that positive emotions function within sport psychology consultations will be explained. It is important to note that emotions should not be solely categorized as either positive or negative. Also, it is useful to understand that emotions serve particular functions, and although these functions may have changed over time they have retained their usefulness from our ancestral past to present day circumstances.

To appreciate the value of emotions in sport, we can consider how sport would be without them; for example, no smiling, no crying, no laughing, no hope, no expectation, and no disappointment. This portrayal of sport is not how we typically think of it, as sporting environments are typically associated with quite contrasting emotions such as sadness and happiness, pride and shame, hope and despair. When consulting with athletes in professional practice, practitioners need to balance their own emotional experiences in that respective context, whilst retaining a healthy perspective for the client's behavior, sensation, cognitions, relationships, and environment. For instance, some athletes endeavor to feel hopeful and inspired because their current (poor) condition has drained the energy they once had to train and compete.

The experience of other athletes presents explicit examples of what is possible despite the perceived impossibility of the current situation. Here is an example: In 1954, the Australian runner, John Landy, ran the mile event on three occasions, each time at 4 minutes and 2 seconds, and he reflected, "Two little seconds are not much, but when you're on the track those fifteen yards seem solid and impenetrable, like a cement wall" (Bannister, 2004, p. vii). Through his medical studies, Roger Bannister knew that this could not be true. And on a wet and windy day in May 1954, helped by his friends Chris Chataway and Chris Brasher, he ran the first sub-four minute mile.

Such sensational anecdotes are great examples of situations in sport where there are diverse emotions, and they offer at least three functions when working with athletes. First, they serve as examples to dispute an athlete's thoughts and feelings about the present situation and probabilities about the future. Second, they present a constructive discussion for the client and sport psychology consultant to explore how emotions debilitate but also facilitate performance and well-being. In this instance, we might explore how an athlete's psychological needs are satisfied or frustrated within sport. Finally, we examine the traits of emotional thinking (e.g., jumping to an opinion, thinking in 'black and white', catastrophic impressions, and irrational judgments) and logical thinking (e.g., rational, evidence-based, maintaining context and perspective), in particular, their roles for our survival and self-fulfillment (Peters, 2012).

Sport scientists seek to unravel the mystery of performance excellence with objective explanations. Emotions, whether positively-valenced or negatively-valenced, filter through our mental lives and by knowing and accepting their worth, we appreciate their functions more obviously (McNulty & Fincham, 2012). This perspective emphasizes that the balance of emotions suitable for performance excellence is different to those for psychological well-being. The emotional mix necessary for performance excellence might contrast with the emotional mix to make new friends. For example, higher levels of anger might profit a performer in combative sport but this level of anger in a social setting is unnecessary (and not appropriate).

Consultations with athletes, coaches, and parents and, thus, the psychological interventions that are developed will all contain references to emotion. Often, though not always, negatively-valenced emotions can be heard in the client's narrative, and so efforts by the sport psychology consultant are aimed at understanding this experience and dealing with the effects of such emotions. Rather than just labeling emotions (and psychological traits and processes) as positive or negative, it seems more sensible to adopt a contextual view of emotions (and psychological traits and processes). In other words, we can understand why we feel as we do in particular surroundings but recognize that the circumstances might change over time. Knowing why we feel happy, sad, or anxious in different contexts can present opportunities for us to choose how we could (prefer to) think and feel in that context in future. For instance, research has demonstrated that interpreting somatic sensations of unwanted anxiety in functional terms aids performance in exams (Jamieson, Mendes, Blackstock, & Schmader, 2010). In sport, early research has similarly shown that athletes can be taught to view their anxiety as facilitative (Hanton & Jones, 1999).

Following this line of thinking, the pursuit of positively-valenced emotions seems obvious if these emotions (e.g., happiness, excitement, enjoyment) serve an advantage in performance settings or psychological well-being. Consultants should be aware of the athlete's personality, sport, gender, and competitive setting to maintain a contextual grip on the information they gather. The ultimate objective is to recognize the emotional needs of each individual within their environment, without trying to apply a predetermined emotional formula for success. For instance, if a golfer smiles after missing a three-foot putt for birdie, we might suggest he does not care about his putting; however, we can only speculate about what he is thinking and feeling about that missed birdie putt. He might be smiling because he knows he cannot undo what he has done or he trusted the line of his putt but the ball did not drop into the hole. To provide the best service to athletes, consultants must accept that there may be several possibilities for athletes' emotional experiences, so it is important to be open-minded when interpreting them.

As suggested above, emotions have survived human evolution because they have retained purpose in our lives and are functional in different settings (e.g., sport, social, family, organizational). However, emotions can be dysfunctional when they prevent us from reaching constructive goals. When we acknowledge, accept, and learn from our emotional experiences, the probability to function productively within and outside sport grows. This enlightenment means that consultants can apply the most suitable resources to help athletes when their emotions are harmful to them. The mechanics of this process might involve the sport psychology consultant inspecting what triggered a particular emotion (e.g., excitement, anger), and establishing how the athlete reacted to and/or dealt with it. This assessment allows the athlete to understand how they're currently thinking and behaving, and so increases the chance that they will make constructive adjustments in future. The ultimate aim is to increase the athletes' self-awareness and ability to reflect on past experiences in order to promote positive emotions and behaviors.

NEEDS AND BEHAVIORS

Self-awareness paves the way to a fuller knowledge of ourselves, a better ability to observe what we need and don't need, and an opportunity for change. We usually become aware of a problem behavior after it occurs. With repetition of this experience, awareness begins to occur earlier and may even occur during the behavior. Eventually, the awareness may occur before the actual behavior, and when this happens, a choice can be made to behave differently. This becomes an opportunity for change (Giges, 1996).

Consider athletes who have low self-esteem because of a strong internal critic. To help them build a sense of their own worth may require decreasing the impact of the self-criticism. Trying to contradict the self-criticism and convince themselves that they are worthwhile rarely has much impact. What sometimes is helpful is allowing some uncertainty to enter the equation, e.g., "Maybe I'm not worthless." Behaviors that would encourage this process and build self-worth would include treating themselves as if they are already worthwhile, such as self-nurturing, self-encouragement, self-support, and self-appreciation. Learning these behaviors might require the support of a clinical or educational sport psychologist.

NEEDS AND SPORT PSYCHOLOGY CONSULTATION

In sport psychology consultation, the relationship between the consultant and the athlete is an important element for understanding the consultative process (Petitpas, Giges, & Danish, 1999). Therefore, it is useful to know something about the origins of a consultant's professional training, to help appreciate what he or she brings to the session. A description of the background and approach of the first author's work is included here to assist readers in understanding its different elements.

The beginning of the above specified work was in medical research, where the emphasis was on the importance of careful observation and evaluation, with the aim toward inquiring about how something worked and what happened that made a difference. What followed, and formed the theoretical foundations of the consultative work, were the study and practice of four major psychological systems: psychodynamic theory, gestalt therapy, transactional analysis, and cognitive therapy. A brief description of each framework is provided below to help understand the range of approaches that can be used when working with clients to address their needs.

The first model, psychodynamic theory, is considered the oldest ("grandfather") of theoretical approaches, and its roots can be traced to Freudian psychoanalysis, of which it is most commonly associated (Hill, 2001). Aspects of this approach have also been developed and adopted into more recent models used by practitioners. This model emphasizes the following principles: (a) all behavior has meaning; (b) past events and unconscious processes influence present functioning; and (c) the relationship between the practitioner and the client is a key element in the work of the consultation process.

In contrast, gestalt therapy highlights the significance of awareness and present experience – or, how the athlete functions in the 'here and now' and the existence of polarities in the same individual (opposite wants, opposite feelings, and opposite thoughts).

"In gestalt therapy, the term 'organismic self-regulation' refers to an internal psychological process consisting of a continuing flow of needs and satisfactions. Specifically, when a need emerges into the foreground of our experience, it can either be satisfied or interrupted. If it is satisfied, it then recedes into the background, allowing another need to emerge. This process continues unless it is interrupted by a troubling thought, an uncomfortable feeling, conflicting desires, or external influences. When this happens, the need remains unsatisfied and interferes with the flow and with optimal functioning until the interruption is removed" (Giges, Petitpas, & Vernacchia, 2004, p. 438).

The third approach, transactional analysis, describes the 'child' and 'parent' within, and their influence on internal dialogue, communication, and relationships. There are two types of child according to this approach: (1) the 'natural child' who is the spontaneous, intuitive, creative, playful part; and (2) the 'adapted child' who is the compliant/defiant, placating, submissive/rebellious part who grows in response to parental and societal demands. Similarly, there are two categories of 'parent': (1) the 'nurturing parent' who supports, nourishes, and protects the child; and (2) the 'critical parent' who reprimands, judges, criticizes the child, and imposes all the 'shoulds'.

The final approach, cognitive therapy, highlights thinking or cognition as the major determinant of feelings and behavior. Thus, faulty thinking or irrational beliefs, become the source of significant problems in communication and relationships (Ellis, 1993). Practitioners who apply this approach operate on the premise that the individual's (internal) interpretation of an event or situation is more powerful than the (external) stimulus itself.

Philosophical Perspective

The culmination and synthesis of the above views represents several years of training, research, and professional practice. These relevant experiences will be unique for each sport psychology consultant, and it would be difficult to overstate the value of reflecting on those experiences as part of the process for helping practitioners to understand the needs of their clients and athletes. The below quote reflects a summarizing of the approaches, training, research, and experiences referred to above:

"Although originally trained as a clinician, with a background in medical research, I've come to see myself more as an educator. This change involved a shift from the medical model of illness and disease to a growth and development model, in which problems are seen as the result of learned thinking patterns. The focus of my work with athletes and others is to help them change those patterns that contribute to distressed feelings or troublesome behavior, and to remove the barriers to their optimal functioning. This focus is primarily on present experience, based on the hypothesis that past negative experiences might recede into the background, were it not for the fact that present patterns of thinking and feeling keep them in the foreground. The language used by the person is followed very closely, because it not only expresses present thoughts and feelings, but also contributes to their development. I believe that what we learned in the past can be changed by what we learn in the present" (Giges, 2010).

A fundamental principle in helping others is that sport psychology consultants must be able to recognize their own needs well enough to assure that the work they do primarily addresses the needs and goals of athletes rather than their own. Mark Young (1998) expressed the idea that the journey of learning the art of helping others is a personal one that requires practitioners to know themselves as they learn to help others. Although our needs are not usually in our everyday awareness, there are many questions we can ask ourselves to increase our awareness of what we feel, want, and do. Answers to such questions will give important information about what our needs are and whether they are being met.

Needs Assessment

With this self-awareness, what can we, as sport psychology practitioners, do to help athletes satisfy their needs? This process begins by conducting a comprehensive needs assessment. The consultant's tools to accomplish this assessment are observation, inquiry, intuition, and experience. We can use these tools to explore several areas of an athlete's function, including work, recreation, relationships, patterns of thinking and behaving, how wants and feelings are handled, and whether needs are being met. Important questions to consider include: (1) What needs are not being sufficiently attended to?; (2) What attempts are being made to satisfy those needs?; and (3) What's in the way of the attempts being successful? When we have some information about these areas and answers to these questions, we will have some ideas about where to focus the work, and begin to address the deficiency.

One of the basic assumptions of this approach is that healing would take place naturally if it wasn't the case that *something is interfering.* Therefore, the direction of the work is to remove the barrier or diminish its impact on the athlete's performance or well-being. Although beyond the scope of this chapter, a detailed discussion of this approach can be found in the chapter, "Removing psychological barriers: Clearing the way" (Giges, 2000). The main elements of the process involve identifying the barriers, exploring their meaning and impact, and initiating change. The barriers may be grouped according to whether they are cognitive, affective, behavioral, or conative (pertaining to wants or desires). They can be identified by carefully listening to the language of the athlete, observing the tone of voice, rate of speech, facial expressions, gestures, or posture. The following are some examples of barriers to athletes' needs being met according to each category: (a) *cognitive*: self-criticism, self-doubt, and unrealistic expectations; (b) *affective*: anxiety, shame, and hurt feelings; (c) *behavioral*: overtraining, impulsiveness, and giving up; and (d) *conative*: low motivation, loss of interest, and conflicting wants.

Once the needs assessment is conducted, athletes are generally unclear about how to begin the process of removing barriers and meeting their needs. Thus, a key role of the sport psychology consultant is to help athletes with this process, which starts with assisting them to initiate change. Two important principles in helping people initiate change are: 1) a change in awareness is often the first step in changing, even before behavior change occurs, and this can be accomplished at the beginning of the work; and 2) beginning change demonstrates the ability to change, and serves as a confidence builder for further change. When athletes engage with this process with the guidance of the sport psychologist, it means they can progress past their barriers, with the objective of ensuring their needs (and perhaps wants) are fulfilled.

CONCLUSION

Athletes' needs and wants form an integral part of their existence, and so meeting these needs is paramount to their growth as individuals and competitors. Working with sport psychology consultants, athletes can learn to recognize what their needs are, and to understand the influence of needs on performance. In order to help athletes to fulfill their potential, it is important to ensure that their identified needs are met, that they can achieve their goals in the context of positive emotion, and ultimately that they learn to self-regulate by maintaining awareness of current needs.

LEARNING AIDS

1. Explain the importance of psychological needs.

    Psychological needs are fundamental requirements of personal growth, health, and well-being. At any stage of development and in any type of activity, these elements exist and influence our functioning.

2. Summarize the differences between basic needs and acquired needs.

    Basic needs consist of the need for security, autonomy, identity, self-worth, mastery, intimacy, belonging, and a sense of meaning or purpose in life. Acquired needs are not really needs, but rather dysfunctional attempts to compensate for the deficiency when basic needs are not met.

3. Discuss how you might help an athlete with a "have to" dilemma.

    Everything we do is connected to something we want. When athletes are not aware of their wants, they may think they 'have to' do something. Helping them become more aware of their underlying wants allows them to realize they have a choice, and thus feel less pressured or victimized.

4. Identify some reasons that athletes might not know what they want.

They may have given up their first choice, have conflicting wants, discounted the importance of what they want, feared criticism for focusing on their want, or not felt deserving of saying what they want.

REVIEW QUESTIONS

1. What are some basic psychological needs?

2. What are some consequences of unmet needs?

3. How are needs satisfied in everyday life?

4. What is meant by acquired needs?

5. What is the relationship between wants and needs?

EXERCISES

These exercises can be used by sport psychology students, beginning consultants, and experienced practitioners to increase their self-awareness.

1. Awareness of Needs: In answering the following questions, spend at least 5 minutes contemplating each answer. Go well beyond your first response. If nothing comes to mind after your first response, allow time for something to come up that you might not have thought about before. Sometimes, repeating the question is useful if no answer comes to mind.

Which basic psychological needs are you aware of? Review this list and select all that apply.

Security Autonomy Identity Self-worth

Mastery Intimacy Belonging Meaning or purpose in life

For needs that you are aware of, answer the following questions:

Which needs are you comfortable with?
Which needs are you uncomfortable with?
What is the nature of that discomfort?
What, if anything, will you do about that discomfort?
Which needs are not currently being satisfied?
What are you reactions (thoughts, feelings, wants, behavior) to that awareness?
What, if anything, do you plan to do about satisfying that need?
Describe what barriers you anticipate in doing that?
What might you do to remove or avoid those barriers?
Read the instructions for Part I(a) above. Review the list of basic psychological needs.
Which needs are you <u>not</u> aware of? Select all that apply. For needs that you are not aware of, answer the following questions:
What are your reactions (thoughts, feelings, wants, and behaviors) to not being aware?
What might account for you not being aware?
Is not being aware something you want to change?
If yes, what might be a beginning to making that change? (This might take more time.)
Is that something you think you will do? If not, what might be in the way of doing it?
If you don't want to change not being aware, what might account for that choice?
What is your reaction to making the choice to remain unaware?
Think of three people who are important to you. For each of them, which needs do you think are not being satisfied?

For each of them, what do you see or hear that accounts for your opinions?

2. Self-Reflection. For each question, look for more than one answer.

a. What are your main sources of enjoyment or satisfaction?
b. What gives you good feelings about yourself?
c. What do you want that you are not currently getting?
d. What need would be served if you got what you want?
e. What are your reactions (thoughts, feelings, wants, behaviors) to not getting it?
f. What might give you bad feelings about yourself?
g. What leads to your feeling guilty?
h. What leads to your feeling hurt?
i. What do you believe is the explanation of your feeling?
j. What leads to your feeling embarrassed?
k. What leads to your feeling ashamed?
l. What do you fear?
m. What do you pretend?
n. Which questions were uncomfortable to answer?
o. What might account for the discomfort?

3. Needs and Activities.

Make a detailed list of your activities for a typical day in your life. Arrange the activities in time segments of 1-2 hours each.

For each time segment, identify one or more basic needs that are being addressed.

Repeat step 1 for what would be an "ideal" day in your life.

For each time segment, identify one or more basic needs that are being addressed.

Compare the typical day with the ideal day.

Identify changes you want to make in the typical day to bring it closer to an ideal day.

Describe what barriers you anticipate to initiating those changes.

Consider what you might do to remove or avoid the barriers.

ADDITIONAL READINGS

Andersen, M. B. (Ed.). (2005). *Sport Psychology in Practice.* Champaign, IL: Human Kinetics.

Van Raalte, J. L. & Brewer, B.W. (Eds.). (2014). *Exploring sport and exercise psychology* (3rd ed.), Washington, DC: American Psychological Association.

REFERENCES

Bannister, R. (2004). *The first four minutes.* Gloucestershire, UK: The History Press,

Beck, A. T. (1967). *Depression: Clinical, experimental, and theoretical aspects.* New York: Hoeber

Berne, E. (1961). *Transactional analysis in psychotherapy.* New York: Grove Press.

Danish, S. J., Petitpas, A. J., & Hale, B. D., (1992). A developmental-educational intervention model in sport psychology. *The Sport Psychologist,* 6, 403-15.

Deci, E. L. (2002). Facilitating autonomous self-regulation through support of basic psychological needs. *Journal of Sport & Exercise Psychology, 24* (Suppl.), S50.

Ellis, A. (1993). Fundamentals of rational-emotive therapy for the 1990s. In W. Dryden & L. Hill (Eds.), *Innovations in rational-emotive therapy.* Newbury Park, CA: Sage Publications.

Erikson, E. (1950). *Childhood and society*. New York: W. W. Norton.

Frankl, V. (1992). *Man's search for meaning: An introduction to logotherapy*. Boston: Beacon Press

Giges, B. (1995). *How People Change.* Keynote address presented at the annual meeting of the Association for Applied Sport Psychology, New Orleans, LA.

Giges, B. (1996). *Self-awareness for sport psychology practitioners.* Workshop presented as part of a Workshop Series on Contemporary Issues in Sport Psychology, Department of Psychology, Springfield College, Springfield MA.

Giges, B. (2000). Removing psychological barriers: Clearing the way. In *Doing Sport Psychology* (pp.17-31), M. B. Andersen, Ed. Champaign, IL: Human Kinetics.

Giges, B. (2010). Retrieved from the website *http://www.burtgiges.com/Home_Page.php*

Giges, B., Petitpas, A. J., & Vernacchia, R. A. (2004). Helping coaches meet their own needs: Challenges for the sport psychology consultant. *The Sport Psychologist*, December, 18, 4, 430-44.

Hanton, S., & Jones, G. (1999). The effects of a multimodal intervention program on performers. II. Training the butterflies to fly in formation. *The Sport Psychologist, 13,* 22-41.

Hill, K. L. (2001). *Frameworks for sport psychologists: Enhancing sport performance*. Champaign, IL: Human Kinetics.

Hoffer, E. (1952). *The Ordeal of Change.* New York: Harper & Row.

Jamieson, J. P., Mendes, W. B., Blackstock, E., & Schmader, T. (2010). Turning the knots in your stomach into bows: Reappraising arousal improves performance on the GRE. *Journal of Experimental Social Psychology, 46,* 208-212.

Maslow, A. (1987). *Motivation and personality* (3 rd ed.). New York: Harper & Row

McNulty, J. K., & Fincham, F. D. (2012). Beyond positive psychology? Toward a contextual view of psychological processes and well-being. *American Psychologist, 67,* 101-110.

Pearson, R., & Petitpas, A. (1990). Transition of athletes: Pitfalls and prevention. *Journal of Counseling and Development, 69,* 7-10.

Perls, F., Hefferline, R. F., & Goodman, P. (1951). *Gestalt therapy: Excitement and growth in the human personality.* New York: Dell.

Petitpas, A. J., Giges, B., & Danish, S. J. (1999). The Sport psychologist-athlete relationship: Implications for training. *The Sport Psychologist, September, 13,* 3, 344-57.

Watzlawick, P., Weakland, J. H., Fisch, R. (1974). *Change: Principles of problem formation and problem resolution.* New York: W. W. Norton.

Young, M., E. (1998). *Learning the art of helping: Building blocks and techniques.* Columbus, OH: Merrill Publishing.

Reprinted, with permission, from Doing Sport Psychology (2000), edited by Mark B. Anderson (Champaign, IL: © Human Kinetics), 17-33.

REMOVING PSYCHOLOGICAL BARRIERS: CLEARING THE WAY

Burt Giges
Springfield College and Westchester Track Club

In sport psychology, performance enhancement generally refers to helping athletes improve, using a variety of methods or techniques referred to as "psychological skills training" or "mental training." These techniques include goal-setting, relaxation, imagery, self-talk, concentration, and others (Cox, 1994; Nideffer, 1985; Orlick, 1986; Van Raalte & Brewer, 1996; Weinberg & Gould, 1995; Williams, 1998). In this chapter, I will describe an alternative approach to performance enhancement that identifies and aims to remove psychological barriers to performance excellence (Giges, 1997). This approach represents a synthesis of different disciplines learned in the course of my professional development. To give in-depth meaning to this synthesis, I will summarize my philosophical perspective, and identify the guiding principles and focus in my work. Examples of the method, selected from dialogues with athletes and graduate students, will then be presented.

PHILOSOPHICAL PERSPECTIVE

What we do as practitioners comes in large part from our training. From my medical research background, I learned the importance of careful observation and evaluation--to inquire how something worked and what happened that made a difference. From psychoanalytic theory, I gained an understanding of the principle that all behavior has meaning, that past events and unconscious processes influence present functioning, and that the working alliance between the practitioner and the client occupies a central role (Greenson, 1967; Munroe, 1955). From gestalt therapy, I developed an appreciation of the significance of awareness, responsibility, and present experience--how the athlete is functioning in the "here and now" (Perls, 1969). From transactional analysis, I discovered the child and parent within, and their influence on internal dialogue and on communication (Berne, 1961). Cognitive therapy taught me to emphasize thinking as the major determinant of feelings and behavior (Beck, 1967), and I regard feelings (affect) as the important mediator between thinking and behavior (Giges, 1995).

Although originally trained as a clinician, I gradually became more of an educator working with a growth and development model (Erikson, 1950; Danish, Petitpas, & Hale, 1992), in which problems are viewed as the result of learning, rather than with the medical model of psychotherapy. The growth model came into prominence as part of the human potential movement in the 1960s, from the seminal work of Abraham Maslow (1954) and other founding contributors to humanistic psychology (e.g., Carl Rogers, Gordon Allport, James Bugental). The growth model includes focusing on developing one's potential, giving prominence to here-and- now experience, encouraging risk-taking behavior, and highlighting choices and responsibility. A basic assumption of the model, as applied in sport psychology, is that athletes inherently have the capacity for optimal functioning, and would be able to do so if nothing were in the way. Removing psychological barriers is an approach that helps release potential and can be seen as "clearing the way." The medical model, in contrast, implies that problems are a result of sickness or disease, and that something is "wrong" with the patient. Helping the patient, therefore, would require interventions by an expert to correct or alleviate the defect or illness.

For me, the greatest challenge in working in sport psychology was the shift from the clinical perspective to the educational one. The most useful idea in making this transition was the concept of psychological barriers to optimal functioning rather than the emphasis on deficits and illness (Giges, 1996a). With this change, concentrating on the present became more important than the past, and opened new possibilities for effective interventions. I had learned from my training that for significant change to occur, it was necessary to have long-term contact. As I began to explore alternatives, I found this idea too restrictive. Working with an athlete about performance is not the same as psychodynamic psychotherapy (Giges, 1996b). In the process of removing psychological barriers, transference, resistance, and early childhood experiences (classic psychoanalytic concerns) are not usually the focus of the work (Giges, 1998). Present functioning and here-and-now experience are the starting points of intervention.

GUIDING PRINCIPLES

In the process of synthesizing the several influences on my present work, there are three guiding principles that help me integrate the concepts and apply them in consultation with athletes: (a) examining present psychological experience, (b) listening carefully to the athlete's language, and (c) using "entry points" to help remove psychological barriers.

Psychological experience

Past negative experiences (a psychodynamic factor)_might recede into the background of our inner world (a gestalt therapy concept), were it not for present thinking patterns that keep them in the foreground (a cognitive therapy principle). For example, past parental ridicule of a young athlete's performance can exert a detrimental influence if the athlete continues an internal dialogue of self-ridicule in the present. This dialogue, which began in the past, now takes place in the present between the critical parent and the child within (a transactional analysis concept), and represents a psychological barrier to optimal functioning. I have found that focusing on removing such present barriers, in this case self-ridicule, has been an effective method in helping athletes improve their performance.

Present psychological experience includes thoughts, feelings, needs, wants, and behavior. Each of these, in turn, consists of many specifics. Thoughts include ideas, opinions, judgments, decisions, and speculations, as well as memories of past experience. Feelings represent the emotional part of an experience, such as fear, anger, sadness, joy, shame, guilt, and embarrassment. Needs are the basic elements of psychological growth, and are broad and enduring (Maslow, 1954). Some examples are the need for safety and security, for self-worth and self-acceptance, and for autonomy and mastery (Maslow, 1962). Others are the needs for belonging, meaning, and purpose (Frankl, 1992), and for intimacy and relationship (Erikson, 1950). Wants pertain to issues of striving or desire, and are the specific ways to meet underlying needs. For example, wanting to do well in competition would help meet the needs for mastery or for self-acceptance. Behavior is the physical bridge between our inner experience and the outer world, and between ourselves and others. Fully understanding an athlete's experience, therefore, involves knowing something about each component of psychological experience, and may be accomplished by exploring feelings when thoughts are described, inquiring about thoughts after feelings are expressed, and in both instances listening for the athlete's wants.

Listening

Words can be clues to inner experience, revealing hidden thoughts, feelings, or wants. We can, therefore, use words in much the same way as we use non-verbal messages, such as voice tone, rate and volume of speech, facial expressions, and body positions or movements, to help understand athletes.

Words, however, not only express experience, they also contribute to it, operating as a feedback loop. An example would be athletes who call themselves "losers." They not only reveal their dissatisfaction and unhappiness, they also reinforce their sense of impotence and undermine their self-confidence. Words that are not spoken can be as meaningful as those that are. A useful clue to something that is avoided is the unanswered question. Not answering a question may indicate an underlying fear, guilt, embarrassment, shame, or other unpleasant feeling or thought.

Entry Points

In describing their experiences, athletes will often say something that the consultant hears as an opportunity for more in-depth exploration. These "entry points" are openings that can be used to help increase athletes' understanding of their experience, such as an unexpressed feeling, an unrecognized want, or an underlying judgment. They allow the consultant to follow the athlete's discussion, and then lead her or him into unexplored areas. For example, if an athlete is describing performance and mentions that he or she does better in practice than in competition, this would be an opportunity to explore the significance of that experience more fully.

REMOVING PSYCHOLOGICAL BARRIERS

Danish, Petitpas, and Hale (1992) have described various roadblocks athletes may encounter in reaching their goals. They stated, "These individuals had to overcome their roadblocks before they were able to work toward their goals. For many, removing the roadblocks became a goal in itself." (p. 409). The process of removing psychological barriers, which is analogous to overcoming roadblocks, involves identifying them, exploring their meaning, and initiating a change that will decrease their impact on athletes.

Identifying Barriers

Psychological barriers include those aspects of athletes' experiences that interfere with the ability to use the talent or skills they have. The barriers may be categorized into the three familiar groups--cognitive, affective, and behavioral, and the one less familiar group--conative (pertaining to issues of striving and desire, i.e., wants). Cognitive barriers include self-criticism, self-doubt, low self-confidence, low self-esteem, unrealistic expectations, and negative thinking patterns. These barriers can be detected in the language used by the athlete, or in facial expressions or gestures. For example, athletes calling themselves "stupid" can undermine self-confidence. Affective barriers might be anxiety, guilt, shame, embarrassment, anger, sadness, disappointment, or hurt feelings. If not directly expressed by the athlete, these feelings often reveal themselves in voice tone, rate of speech, or in bodily gestures or positions. Behavioral barriers could be overtraining, pushing too hard, impulsiveness, giving up, communicating poorly, or other self-defeating behaviors. Examples of conative barriers are low motivation, loss of interest, or conflicting wants between sport and other interests, or between what the athlete wants and what others want. In the course of identifying which barriers are interfering with performance, it is important to be as specific as possible. For example, if an athlete is vague in describing an upset, helping remove that upset may require knowing whether the upset feelings are sadness, anger, fear, shame, or some combination of several feelings. Specificity is preparation for the next step, and that is examining the meaning given to the identified barrier.

Exploring the Meaning

In the process of removing a psychological barrier, it is often necessary to examine the meaning given to it in some detail. This examination could begin, for example, with the question "What would it mean for you to perform poorly?" Examining meaning also involves: (a) describing the content of the barrier (e.g., "I'll never be able to do it," "I'm not good enough"); (b) determining how much power or intensity it has, its impact (e.g., how much of a grip it has on the athlete, how strongly it is believed); (c) considering the context (e.g., whether it is part of a larger issue, such as entitlement, assertiveness, or self-concept); and (d) if necessary, identifying its origin, such as when, how, or where it began, or who might have believed it in the past. This last step may be useful if the previous information is not sufficient to make an effective intervention.

Initiating Change

Having some understanding of the meaning given to the barrier paves the way for initiating a change in that meaning, so as to diminish its impact on the athlete. The purpose of this change is to help athletes alter the habitual patterns that lead to distressful feelings or troublesome behavior. The "entry points" mentioned above may be used to create a shift in the athlete's experience. Examples of ways to initiate change include: (a) exploring behavioral options; (b) helping the athlete recognize "all or none" thinking; (c) identifying the athlete's pessimistic anticipations, such as "what if..."; and (d) comparing reality and fantasy, (i.e., the actual experience with ideas about the experience). These examples are not, of course, unique to this approach. Whatever changes are initiated usually require practice and persistence in order to be maintained and strengthened. As illustrated below, however, some shifts in experience can occur relatively rapidly and can be of lasting benefit.

CASE ILLUSTRATIONS

The following are illustrations of removing psychological barriers, drawn from sessions conducted either in an office setting, or from workshops in sport psychology. As stated in the introduction, sport psychology services are delivered in a variety of settings. Besides holding sessions in my office and conducting workshops, I also deliver service at the sporting venues during practice and competition. Office settings allow for maximum uninterrupted privacy, and at times that is exactly what athlete needs. Field settings allow for interventions in the real world, and are the time for putting what was discussed in the office into practice (literally).

In the Office

The duration of a first session is usually about an hour and a half, and subsequent sessions often last at least an hour. The four examples selected in this section illustrate several psychological barriers commonly seen in consultation with athletes.

An Anxious Young Athlete S. is a high school junior and a member of the swim team. His mother called to ask if I would see him because he was unhappy about his swimming. I saw him for three sessions of 60 to 90 minutes duration. The following excerpts were taken from each session, and were selected to illustrate the problem, how it was approached, and the result.

Session I

B. Your mom told me on the phone you were unhappy about your swimming.
S. Yeah.
B. Would you tell me more about it?
S. I haven't been doing too well.
B. In what way?
S. My times are terrible.
B. Would you fill me in on the details?
S. Whatever I race.
B. What do you mean?
S. It doesn't matter whether it's the 100, the 200, or the 400.

B. Is this happening just in competition?
S. I don't know...I guess. I do better in practice.

His response is an example of an entry point--an opportunity to go beneath the surface for a clue in identifying the barrier, or perhaps removing it. I note that his answers are quite short, and then he waits for the next question. He may be guarded because he feels unsafe or be concerned about how he will sound, or he is demonstrating a passive compliance. At this point I'm not sure if I will be able to help him alter his pattern and become more active in the session.

B. What's different about practice?
S. I don't know

This "unknowing" is a common first response to questions. It often says more about reluctance or even a disinclination to think about an answer, rather than a lack of information. So I persist.
B. Can you recall a recent practice?
S. ...Yeah.
B. Would you describe it to me?
S. What do you want me to say?

His response cautions me not to make indefinite requests. To answer his question with a specific instruction might continue his pattern of short replies followed by waiting for the next question, and not being actively engaged. An unstructured reply, such as, "Whatever you want," invites another "I don't know what to tell you." So I decide to change from a question to a more structured intervention, a guided fantasy, which can be particularly useful in working with what someone remembers or anticipates. Its value is in stimulating the thoughts, feelings, or desires that are part of the event, thereby bringing past or future experience into the present.

B. I would like to ask you to try something using your imagination. Would that be all right?
B. Okay, would you close your eyes for a few moments? ... Now imagine yourself at practice. Can you do that?
S. Yeah...I'm seeing myself at the school pool
B. What's happening?
S. Well, it's noisy.
B. Go on.
S. It smells of chlorine.

Although he's not really talking about swimming yet, he is giving olfactory and auditory confirmation of his imagery, and this response is an indication that he is becoming involved in the process.

B. What's in your head?

Usually I would ask, "What are you thinking?" but it seemed better to be concrete with him because of his previous responses.

S. I'm getting ready.
B. How are you doing that?
S. I'm looking at where I'll dive in.
B. What's going on in your body?

Usually, I would ask "What are you feeling?" but the concrete question seemed to be working.

S. I feel loose, ready to go.
B. Okay, now would you please come back to the room and open your eyes...What did you notice?
S. What do you mean?
B. How were you feeling?
S. I wasn't under any pressure.
B. How come?

S. Well, nobody was expecting anything. I hate it when that happens.
B. What makes pressure bad?
S. I get so tense and anxious. I can't concentrate when that happens. I get afraid I'll do too much, you know, go out too hard, and then not have anything left at the end.

His short responses are changing. Without my having done anything direct to help him change his way of answering questions, he has became more open about expressing himself. This change may represent a beginning trust. The idea of others' expectations may be a clue to removing the barrier of pressure. He may also have a strong internal critic. I continue in the direction of exploring the effect of others' expectations.

B. Let's do another one, okay?
S. Another what?
B. Another imagery with your eyes closed.
S. Okay.

The working alliance is forming; the athlete is engaging in the process, and a "we" is being established (i.e., "Let's do another one"). As the "we" develops, the dialogue becomes more of a two-way conversation with both the athlete and consultant engaged in examining his performance.

B. Close your eyes again. This time imagine you're at a swim meet.
S. Yeah.
B. Tell me what's going on.
S. Okay. I'm at the start of the 100, my first event...I'm very jittery...All I can think about is not letting the coach and my folks down...I'm hoping I don't go out too fast...I wish nobody knew me here. I can't stand people expecting me to do things.
B. Let yourself imagine that nobody knows you.
S. Okay.

B. What are you feeling?
S. I don't know...I guess I don't feel as much pressure [opens his eyes]. Boy, I wish that would happen at a meet.
B. When is your next meet coming up?
S. Actually, I have one coming up this weekend.
B. Do you suppose you could pretend that you don't know anybody when you're there?
S. I could try. Do you think that will help?
B. I think it's worth a try. You might not feel as much pressure.

The psychological barriers at this point were his anxiety and his concern about not living up to others' expectations. It may become necessary to address this latter barrier first before his anxiety could be decreased.

Session II

B. Hi, how did it go?
S. Well, I did pretty well in the first race. Then I did poorly.
B. Let's start with your telling me about the first race.
S. I wasn't too anxious at the start. I was thinking about not going out too fast, and I was able to pace myself during the race so I had something left at the end.
B. Did you pretend you didn't know anybody?
S. Not when I was at the start. I did that before the race.
B. What happened after the first race? [In the meet he had four races.]
S. I was afraid I did too much, that I wouldn't have anything left for the other races. Well, in the next race I did poorly, and then I started to lose confidence. So I thought I better hold back until the last race.
B. What happens when you lose confidence?
S. I get more nervous. Then I get angry at myself for not doing well.
B. What do you say to yourself when you get angry?
S. You're a screw-up! You're no damned good!

There were several barriers to his performing well: his thought that he has to do well, his worry about not living up to others' expectations, his anxiety, his low self-confidence, and his anger. This combination adds to the likelihood of him having a strong internal critic. What helped me decide which to explore was noticing that he was tentative and almost apologetic in talking about most of these issues. In contrast, when expressing his anger, he came alive, and seemed more powerful. Therefore, I decided to use that strength to help change his experience of not swimming well. This change was accomplished by leaving the anger unchallenged, and helping him shift its target. The goal was for the anger to become an ally rather than a barrier.

B. So let me go over what you've told me. When you get anxious you swim poorly. Then you lose confidence. Then you get more anxious, swim poorly again, and get angry at yourself.
S. Yeah, it sounds kind of stupid when I hear you repeat it.

If he had demonstrated more interest in self-examination, I might have commented on his self-critical remark, and discussed the effect it could have on his self-confidence. In this situation, I decided to focus directly on his performance.

B. I think you can put the anger to better use.
S. What do you mean?
B. Imagine that the anger is raw energy that's available to you before a race.
S. Yeah?
B. Maybe you could use it to help you.
S. How?
B. The way some athletes psych themselves up at the start of a race.
S. Like "Damn it, Go! You can do it!" [said with emphasis].
B. How does that feel?
S. Great!

B. Would you be willing to do that at your next race?
S. Sure.

Between sessions, his mother called to tell me he had a very good meet, which he believed was the result of his sessions. I was not clear about why she called, but decided to wait until his next session, rather than go into it with her. I did, however, feel some immediate relief that he had a good meet. The relief I felt was related to my concern about the effectiveness of the previous sessions.

Session III

S. [Smiling]. I had a great meet!
B. I'd like to hear about it.
S. Well, I used the "You can do it!" and had a good first race.
B. How were you able to keep it going?
S. I felt confident, stronger. I kept using, "You can do it!" and took two to eight seconds off all four races. That's never happened to me before in one meet. I felt great!

Toward the end of his third session, we discussed other aspects of his life--his schoolwork, social life, relationships with his parents, and plans for the future. He felt very satisfied about his visits, and quite comfortable ending them. He thanked me and said he'd be back if he ever needed it again. I heard a year later that he had used what he learned on several occasions and that he had continued to improve. If he had come for therapy, we could have dealt with his low self-esteem, his self-criticism, his need to please, his fear of letting people down, and his fear of failure. In the presence of these problems, it would have been easy to focus on the underlying issues. That was not, however, why he came. It is still a bit of a surprise to me that focusing on performance concerns can suffice in the face of several intrapsychic issues.

An Angry Amateur Athlete G. is a business man and a very competitive athlete, to whom sports have been important all his life. He came to see me because he had become enormously frustrated with his golf game. He previously had been a swimmer, tennis player, runner, and skier. An excerpt from the first session follows.

G. I'm ashamed to be here--a grown man acting like a baby.

This comment already reveals a harsh internal critic and strong disapproval of his display of intense emotion.

B. What do you mean?
G. Well, when I play well there is nothing in the world that's better--not even a woman. But when I don't, I get crazy.
B. In what way?

G. I can't seem to play a single game without getting so frustrated that I throw the damn golf balls into the woods, and it's even gotten worse; I've broken golf clubs after really bad shots.

Before going further with the problem, I wanted to get a broader picture of his life as a golfer to explore whatever strengths he might have that would help him confront the problem.

B. Tell me more about yourself as a golfer.
G. Well, about six years ago I came back to playing golf after years doing other sports. It's a stupid game, but I love it--and I hate it. I was able to lower my handicap to twelve, not only by playing a lot, but also by studying the game, reading about golf technique, about the pros and the games they played. I took lots of lessons and I bought the best clubs.

He seemed to take pride in being a student of the game, and I saw this as a possible entry point for removing barriers. I returned to the present.

B. What's been happening more recently?
G. I've been playing lousy golf. It began by my getting upset after a few bad shots, then my handicap started creeping up. First I just got angry, then things got out of control. How could I behave this way? It's stupid! The last thing I want is to be like my father on the golf course. He was a lousy player and used to go nuts when he played.

Several barriers can already be identified in this first interview: his anger at hitting poor shots, his self-criticism for playing the "stupid game," his shame at losing control, his fear of being like his father, his uncontrollable behavior, and his judgment of himself when he plays poorly. There are, therefore, many possible approaches to helping him. He could be taught relaxation techniques, better pre-shot routines, or imagery to visualize the path of the ball. Helping him manage his anger would appear to be important as well. He could explore why his game has changed, what else is going on in his life, or how his relationship with his father may be affecting his game. Discussing how his self-esteem seems tied to his golf score might help him be less driven. Each of these might lead him to a better experience with his golf game. Because he took pride in being a student of the game, using this strength might be a way to make a shift in his perspective. Instead of criticizing himself for poor performance, he might then appreciate himself for his ability to learn. I believed that with more self-appreciation, he would be able to decrease the influence of his psychological barriers.

B. Let me go back to something you said before. As you were telling me about your studying the game, and learning more about strategies and techniques, you seemed proud of your ability to learn. Is that true?
G. Yeah! Whenever I do something difficult, I love to research it, study it, learn everything I can about it. I feel great when I'm really into that.

B. Maybe you can use that in your golf game.
G. Well, I've already done that.
B. I mean in the game.
G. I don't understand.
B. Okay, how do you know when you haven't hit the ball right?
G. [With a puzzled expression]. Obviously, it either hooks [goes left] or slices [goes right].
B. How can you tell?
G. All I have to do is watch the ball!
B. So the ball tells you when you didn't hit it right.
G. Sure.
B. In a way, that ball is your teacher. It lets you know that some adjustment needs to be made in the way you're hitting it.
G. I never thought of it that way.
B. Now if you want to apply what the ball taught you, you'll obviously need your clubs.
G. Of course.
B. So they could be your allies.
G. Wow! All this time I've been throwing away my teachers and busting my buddies [laughing]!

At this point, there is a shift in his perspective and he can laugh at himself. The next questions are intended to reinforce his new experience by helping him describe his reaction in more detail.

B. What do you feel right now?
G. I feel good. I'm even a little excited.
B. What would you like right now?
G. I'd like to get out on the course and see what happens.
B. What do you think might happen?
G. Right at this moment, I don't think I'd throw my teacher away or break my friends. But I don't know for sure. I've been doing this sort of thing for quite a while. Can it just change?
B. It might. We'll see.

In the next session, he said he played poorly but he did not "get crazy." He did have the urge to throw a golf ball and break a club, but he did neither. He was also surprised to feel some enjoyment about being a student of the game even though he did not play well. The following weekend he played "so-so," and again did not lose control. After that, he played "okay" in some games, and was able to manage his upset when he did not. He called a few months later, and reported that there had been no recurrence of his problem behavior, and that the urges to throw golf balls and break clubs had subsided. The work on his performance difficulties was helpful, even in the presence of a multitude of other psychological issues (Giges, 1998). Although I have seen this relatively simple reframing intervention work many times, I continue to be somewhat surprised when it happens, and wonder how long the good result will last.

An Elite Athlete L. is a middle distance runner whom I had known for about a year through my weekly attendance at track practice, before she came to see me. In local and regional races she usually expected to finish in the top three. The coach suggested she talk with me because she had recently been dropping out of races before the finish.

B. The coach told me it was his suggestion that we talk.
L. Yeah and I thought it was a good idea, too. In fact, I'm kind of relieved he did.
B. Tell me more about it.
L. I'm not racing well.
B. How so?
L. I've dropped out of a few races before finishing.
B. Is that a new experience?
L. Yeah, I've never done that--until recently.
B. What do you think is going on?
L. I don't know. I've tried to figure it out, but nothing seems to fit. I'm in good physical shape. Training has been going well. I'm enjoying running. I really don't have a clue.

B. Anything outside of running causing you trouble?
L. Not really. My boyfriend and I have been fighting lately, but that started after my dropping out. I think I'm taking it out on him. I'm feeling kind of down and discouraged, and it makes me irritable.

Here was an opportunity to explore her "down" feelings in more depth. Because this session was not psychotherapy, I decided not to unless it became important in helping her remove the psychological barriers to her performance.

B. Tell me about the last time it happened.
L. Well, just last week again, in the mile. I was running well and feeling strong. I was leading for most of the race. Then someone passed me near the end of the race, and I just quit.
B. What happened?
L. I don't know.

At this point, I thought the question/answer approach might not be the most effective way to identify the barrier. Her last comment about someone passing her seemed like an entry point, and I decided to follow it.

B. Would you be willing to go back to that race and tell it to me as if it's happening right now?
L. OK.
B. Would you close your eyes? Now go back to last week's race, and picture yourself before the race.
L. I'm there.
B. Tell me what's going on for you.
L. I'm a little nervous. I know a couple of the runners, and one of them is pretty good. I've beaten her in the past, and that helps my confidence.
B. OK, take me through the race.

This comment is asking the athlete to help me understand her experience--it is part of building the working alliance.

L. Well, I decide to go out fast and take the lead. I figure I can put some pressure on the others that way...I'm not going too far ahead, and I'm still leading the pack after the first lap....I feel strong, so I pick up the pace a little, and at the half I've increased my lead....In the third lap I'm getting a little tight, and the runner I told you about is closing the gap....At the three-quarter mark, she is almost up to me....As we go down the back stretch, she pulls even, is right on my shoulder, and on the turn she goes past me....I'm slowing down....I can't seem to run any more...[She looks puzzled].
B. Hold it right there. What just happened?
L. [Long pause...eyes still closed]). I feel so ashamed!

Shame can be a substantial barrier. It is a powerful emotion with deep-seated roots. Because this is not psychotherapy, I am reluctant to explore it with her more deeply. It would change the original purpose in her coming, and probably involve a longer period of time than dealing with her performance problem. It might, however, become necessary. I decided to ask her about it, without intending a deep exploration.

B. Is this something you've felt before?
L. [eyes open]. Not since I was a little girl.

I am treading on thin ice here. Discussing a childhood memory of a significant emotional experience brings me back to when I was a psychoanalytic psychotherapist. Yet something inside me says, "Go ahead. Just because it feels similar doesn't make it the same." I will try to stay focused on her performance issue.

B. Was that situation also about your performance in sport?
L. As a matter of fact it was. I was just a kid, and we were playing soccer. I was one of the fastest kids on the team, so when I got out ahead, nobody could catch me. I was going for the goal with the ball when I tripped and fell. My father, who always

came to our games, yelled at me about how clumsy I was, in front of everybody. I was so ashamed! He was always doing something like that. I felt like nothing.

The therapist in me was certainly tempted to look further into her past and present relationship with her father, its connection to her self-worth, and its implications for her sport performance. It was something I would not be doing unless it was at her request (Giges, 1995).

L. So what do I do about that now?
B. Is there something you want to do about it?
L. No. It's past and I'm done with it. Or at least I thought I was done with it. Do you think it has something to do with my dropping out of races?
B. Maybe--but sometimes becoming aware of something from the past is enough to change its influence on us. Let's see what happens. Would you close your eyes again, and go back to last week's race? Describe the race again.

I was interested in seeing whether that emotional connection to the past would have any effect on her description of the race. She began to describe it in the same way until the final lap.

L. ...As we're going down the backstretch, she's pulling even. She's passing me... [pauses]...
B. What's happening?
L. [eyes still closed] Well, it didn't really happen this way, but I'm still running. Around the turn, she pulls ahead, and I'm right behind her. Down the stretch, she pulls away and wins, and I finish second. [opens her eyes].
B. What seemed to be the difference between the two descriptions?
L. This time I didn't feel that overpowering shame. I just kept racing. I wish that were real.

B. Even though that was a fantasy, you might be able to make it real in your next race.
L. I hope so.

In the four years that I continued to see her race, dropping out did not recur. What accounted for the change is not exactly clear. One possibility is that the fantasy experience was like hypnosis, and the result resembled post-hypnotic suggestion. Another is that she formed a positive transference with her new father (me), and continued to try to please "him" by not dropping out. A third possibility is that her shame was reconnected to its origin, and, therefore, had less impact on her present experience. Each of these, as well as others, may have contributed to what was a significant and lasting effect. During the session, what had seemed like therapy remained focused on her sport performance.

A Changing Competitor P. is a young adult tennis player who graduated from college two years before he came to see me. He was unhappy about the way he was currently playing. Excerpts from two of his sessions are described.

Session I

P. I'm very frustrated about my playing. I just haven't been doing well this past year. I can't seem to concentrate or stay focused during my matches.
B. What do you think is going on?
P. I've been getting injured a lot lately. Nothing major, but I'm afraid to go all out. I'm not playing up to my ability, and I'm not enjoying it any more.
B. Is that the situation in all your matches?
P. Actually, the more competitive it gets, the worse it is. If I win, I think, "I should have beaten him by more." If I lose, I think, "I didn't play as well as I should have." Then I get angry at myself.

B. Any ideas about why this is happening?
P. I don't really know. One thing I've been noticing is that I'm starting to worry that I won't look good. Lately I seem to be more caught up in looking good than in playing good.

A few barriers can already be identified: difficulty concentrating and staying focused, distraction by thoughts about how he looks when he's playing, and holding back because of fear of injury. His comment about looking good stands out, suggests a strong internal critic, and may be a useful entry point. It also indicates a capacity for insight that augurs well for our work together.

B. Who watches you when you play?
P. It doesn't seem to make any difference. Sometimes my parents come to a match, sometimes they don't. Sometimes I don't really know anybody in the stands, and I'm still worried about how I'll look.
B. What do you think about that?
P. What do you mean?
B. Got any ideas about worrying how you look even when nobody you know is in the stands?
P. I guess I'm the one that's looking.

This last comment again shows some ability for self-reflection, and may provide a clue about which barrier to address. I explore his comment a bit further.

B. What do you notice when you see yourself playing?
P. It seems like I'm not really into it. I don't have the drive I used to have.
B. What's your reaction to that?
P. Maybe it means I'm lazy. Maybe I've become a loser.

His self-criticism is more apparent. It is not surprising, therefore, that he would expect criticism from others, especially because the source of his internal critic was from others (i.e., his parents). In his situation, reassurance with a statement of affirmation would probably have little effect. Because his agenda is performance improvement, it also did not seem appropriate to explore the origins of his self-criticism. Starting where his attention is focused (i.e., the critical audience), I tested the possibility of shifting his negative expectations to a positive experience.

B. Who in your life is most accepting of you...someone who appreciates you for yourself, not just for what you achieve?
P. I don't know...I do have three great friends that I'm very close with. No matter how bad I play, they still want to go out with me and have fun.
B. Would they judge you as lazy or a loser?
P. Never in a million years!

The relationship he has with these friends might be able to influence his negative view of himself enough to lessen its impact on his performance.

B. Are you up for doing something different right now?
P. What do you mean?
B. Instead of me asking you more questions, how about if I guide you through an imaginary scenario?
P. That's fine with me.
B. So, would you close your eyes now? Recall the match that you recently played....Before the match starts, imagine that your three friends are in the stands....Can you do that?
P. Yeah, I can see them right at mid-court grinning at me.
B. Now allow their feelings and thoughts about you to be with you as you begin to play the match....Describe what's happening.
P. I'm kind of smiling inside....I feel nice. As I'm starting to play I notice my legs don't feel as heavy as they did in the real match....I'm a little faster on my feet....I'm beginning to make points I didn't make before....I seem to be playing better.

His imagery continued in a positive frame of mind, and at the end he described feeling warm and confident. Before the next visit, he was to play in another tournament.0

Session II

B. How'd it go?
P. Well, I played OK, but I lost.
B. What else happened?
P. I was surprised. But I noticed I wasn't as worried about how I looked. I still didn't play with the intensity I had in college.
B. What do you think about that?
P. Well, one thing I realized was that playing tennis was not as important to me as it used to be.
B. Is that OK with you?
P. I guess so, because what's really important to me right now is going to med school. The only reason I played this last tournament was because I had signed up for it a while back.
B. It's good to realize that. Does that create any problem for you?
P. Well, I'm worried that I'll be letting my parents down. They put so much into my playing.
B. How do your folks feel about you going to med school?
P. Oh, they're very happy about it.
B. Do you think they would be upset if you gave more importance to med school than to tennis?
P. No way! I guess I'm not really letting them down....I'm moving up.
B. You also sound as though you're more accepting of the change you're making.
P. Yeah, I feel good about it.

In this instance, the performance problems resulted in part from a changing interest (from tennis to medical school), which created the psychological barriers of guilt and fear about not living up to the expectations of others. Guided fantasy can be a useful intervention because it allows the athlete to re-create a past situation that was unpleasant or upsetting, and alter the experience or the outcome. This alteration can be accomplished by a change in perspective, in feelings, or in attitude, and followed by a change in behavior.

From Workshops in Sport Psychology

The first example in this section was selected from a university workshop on "Psychological barriers to excellence in sport performance," in which, after I gave a lecture on this topic, one of the graduate students in sport psychology volunteered to work on an important performance issue. The workshop participants were current and former graduate students, and members of the faculty; all agreed that the contents of the interview would remain confidential.

A Student/Dancer/Teacher D. is a life-long dancer who became interested in teaching and helping others to dance. Recognizing that psychological factors were important in performance, she decided to study sport psychology.

B. Where would you like to begin?
D. I have a performance problem, and I feel stuck right now. Dancing is something I've been able to do all my life, and technically there shouldn't be anything holding back my performance now.
B. What do you mean there shouldn't be anything holding back your performance?
D. I was hit by a car almost three years ago, but I didn't have any broken bones or anything like that. I was told I could go back to class and work the way I had been working. But I couldn't do it. Something occurred during the warm-up, while we were on the floor. I started feeling strange.

B. Strange in what way?
D. Physically, something didn't feel right on the left side of my neck. I wasn't sure what was going on. I got scared and started to hold back. I felt like I was going to fall. I thought I couldn't hold my balance on my left side. The next morning I had such a severe pain I went to the E.R. The doctors thought it was a migraine, but I never had one before.
B. What happened after that?
D. Well, since that experience I haven't gone back to jazz class. I went to a couple of ballet classes, but I didn't do any jumps, and the turns have me terrified. I don't know if I'm holding myself back or if there is a legitimate cause. I'm too chicken to try it.

The intensity of the fear did not appear to be fully explained by the physical injury. I believed there was an important psychological cause of such anxiety, namely a threat to her identity as a dancer. Because dancers do not hold back, her holding back meant to her that she was not a dancer. So I began with her judgment that holding herself back was not a "legitimate cause" for her behavior.
B. Does that imply that if you're holding yourself back, it's not legitimate?
D. I would hate to think that I'm afraid of something I've done all my life.
B. Let's suppose both are true--you have what you call a legitimate cause and you are holding yourself back. Since you mentioned before that you are afraid, which of these do you want to focus on now?
D. I think I'm afraid I'm going to wind up back in the E.R. But the thing is I can't even bring myself to try it--any turns or leaps.

A physical cause seemed less likely to me at this point. If fear were the main psychological barrier, there are different ways to approach trying to lessen its grip on her: (a) explore why she's afraid, (b) use imagery to decrease the impact of the fear, (c) do a relaxation exercise, or (d) experiment with doing what she fears in small increments, as in desensitization techniques. Her emphasis on not being able to try turns or leaps led me to start with the last one.

B. Would you be interested in trying a turn or leap now?
D. I'm not sure, because after this much time, I'm afraid I've even lost the technique.

Because her reluctance was expressed by another fear, I decided to postpone any direct experiment with jumping or turning.
B. So, in addition to your fear of injuring yourself, there is also a fear that you won't know how to do it. Is that correct?
D. And the really big one is I don't want to look stupid, especially after the career I had before.

At this point, I decided to do more preparation before encouraging her to take any risks. Because there is evidence of significant self-criticism, I began to address this barrier of judgment against herself.
B. What would looking stupid consist of?
D. I guess people who knew what I've done in the past would see me working at a much lower level.
B. And they would say that's stupid?
D. No. Well, maybe stupid is the wrong word.
B. It may not be the wrong word; it may be your own thought. So what would be stupid about your performing at a lower level from your point of view?
D. It would be embarrassing.
B. Because...
D. Well, because of the level I was at before.
B. You were at a much higher level, sustained an injury followed by severe pain, and now perform at a lower level. What is embarrassing about that?
D. If I do a turn, I might fall out of it, or it might not look as clean as it used to, or I won't spot it correctly. If I'm demonstrating in

the jazz workshop I'm doing, and I'm holding back, I don't want my students to think I can't do it.
B. What do you imagine they would think?
D. Something like, "Why isn't she doing it? Why isn't she showing us?"
B. How do you think they would answer those questions?
D. Some of them know about the accident, and some of them don't.
B. What might those who don't know about it be thinking?
D. I've never thought about that.
B. Well, would you think about it now?
D. They might think I'm not good enough.
B. Do you have any clues that they do think that?

The issue of low self-worth would be important to pursue in depth if this were psychotherapy. It cannot be avoided, however, in exploring the performance barrier.

D. No, none at all.
B. But you think they would?
D. Right now, yeah.
B. So, whether they actually do or not, you think they do?
D. I guess so.
In working with barriers such as low self-esteem, low self-confidence, or low self-worth, it is important to clarify the basis for these ideas, as specifically as possible.
B. In what way do you think you're not good enough?
D. Oh, there's a laundry list of ways.
B. Tell me what they are.
D. Double turns, chain turns across the floor, grand jeté, which is a huge split leap in the air, rapid jumps, doing a layout, which requires arching the back, keeping the leg high, and leading with it.

She is quite specific about which techniques she fears. It began to sound as if she wanted to do these movements so badly she could almost "taste" it. I decided to press a little.

B. What seems to be in the way?
D. I'm afraid I'll fall.
B. And if you fell?
D. That's not an acceptable option.
B. To whom?
D. To me.
B. What makes falling unacceptable?
L. I've never done it before. I've never fallen out of a turn or a jump, or from a layout.

Here is an example of an unanswered question mentioned previously in the Listening section. What is avoided is not clear, so I ask again.

B. And what makes it unacceptable?
D. I was really good at it. I don't like the idea of not being really good.
B. I realize that you have never fallen before, and that you don't like the idea of not being really good, but what is it that makes falling unacceptable?
D. The feeling that I'd get from falling. I'm not even sure what that would be, but just the idea of it gives me the creeps. Based on what I've done in front of an audience in the past, it's way below the level I know I'm capable of.
B. And therefore...
D. And that...it's just...I can't...I guess I can't accept the idea that I'm less than I was.
B. And if that's true, what makes that so difficult for you?
D. What I was...meant the world to me.
B. So if you're not at that level, then...?
D. I guess part of me feels that I'm no longer a dancer.
B. And if that's true, then...?
D. It's kind of like something in me died. It gets me emotional.
B. What kind of emotion?
D. Loss...Big loss...knowing I could do it...I was secure doing it. I got paying jobs doing it. I knew I was better than most other

people doing it. I wish I had it back...the people I worked with, the experiences I had. It was so much fun. It wasn't work. I wish I had it all back.
B. It sounds like it was more than just fun. It sounds very important to you.
D. It was pretty much my whole life!

Certainly D's identity is significantly involved with being a dancer. The idea of no longer being one is frightening for her to anticipate. Because this was a workshop interview, I wasn't sure that a significant beginning could be made toward changing her perspective and removing the barriers. I decided to explore this possibility with her

B. What's your reaction to hearing yourself say that?
D. I never talked much about it, but I always saw myself as a dancer. I didn't feel a need to talk about it. I just did it. People would ask "What do you do?" and I'd always answer "I do shows" or "I go to class." I always felt, no matter what, I had a chance to get better, because I knew I was good. I knew I was a dancer. And it was more than that....it was being a performer....you could dress up, become someone else....you could do anything.

She began to be more animated. I could really sense how much it meant to her, and this strengthened my resolve to do what I could for her in this situation.
B. How is it different now?
D. I haven't been back in the studio. I grew up in the studio. From the time I was able to walk, I always danced. By the time I was five years old, there wasn't a week in my life when I wasn't in the studio for at least one class. And by the time I was in high school, I was at the studio five to seven days a week. If I wasn't taking a class or teaching a class, I was at the desk. I can't tell you what the smell of rosin

does. You know, you combine rosin, sweat, and humidity, and that's life.
B. I have a sense of what it meant to you, and what it still means to you. What feelings do you get with not performing at the level you used to?
D. I'm angry.
B. At?
D. At the fact that I can't do it.
B. And at whom are you angry?
D. I'm very angry at the people who caused the accident that did this to me.
B. Is there any anger at yourself?
D. Yeah. It's the "what if" thing. If I hadn't gone to get a bagel and tea, if I hadn't been standing on the corner, if I hadn't crossed the street, this never would have happened.
B. That may be true. If it is true, how would that make you angry at yourself?
D. I should've stayed inside stretching, getting ready for class. I should have been doing something different. I should've been getting the music ready. I should've been working on the last sixteen counts of the combination. If I had done something different, then I could still be doing what I love more than anything.

Self-blame and more self-disapproval make it difficult for her to forgive herself.

B. If you should have been doing all those things and weren't, does that say anything about you?
D. It says I wasn't being as responsible as I should have been for class. And because I made the decision I did, I'm not what I used to be.
B. If you're not the dancer you used to be, what does that say about you?
D. I keep thinking that maybe my talent was all in my head.

B. That you never were what you thought you were?
D. Yeah, because I can't get it back!
B. So if you can't get it back, it means you never had it?
D. Well, I know I had the experiences; and I know I had the feedback. But since some of the best stuff I did is not on film, I don't really know for sure.

The dialogue that begins with "what if" illustrates the tenacity of negative thinking, even leading her to doubt her own experience. I decided to introduce a lighter note to see how much of a hold this self-doubt had on her.

B. Well, at least you never fell.
D. No, I never fell...Wait, I take that back. I did fall once, but it was absolutely nothing I did. Someone washed the floor in the studio, and this is something you never do because when you wash a wooden dance floor, it's like an ice skating rink--very slick. When I went into a move, my foot slipped out from under me because of the floor. But that was the only time ever.

Her comment about that being the only time she ever fell suggests a lot of control, a great deal of caution, or difficulty remembering what might threaten her image of herself.

B. Were you angry at yourself for falling?
D. Actually, I was laughing because we all knew the floor had been washed, and were taking really good care not to fall. The way it happened looked really comical.

In discussing her present experience, it became apparent that she had given up trying to come back. I believe this was partly from the fears she described, partly from her pessimism about the outcome, and mainly from the threat to her identity as a dancer. She no longer did even gentle practicing when she was by herself. I was quite moved in hearing this, and decided to try to help her clear the way to begin doing so by providing an opportunity and direct physical support.

B. Would you be willing to do some practice jumps right now?
D. [laughs] Well, OK...
B. Come, let's work together on this. I'll hold your hand while you take a practice jump.

What followed was a first jump with her holding my hand, then several off balance jumps by herself. I noticed that she began her jumps without getting ready, and suggested that she get set before jumping. During the jumps she had some shortness of breath and felt anxious. After encouraging deeper, slower breathing, I suggested that, in addition to getting set physically, she do something that represents getting set mentally as well. She then went over to the opposite wall and drew a spot to focus on. This was something she frequently did when jumping, and was an indication of her focus in getting mentally ready to jump. She then performed several more jumps. We concluded the interview with her decision to continue the practice she had just begun. I asked her where she would be doing it, and when, and sensed her determination to do so. Several months later, she told me that her "life had gotten back on track," and she felt very satisfied with the work she had done in the interview. This example illustrates that even when important psychological issues exist and interfere with performance, these issues do not always require in-depth exploration in order for performance to improve.

Several factors may have contributed to the good result. Her volunteering in the workshop suggests that given the right conditions she was ready for change. During the interview, I was aware of a strong bond between us, working together to accomplish a difficult task, which I think was an important element in helping her overcome a barrier. This bond consisted of my being quite eager to help her, partly because we had gotten to know each other at sport psychology conferences for several years, and partly because I felt fatherly toward her. Her contribution to the bond was the considerable trust and respect that she felt toward me. My willingness to address her difficulty in physical as well as emotional ways (by holding her hand and supporting her first jump) must have been important to her, a woman who has danced all her life. For someone who is quite self-reliant, accepting help was difficult, and overcoming that difficulty was quite rewarding. I also think the presence of the "audience" worked in her favor, not only because she was a performer, but also because this particular group was part of her support network (fellow students).

A Competitive Student T. is a graduate student in sport psychology who volunteered in a seminar in sport psychology to discuss a problem he has been having in his tennis game. The seminar was an hour long and included 12 students and a faculty member. I was invited to present how I work with athletes who have some psychological difficulty with their performance.

B. How would you like to begin?
T. Well, I'm a tennis player, and I've played my roommate many, many times over the past few years...probably over 100 sets... and I've never beaten him.
B. What is your explanation of that?

Ordinarily, I would not start an interview with this question, but in this instance, I sensed he had spent a lot of time thinking about it, and had a response ready to go.

T. Overall he is a better player than I am, and he started playing at a much younger age. In order to beat him, I have to play very well and he has to play just average, but I have never been able to put it all together. Several times I've come close, like 6-4, 7-5, but I can't seem to overcome all the factors. One

particular incident stays with me, and is the primary reason for my volunteering in this session today.
B. I'd like to hear more about it.
T. A couple of months ago, we were playing just one set. I was playing great, and he was playing poorly. The next thing I know, I am up 5-0 and serving for the match [they played one-set matches]. Then things went downhill from there.
B. Describe what happened.
T. Well, at that point my play became very tentative, and my thoughts drifted away from the task.
B. What were your thoughts?
T. I began thinking about who I'd call when I won, and how great it would be to finally beat him. I had trouble concentrating on the match after that.

One barrier would be loss of concentration resulting from thinking about bragging after the match. It was important to get more specific information about how his performance was affected.

B. How did your performance change?
T. Well, I started to play "not to lose" and he seemed to sense this. As I became more distracted, his play gained momentum. I started hitting the ball short, and he consistently put the ball away. I also had several double faults. He very quickly evened the score at 5-5, and I was in shock.
B. What do you mean?
T. I couldn't believe how quickly the tables had turned...one moment I'm serving for the match, and a few minutes later I'm serving to just stay in the match. My head was filled with thoughts and concerns about losing the match after being up by five games.
B. What did you do then?
T. I tried to recycle several times and say "let's go!" to myself, but I got too caught up in the pace of his comeback. After being up, I let him dictate the rest of the match, and I didn't feel in control.

B. What interfered with you staying in control?
T. I lost confidence in myself, and I felt discouraged. I was unable to stay positive, and was losing my incentive. Then my energy and enthusiasm started to go down.

Several additional barriers are present at this point, such as worry about losing, loss of confidence, loss of control, discouragement, and loss of incentive. Although any of these could have been pursued, they were described without much emotion. I was waiting to hear something that had more personal involvement to use as an entry point.
B. What might have helped pull you up in that situation?
T. I don't really know. I felt pretty alone out there.

His facial expression changed to a slight frown, suggesting that being alone might be an important issue for him. As I pictured him out there all alone, I imagined that he had difficulty supporting himself, being on his side, rooting for himself. Because focus on present experience is an important component of my working with athletes, I chose his feeling alone as an entry point.

B. What are you feeling right now?
T. I'm not sure...maybe I felt a little lonely when I said that.
B. Would you be willing to do something a bit different at this point?
T. Sure. What do you mean?
B. Instead of my asking you more questions right now, would it be OK if you closed your eyes? Now I'd like you to imagine that you're back in the situation you were just describing. Can you do that?
T. Yeah. I see him waiting for my next serve.
B. Let the match be at the point when the score is 5-5, and you are discouraged...losing energy...losing incentive...going down...feeling pretty alone out there. Are you there?
T. Yeah.

B. Now with that picture still in mind, imagine that you are also a cheerleader at the match, leading a cheer for you on the court.
T. Hmmm...I don't know...I've never been much of the cheer-leader type.
B. Well let's see how it goes. See if you can make up a cheer to encourage you on the court...How would you like it to go?
T. How about "Go!"
B. Go whom?
T. Go T.
B. Now do that as a cheerleader.
T. Go T.! [A little louder but without enthusiasm].
B. Notice the low energy in the cheer. Try this...turn to the group as if they are the stands, and lead them in the cheer... and stand as you lead them.

T. [to the group]. OK guys, are you ready?
Group. Yeah!

T. [stands up hesitantly]. We're going to cheer "Go T."...and raise your hands on "T."...like this. Ready...Go T.!...
Group. Go T.! [With enthusiasm].
T. Nice job.
B. [To T.] OK. Now do it again without holding back.
T. [standing]. GO T.!!!
Group. GO T.!!! [very enthusiastically].
B. [To T.] How did you do?
T. They did really well.
B. How did you do?
T. Pretty well, I guess.
B. Only pretty well?
T. I'm not sure. I'm not used to being a cheerleader for myself.
B. It seems difficult for you to root for yourself. Is that true?
T. I guess I've always been more comfortable telling others they did a good job than telling myself the same thing.

B. Is that something you would like to change?
T. I guess.
B. You sound uncertain.
T. Well, wouldn't that be boasting?
B. Some people might see it that way. Others might see it as you being on your own side. Would that be OK if it weren't at somebody's expense?
T. Yeah, that would be OK. In fact, I'm going to try it.

If this session were just the two of us, I might have explored further his difficulty being supportive to himself. Because it was a time-limited demonstration, I asked if it would be OK if we stopped here and he agreed. Months later, the idea of being his own cheerleader was still with him. The purpose of performance enhancement is usually improvement in some objective, quantitative result, such as running faster, hitting the ball further, jumping higher, throwing further, or shooting more accurately. It can also be improvement in the subjective, qualitative experience of performing, such as more enjoyment, increased motivation, better attitude, or more satisfaction. In this interview, the latter type of benefit, improved self-support, may have been initiated.

SUMMARY

My approach to the process of removing psychological barriers in sport performance includes theory and techniques drawn from psychoanalytic psychotherapy, gestalt therapy, transactional analysis, and cognitive therapy. Each of these approaches contributes an essential component to my work with athletes. From psychoanalytic theory the component is that all behavior has meaning; from gestalt therapy it is a focus on the here-and-now; from transactional analysis comes the concept of the internal child and parent; and from cognitive therapy the principle that thinking is the major determinant of feelings. These several theories exert their influence on my work, which is grounded in humanistic psychology, in particular, a growth model of human development.

Some of the more common psychological barriers seen in sport performance are anxiety, low self-confidence, anger, self-criticism, low self-esteem, shame, loss of incentive, and difficulty staying focused. Each example in this chapter illustrates one or more of these barriers, as well as the methods and rationale for the particular interventions. More specifically, guided fantasy is a major technique that plays a central role in removing psychological barriers. It is a means of re-constructing an athlete's experience to help remove or decrease the impact of the barrier, and enable the athlete to move more easily into an effective mind-set for approaching competition.

REFERENCES

Beck, A. T. (1967). *Depression: Clinical, experimental, and theoretical aspects.* New York: Hoeber

Berne, E. (1961). *Transactional analysis in psychotherapy.* New York: Grove Press.

Cox, R. H. (1994). *Sport psychology: Concepts and applications.* Dubuque, IA: Brown & Benchmark.

Danish, S. J., Petitpas, A. J., & Hale, B. D., (1992). A developmental-educational intervention model in sport psychology. *The Sport Psychologist, 6,* 403-415.

Erikson, E. H. (1950). *Childhood and society.* New York: W. W. Norton.

Frankl, V. (1992). *Man's search for meaning: An introduction to logotherapy.* Boston: Beacon Press.

Giges, B. (1995, September). *How people change.* Keynote address presented at the annual meeting of the Association for the Advancement of Applied Sport Psychology, New Orleans, LA.

Giges, B. (1996a, May). *Beyond psychopathology: An alternative to the medical model in sport.* Paper presented to the International Society for Sport Psychiatry at the annual meeting of the American Psychiatric Association, New York.

Giges, B. (1996b, Fall). Commentary. *Newsletter of the Association for the Advancement of Applied Sport Psychology, 11*, (3), 24, 27.

Giges, B. (1997, February). *Psychological barriers to excellence in sport performance.* Keynote address presented at the Southeastern Region Sport and Exercise Psychology Student Symposium, West Virginia University, Morgantown, WV.

Giges, B. (1998). Psychodynamic concepts in sport psychology: Comment on Strean and Strean. *The Sport Psychologist 12*, 223-227.

Greenson, R. R. (1967). *Technique and practice of psychoanalysis.* New York: International Universities Press.

Maslow, A. (1954). *Motivation and personality.* New York: Harper & Row.

Maslow, A. (1962). *Toward a psychology of being.* Princeton, NJ: Van Nostrand.

Munroe, R. L. (1955). *Schools of psychoanalytic thought.* New York: Dryden Press.

Nideffer, R. M. (1985). *An athlete's guide to mental training.* Champaign, IL: Human Kinetics.

Orlick, T. (1986). *Psyching for sport: Mental training for athletes.* Champaign, IL: Human Kinetics.

Perls, F. (1969). *Gestalt therapy verbatim.* Lafayette, CA: Real People Press

Van Raalte, J. L., & Brewer, B. W. (Eds.). (1996). *Exploring sport and exercise psychology.* ashington, DC: American Psychological Association.

Weinberg, R. S., & Gould, D. (1995). *Foundations of sport and exercise psychology.* Champaign, IL: Human Kinetics.

Williams, J. M. (Ed.). (1998). *Applied sport psychology: Personal growth to peak performance* (2nd ed.). Mountain View, CA: Mayfield.

Personal Growth, Encounter and Self-Awareness Groups

Burton Giges and Edward Rosenfeld

PERSONAL GROWTH can be viewed as making new connections in any of several directions: upward, to achieve one's full potential; outward, to make contact and encounter others; inward, to increase our awareness of who we are, and what we want, need, sense, feel, think, and do; and downward, to touch earth, to be grounded, and to connect with the universe. Such growth involves increasing the range of perceptions, thoughts, and feelings we experience, developing new ways to express them, and making choices and decisions about the direction in which we wish to move. This leads to increased flexibility as we create and recognize our alternatives; greater spontaneity as we stretch our boundaries and free ourselves from fixed patterns of behavior; and enhanced self-esteem as we begin to sense our mastery, use our ability to effect change, and take responsibility for the outcome. Ultimately, these processes lead to in-, creased acceptance of ourselves and others, as we come to know who we really are and where we want to be in this universe.

The purpose of this chapter will be to show how these processes are enhanced and facilitated by a variety of approaches, methods, and techniques generally referred to under the grouping of the *personal growth movement* or the *human potential movement.* Elements of these approaches embrace self-awareness, living in the here and now, body work, movement, play, meditation, and encounter.

The origins of group psychotherapy, in general, and the personal growth movement, in particular, can be traced back to the nineteenth century. However, the real emergence of these movements begins following World War II.[1] The aftermath of the devastating global warfare brought many serious thinkers into profound consideration of basic questions and facts of individual existence.

Existential Origins

The burgeoning of intellectual interest in phenomenology and existentialism created an intense and fertile environment for the development of new psychotherapeutic tools. The post-war existential vantage point was of a world never again to be safe from the threat of total and instantaneous holocaust. Thus the daily life of an individual is a microcosm of potential oblivion and, conversely, of potential joy.

Philosophers and psychotherapists alike began to reexamine the very stuff of existence, the moment-to-moment phenomena of daily life. Rather than attending only to the client's verbal report, therapists began to emphasize other perspectives of the client: style, manner, and, most especially, the body. Soon after the war, Sheldon pointed to the possibility that the body may be what psychoanalysts called the unconscious.[2]

By attending to the obvious, the a priori given of daily existence, therapists began breaking ground in a new, decidedly phenomenological field: the field of awareness. The attention of the developing therapies in the personal growth movement was centered on awareness of the present, the here and now. Such awareness does not ignore the past and the future. It integrates them with the knowledge that cognizance of the past (memory) occurs in the present as does expectation of the future. Thus the present is seen to include representations of the past and the future.

By focusing on the present, and introducing techniques for developing and enhancing awareness, the therapies of the personal growth movement developed a new style of helping the client that has come to be known as the *safe emergency*. The safe emergency lets a client experiment with awareness of his feelings, awareness of his life style, and new ways of being within the context of the therapeutic situation. By experiencing his new ways of being and integrating feedback from the therapist and the group, the client has a base from which to operate when taking this new behavior out into the world at large. By being themselves, by being real in an experimental situation first, clients can safely approach new ways of being.

Authenticity

The concept of authenticity is fundamental to understanding what is meant by *being oneself* or *being real*.[3] To be authentic requires an awareness of one's deeper feelings and needs, those which may have been buried early in life, behind a facade that was more palatable to others or less uncomfortable for ourselves. Everett Shostrom[4] focused attention on how this leads to manipulations; Eric Berne[5] introduced the concept of games; Ronald Laing[6] and Arthur Janov[7] described the unreal self, the facade we develop to hide the pain we originally felt.

To know what one really wants is not always immediately apparent. Being authentic is not necessarily presenting ourselves with our first feeling. Sometimes we may wish to cover our deeper feelings to avoid embarrassment or anxiety, or we may express anger to cover hurt feelings, irritation to cover sadness. It is erroneous to equate authentic behavior with immediate gratification. Authenticity often leads to a choice which may postpone being satisfied immediately. The first feelings we are aware of may not be any truer than those which emerge if given time. Hugh Prather[8] expresses it this way:

At first I thought that to "be myself" meant simply to act the way I feel. I would ask myself a question such as, "what do I want to say to this person?", and very often the answer was surprisingly negative. It seemed that when I looked inside, the negative feelings were the ones I noticed first. . . . But I soon found that behind most negative feelings were deeper, more positive feelings—if I held still long enough to look. The more I attempted to "be me" the more "me's" I found there were. I now see that "being me" means acknowledging all that I feel at the moment, and then taking responsibility for my actions by consciously choosing which level of my feeling I am going to respond to.

An authentic relationship is one in which each person is seen as separate, and acknowledged as having his own needs and feelings, rather than merely being the object of the other's needs or feelings. Martin Buber[9] identified the former as an *I-Thou* relationship, a mutual attempt to know and be known, and the latter as *I-It*. The I-Thou is the core of a meaningful encounter between two persons. To allow another to be different and to accept that difference forms the basis for an authentic relationship, one in which intimacy becomes possible. George Land calls this ability to accept differentness the *mutual phase* of growth. In this phase, one can use similarities as a beginning basis for a relationship, and differences to deepen it and allow for mutual growth.[10]

Personal Growth

Being authentic is an aspect of personal growth emphasized by Carl Rogers.[11] He describes such growth as moving away from façades and *oughts*, being self-directed, opening to inner and outer experience, being capable of intimacy, with sensitivity to and acceptance of others. The aspects of personal growth which Jack Gibb[12] considers as central and of critical importance are trust, openness, realization (what I want to become), and interdependence. He believes that the basic dynamic process of growth is the change from fear to trust, and that progressive changes in the other aspects can be described as fulfilling, emerging, and becoming.[13] These processes are characterized by an increased capacity to express love and warmth, an enhanced sense of power and influence, a greater freedom from role, and increased ability to live fully in the present moment.[14]

The ability to initiate action is emphasized by William Schutz and Charles Seashore[15] as an essential element in personal growth. This requires a heightened awareness of alternatives which provides the opportunity to make decisions. In developing the concept of self-actualization, Abraham Maslow[16] states that we are capable of functioning with far more intensity, creativity, and vitality than we realize. He sees personal growth as the process by which we can approach our full human potential. While he describes growth as intrinsically rewarding and delightful, he recognizes that it requires effort and self-discipline, and may involve pain and sorrow.

According to Clark Moustakas, [17] personal growth has two major components: self-growth and growth in human relations. The former requires self-awareness and self-understanding, and often leads to periods of loneliness and solitude; the latter becomes possible when each person recognizes others as they are and accepts their otherness. Sidney Jourard[18] writes that "growth is the disintegration of one way of experiencing the world, followed by a re-organization of this experience, a reorganization that includes the new disclosure of the world." He believes he has personally grown when he perceives changes that have occurred, decides how he wants to be in this world, how he wants the world to be for him, and then acts.[19]

In thinking about his own personal growth, Moustakas[20] writes:

Many times in my life I have overcome obstacles to my own growth (after) I discovered resources when none appeared available. Many times, too, I have felt emptiness, boredom, triviality, repetitiveness, sterility and meaninglessness—momentarily; but when I transcended the mood or feeling or situation, when I became involved, spontaneous and free, suddenly I was seeing with different eyes and hearing with different ears . . . boredom dissipated into interest, sadness into joy, and emptiness into excitement.

Alan Watts[21] has also commented on the ever changing process involved in feelings, and the importance of allowing a natural flow from one to another. To allow this flow requires awareness and acceptance of these feelings as a natural part of one's moment-to-moment existence.

Awareness

We believe that awareness is central to the concept of personal growth: awareness of feelings, thoughts, needs, senses, and bodily messages. In gestalt therapy, awareness = experience = reality = now.[22] If awareness is blocked, growth stops. Awareness is essential in enabling us to deal with whatever the most important unfinished situation is from moment to moment.[23,24] It is necessary to provide us with the opportunity to see alternatives and make choices,[25] and to develop self-understanding and self-acceptance.

Awareness can be developed and expanded through fantasy and imagery, through focusing attention on body parts, positions, and movement, through exposure to sensory experiences, and through feedback from others. Using fantasy and imagery, one is able to get in touch with thoughts and feelings which may have been hidden, either because other ideas pressed for attention or because too much discomfort would accompany their direct expression. Fantasy also makes possible the clarification of how we experience a current situation, or facilitates the emergence of inner resources and wisdom of which we were unaware.[26]

Muscle tension and limitation of motility are related to decreased self-awareness, according to Alexander Lowen.[27] In bioenergetic analysis, he attempts to integrate body function and emotions by removing the blocks to the free flow of energy. Charlotte Selver[28] emphasizes the importance of sensory awareness, which she describes as a "gradual unfolding and cultivation of sensibility, of a greater range and delicacy of feeling, which brings about concurrently the awakening and freeing of our innate energies." She believes it is necessary to restore the smooth and effective functioning of our body to allow those natural responses which have been covered over to be reawakened. Bernard Gunther[29,30] has developed a series of exercises as part of a process called sensory awakening, which leads to heightened awareness and contact with one's world, and which removes the dulling effects of our past experiences. They involve movement, breathing, massage, and other exercises to stimulate the senses.

Gestalt Therapy

Now that we have discussed a historical perspective and some theoretical roots, let us go on to consider some specific elements of the personal growth movement in a more detailed discussion.

A good beginning is the career, thought, and influence of F. S. "Fritz" Perls. As a medical doctor in Germany, prior to World War II, Penis had been an assistant to Kurt Goldstein. As a psychoanalyst, he had been in training with Wilhelm Reich and under the supervision of Otto Fenichel and Karen Homey. Perls escaped Germany in 1933 and, with the help of Ernest Jones, took a position as a training analyst in South Africa the following year.

In 1942, Perls published *Ego, Hunger, and Aggression: A Revision of Freud's Theory and Method.*[31] In this work, Perls started to develop a theory that would move past psychoanalysis, a theory that would integrate many influences on his life and thought. Among these were: gestalt psychology, existentialism, Reich's attention to the body, and elements from Eastern philosophical systems.

In 1946, Penis came to the United States, and settled in a number of communities across the country during the 1950s and 1960s. His work in New York City had a strong influence on Paul Goodman. Similar residences in Miami and Cleveland left trained practitioners in gestalt therapy like Marty Fromm and Erving and Miriam Polster.

But it was in California that Perls' influence was most astounding. In 1964, Perls came to Esalen Institute at Big Sur, one of the first centers of the personal growth movement. He stayed on as a psychiatrist in residence, and as the popularity and recognition for Esalen grew, so did the acknowledgements of Fritz Perls and gestalt therapy.

Gestalt therapy usually takes place in a group setting, and is conducted on a one-to-one basis, with the therapist and the client encountering each other in an I-Thou situation. Perls would work with one client at a time, while the other members of the group listened and, hopefully, did their own silent self-therapy. After a client finished some therapeutic work, other members might then be invited to share their own self-recognitions with the rest of the group.

The theoretical basis of gestalt therapy begins with the situation of the organism as a being in relationship with a constantly changing and emerging environment. The organism is constantly striving to complete situations and to maintain a balance, or homeostasis, with its context in the environment. Perls paid particular attention to helping the client (the organism) come to awareness of how he was functioning in relationship to his environment. Perls noted that the client attempted to manipulate the environment for support. Perls' definition of maturity was the transition from environmental support to self-support, when the client would take full and complete responsibility for all of his actions and behavior.

Among the many ways that the client would experience himself and his environment, Perls noted that transactions might be a) projections: the client's attempt to attribute his own thoughts or feelings to another (person or thing or situation) in the environment; b) introjections: the client's attempt to make something outside him his own; and c) retroflections: the things the environment bent back to the client after the client had directed that same thing outward. For example, narcissists, persons who, instead of directing their love outward to an object, fall in love with themselves.[32]

Some of Perls' most exciting work came out of therapeutic investigation of dreams. He believed that a client's dream was an existential message of the client's life situation experientially, at the time of the dream. In order to work on the dream, Perls would direct the client to act out, in psychodrama form, each element of the dream: all of the characters, objects, and occurrences in the dream. In this way, the client would come to experience the fact that he was the whole dream, rather than just one character or symbol in the dream.

An important element of Perls' theoretical viewpoint was that a client cannot *get well* without becoming whole. The basic road to wholeness in gestalt therapy is through the integration of the disowned parts of the self. Perls would have the client experiment with a dialogue so that the disparate elements of the self could encounter each other.

Perls found that these elements of the self often grouped themselves into two distinct characters. Perls named these characters *top dog* and *under dog*. Top dog is authoritarian, impatient, proper, rigid, and often uses the expression "you should" when barking his commands at under dog. Under dog is apologetic, manipulative, and usually wins most arguments in the top dog/under dog dialogue through deviousness and subterfuge. Under dog often says: "I know, I should have, I'm sorry. I'll do better tomorrow."

A good deal of the effectiveness of the gestalt therapy approach is found in its reliance on an intensive dynamic in the relationship between therapist and clients, which involves a process relationship that evolves over time. This duration allows the insights and awarenesses that occur during the course of the therapy to be integrated into the life style of the individual client.

Though Perls gave demonstrations and one-day workshops, the bulk of the work that goes under the name gestalt therapy takes place in an intensive group atmosphere. Groups extend in time for a year or longer and the client is making a commitment to a process that will involve him in such a group experience that will aid him in new awareness, new recognitions, and new life possibilities.

Perls perceived living as a series of situations, or *gestalten*, in process from being incomplete to being completed. When a situation has been completed, another situation that was in the background will move into prominence to become figure and demand attention for completion. This never-ending series of situations applies to the therapeutic encounter as well. As Perls wrote in *The Gestalt Approach:*[33]

Self-support is very different from self-sufficiency. When patients are discharged from therapy they will not lose their need for other people. On the contrary, they will for the first time derive real satisfactions from their contact with others.

At the same time that Perls and Esalen were coming to national prominence, another Esalen-enhanced technique was gaining adherents: encounter. Kurt Back cites August 1946 as the birth date of the encounter movement.[34] Others point to encounter as an outgrowth of the sensitivity training laboratories at NTL in Bethel, Maine. No matter what its real origins, encounter has changed the face of contemporary psychotherapy, with particular reference to the intensive small group experience.

Group Experience

The intensive small group—sometimes called encounter group, sensitivity training group, or human interaction laboratory—can provide a unique opportunity to facilitate personal growth by stimulating the development of awareness of how we feel, how we perceive and react to others, and how others perceive and react to us. It also affords us the chance to make a fundamental connectedness with others, to express feelings openly and honestly, to experiment with new behavior, and to experience others un-encumbered by our usual role restrictions. Most such groups are not designed to solve problems directly, but to develop skills and an approach to deal with such problems. Jack Gibb believes that "there is no substitute currently available for the intimate personal group experience as a medium . . . for creating the capacity to produce an enhancing and facilitative interpersonal environment".[35] He says that "those who commit themselves to group experience can grow significantly," and for them "the small group experience means growth."[36] William Schutz writes that such groups are oriented toward the development of the full potential of their members, involving the physical, emotional, intellectual, social, and spiritual aspects of each.[37] According to Sidney Jourard, these groups are "places and times for each who is present to disclose himself as he now is, and for each to respond, truly respond to what has thus been revealed."[38] Clark Moustakas points out that the intensive group experience provides an opportunity to share joy and pain, happiness and sorrow, anger and excitement.[39]

Expressing Feelings

The expression of feelings in the group involves a sequence of awareness, decision, action, awareness, decision, and reaction. Figure 1 shows this with just two persons involved. Beginning with an awareness of how I feel about you or how I feel about myself, an action may follow. This leads to additional feelings about myself or stimulates feelings in you about me or about yourself. Another action may follow and begin the sequence over again. If either of us is concerned only with our own feelings, our involvement with each other may be terminated, as we drift into a smaller cycle with only ourselves, depicted on the right side of the diagram.

FIGURE 1 **A Two-Person Interaction**

```
        How I feel about you How I feel about myself
                      ↘                 ↙↗
                           How I act
                        ↙              ↘
    How you feel about me How you feel about yourself
                      ↘                 ↙↗
                         How you act
```

If another person reacts to my action toward you, our involvement with each other may be interrupted, and multiple interactions may quickly follow. The complexity of involvements in a group situation is illustrated in the following excerpt from one group of eight members. This example involved four members of the group and lasted about one minute.

Betty has been speaking to Frank at length, telling him how he should behave in the group. Warren gets impatient and says to her:

Warren (to Betty): Stop lecturing to him.
Jill (to Warren): Don't be so critical all the time.
Betty (to Jill): Thanks for defending me.
Jill (to Betty): I didn't really defend you. I got scared.
Frank (to Warren): Well, anyway, I appreciate your taking my side.
Warren (to Frank): I wasn't taking your side; I was getting very impatient.

Since an interaction between two members can quickly involve others, chaos could replace communication, if everyone were to express all their thoughts or feelings all the time. To avoid this, the concept of a threshold and of making choices becomes useful. This would involve a person expressing a feeling when the need or wish to do so is greater than the need or wish not to. Sometimes one may decide not to express a feeling when there is another feeling that interferes; that is, not expressing anger be-cause of fear of retaliation, or not expressing hurt feelings because of intense embarrassment.

Expressing a feeling fully primarily serves the needs of the person who has the feeling, and not necessarily the one to whom it is expressed. Feedback, on the other hand, can serve the needs of the person to whom it is expressed, by providing useful information which can be the basis for new learning. To attempt both at the same time rarely accomplishes either purpose adequately: either the feelings are not fully expressed, or the ideas communicated are contaminated by the affective message. Making a choice to do one or the other will lead to a more satisfying expression of feelings or a clearer communication of ideas. In an attempt to improve a relationship, it may also be useful for each person to make clear what they want or need from each other. This kind of communication is different from either expressing a feeling or providing feedback, yet is an essential component in developing an authentic relationship.

Encounter

By providing a setting for obtaining feedback and expressing feelings, the encounter group became an opportunity where new kinds of behavior could be tested, and where participants might have an intensive group experience.

Back[40] traces three distinct theoretical foundations to the encounter movement: training laboratories, personal growth centers, and the English (Tavistock) model. The training lab aims at using the group to facilitate the experience of change. In this model change is of paramount importance, as is the group as a whole rather than the individual.

The growth center paradigm is much more concerned with the individual and his ability to function more fully, more toward the limits of his potential. The English groups, mainly those known under the Tavistock name, are concerned with the group, with much more emphasis on the relation of the individual to authority, involving a heavy psychoanalytic orientation. Here we are most concerned with the personal growth approach to encounter techniques. One of the most wide-ranging definitions of en-counter comes from Schutz:[41]

Encounter is a method of human relating based on openness and honesty, self-awareness, self-responsibility, awareness of the body, attention to feelings and an emphasis on the here-and-now. . . . Encounter is therapy insofar as it focuses on removing blocks to better functioning. Encounter is education and recreation in that it attempts to create conditions leading to the most satisfying use of personal capacities.

Gerald Haigh considers encounter to be the antidote to alienation. He sees encounter occurring when the blocks to self-disclosure have been removed from a therapeutic relationship.[42] Carl Rogers notes that the removal of such blocks may make the first expressions of significant feelings, within the encounter process, negative expressions directed at the group leader or other members of the group.[43]

In a typical encounter group, emphasis is given to the *here and now*, to experiential learning, and to participants' feelings. By here and now is meant the experiences, relationships, and feelings occurring during thy course of the group, rather than the narration of outside or past events. Experiential learning is that which occurs during the process of doing, rather than by merely talking about doing. Frequently, it is nonverbal and involves use of the body as well-as of the mind. Feelings occurring in a group member or between members are given priority over ideational or cognitive material. Further, the gestalt therapy principles of making statements instead of asking questions, changing generalities to personal comments, and confronting someone directly rather than talking about them also facilitate a more intensive experience.

The encounter group leader has in mind the goals of increasing awareness and encouraging new behavior (*risk taking*). He may make interventions by modeling behavior of group members, providing feedback to others, disclosing something about himself or herself, being open and honest, offering acceptance or support, or encouraging others to do so. He or she may also invite group members to carry out a structured exercise or experiment as a way of assisting them to "stretch their boundaries," that is, to go beyond the restrictions they usually place upon themselves.

To be effective, such experiments must be specific for the person, time, and situation, and frequently modified to meet individual needs. Routine exercises, mechanically administered, do not facilitate growth, and often decrease a leader's effectiveness. When considering which particular experiment would be most useful, a leader will evaluate whether to use the group as a whole to focus on an interpersonal issue—that is, clarifying feelings or improving communication—or to concentrate on working with a single group member. The leader must also take into account what is possible and appropriate in the particular setting, the readiness and willingness of the individual, the readiness of the group to tolerate the intensity of the experience, and whether a better resolution might be attained with no intervention at all. He or she must also know when to encourage a member to go further and when to stop. To do these, leaders must have a thorough understanding of individual and group dynamics; with these skills, the encounter group leader can significantly enhance the intensity of the group experience. Encounter groups have been linked to a variety of other theories, techniques, and methods. Rosenfeld[44] describes 252 ways of altering consciousness without drugs, with almost one hundred of the techniques in some way related to the personal growth movement.

Growth Approaches

In *A Catalog of the Ways People Grow*, Severin Peterson describes more than forty ways people can pursue their personal growth.[45] He says, "Each person is his own way of growth," and emphasizes that personal involvement is basic, commitment and perseverance essential. The various processes listed are considered auxiliary. Any of them may lead to growth by extending one's boundaries beyond the limits previously established. If we can learn to use our senses more acutely, increase the range of our feelings, develop more understanding of ourselves and of others, stimulate our bodies to feel more alive, or mobilize our inner energies, then we can expand the space in which we live and broaden our experience—we can grow. In his directory of ways people grow, eight major categories are listed, according to the predominant element in the approach described: physical functioning, feelings and relationships, action and behavior, motivation and willing, suggestion and altered states, imagination and symbols, spiritual concerns, and environment. Examples of two of the major categories are:

Physical Functioning and Sensing: Alexander technique, bioenergetic analysis, body awareness, breathing therapy, hatha yoga, massage, movement, sensory awareness, structural integration, tai chi ch'uan, etc.

Feelings and Relationships to Others: Client-centered therapy, encounter group, gestalt therapy, logotherapy, psychoanalysis, psychodrama, psychotherapy, sensitivity training, theater games, etc.

Since many approaches overlap any single category, no classification is completely satisfactory. Some methods which emphasize physical functioning also involve feelings; some which focus on feelings and relationships also deal with action and behavior; spiritual approaches may involve altered states of consciousness or physical functioning; and so on. Whatever the approach, virtually all utilize the concept of energy flow, most recognize the importance of understanding body messages, and many emphasize our oneness with the universe. We believe that the greater the diversity of methods available, the better is the opportunity to find an approach useful for each person. William Schutz[46] states, "The fact that no one method works well for everyone creates a need for a multiplicity of methods. By having a wide variety of approaches, it is more likely that each person can find one or more techniques that he can work with profitably." As indicated above, the intensive small group experience creates a particularly effective setting in which personal growth can occur.

Questions have been raised about how one can hope to achieve authenticity with the use of techniques.[47] Such techniques do not *produce* authenticity; they facilitate its emergence.

By assisting a person to enter the space behind the façade which has been defensively erected, they enable an individual to avoid the habitual response. What may often appear as a spontaneous reaction may be a stereotyped pattern of functioning which prevents intimacy and authenticity. The usual response in a new situation is to repeat what is familiar, rather than risk a new and perhaps threatening behavior. Maslow describes the choice one has: either to go back toward safety or forward toward growth.[48] Encounter "gimmicks," if offered to fit individual needs and situations, can reveal the "phony" ways of relating to others, and allow the authentic self to emerge and an authentic relationship to develop. Soren Kierkegaard wrote:

> Sometimes when you have scrutinized a face long and persistently, you seem to discover a second face hidden behind the one you see. This is generally an unmistakable sign that his soul harbors an emigrant who has withdrawn from the world . . . and the path for the investigator is . . . that he must penetrate within if he wishes to discover anything.[49]

It is not only important to have several approaches available; it is also useful to offer different opportunities for personal growth. Given the objectives and characteristics of the growth process, the intensive small group experience may be modified as to duration, frequency, and length of session, as well as content. The full range varies from those which meet regularly, usually weekly, for 1½ to 3 hours, to marathons which last 15 to 48 hours (the longer ones breaking only for eating and sleeping), to those which meet daily for 5 to 7 days or longer. Weekly groups may continue for a specified number of sessions or be open-ended, with new members entering as others leave.

Whatever structure is utilized, we would emphasize the importance of repeated experiences, since originally established patterns of behavior and ways of relating to others tend to return. Elizabeth Mintz[50] has suggested that marathons can be useful in conjunction with therapy. We agree, and further believe that the combination of an intensive short-term experience and a continuing opportunity to integrate affective and cognitive input in an ongoing group is more effective than either alone. The gains achieved in a marathon frequently require reinforcement for those whose behavior patterns have been dysfunctional for prolonged periods; and the work done in an ongoing group can often be enhanced by the more intense experience of the marathon.

Sensory Awareness

Aside from marathons, and the other approaches referred to above, many theories, methods, and techniques are deserving of a more complete treatment for better understanding of their place in the personal growth movement.

Sensory awareness is often used as an adjunct to the personal growth experience. Sensory awareness has been almost singlehandedly introduced to the American public by Charlotte Selver. She in turn traces the roots of her theories and her work back to the early twentieth-century efforts of Elsa Gindler in Berlin and Heinrich Jacoby in Zurich.[51] Sensory awareness concerns the reeducation of sensory usage so that sensitivity to both internal and external stimuli is enriched.

In general the work may be described as the gradual unfolding and cultivation of sensibility, of greater range and delicacy of feeling, which brings about concurrently the awakening and freeing of our innate energies. This we practice through the *activity of sensing.*[52]

Selver has developed a group of exercises and experiments that allow the client to use his senses in a new, focused way. The simple process of concentration on sensory input can reveal a myriad of details often over-looked in the ebb and flow of daily existence. Often colors are enhanced, sounds seem richer and deeper, and complex inner emotions are encountered in a different light.[53]

The commitment of the client to sensory awareness work in an intensive group experience can lead to new, rich material for consideration.

Body Work

Encounter, sensory awareness, and gestalt therapy all share a common attitude that the human is more than just a mind; that humans are whole systems composed of minds *and* bodies. Many group leaders in the personal growth movement share the perception that we do not *have* bodies, but we *are* our bodies.[54]

With this new set of perceptions, a variety of new approaches to human functioning have begun to receive increasingly serious attention in the psychological community. These approaches include rolfing (structural integration), the Alexander technique, the Feldenkrais method, and bioenergetics.

Central to all of these approaches is the perception that the treatment of a client's problems or disorders must include awareness and treatment of the client's physical structure. As Ida Rolf observes:

Behavior bears witness to a given structure. Structure, here, means relationship in space. And structure (relationship in space) on another plane, in another dimension, is behavior.[55]

Ida Rolf developed structural integration, now commonly known as *rolfing*, in order to free habitual patterns deeply ingrained in physical structure. Rolfing is a system of deep muscle manipulation and realignment. The nature of the manipulation is based on the way the rolfer *reads* the structure of the client's body in its relationship to the environment. Particular attention is paid to the relationship between gravity and the body. Rolfing emphasizes that the client's body is a mirror of past experience. Emotional and physical trauma leave deep impressions in physical structure. A perfect example is fear.

When children are scared and become anxious, they depress their breathing, collapses their diaphragm, and foreshortens the muscles in the upper chest. Repeated experiences of fear perpetuate this habit and the muscular response that accompanies it. Eventually the physical condition cannot be corrected simply by standing up straight, as children's parents are wont to tell them.

The foreshortened muscles include the fascia or sheathing that encloses the muscles. Rolf believes that only through manipulation of the fascia can (potential) restructuring be achieved. A rolfer will realign the muscle fascia so that the client has the potential for a new structural response and true structural integration.

In order that some of the potential for new structural alignment can be achieved, Judith Ashton, working with Dr. Rolf, developed a series of exercises to facilitate the changes that rolfing makes possible. Called *structural patterning*, the Ashton exercises can be used in conjunction with rolfing to keep the client's body from reverting to old patterns and habits.

Rolfing involves deep muscular manipulation of the client by the practitioner. By contrast, practitioners in the Alexander technique touch their clients softly, if at all. Any deep muscle work that is done is an adjunct to the technique rather than part of the method itself.

F. M. Alexander was an orator at the end of the nineteenth century. One day he lost his voice, which was the equivalent of losing his livelihood. He went from doctor to doctor and was continually told that if he stopped speaking his voice would return. He tried this several times only to find that after returning his voice would once again disappear.

Rather than consulting more physicians, Alexander decided to try to cure himself. He spent long hours in front of a mirror studying *what* he did when he spoke. From this awareness, he was eventually able to cure himself, after he noted a three-part process that preceded his every attempt at speech. As he began to talk, Alexander would throw his head back, gasp a breath, and depress his larynx.

However, before he was actually able to cure his loss of voice, Alexander made a variety of discoveries on the relationship between awareness and change, and on the relationship between head and neck. What developed from his new awareness was the knowledge that his loss of voice was a problem that included his entire body and not just his throat.

After Alexander regained his voice, he continued his work as a recitationist. He worked on the development of his method for curing his own problem for over ten years. His work on the stage drew many who were amazed at his control of his breathing. He became known as the "breathing man" and many would come to see him on stage.

This led to Alexander teaching a number of students the method he had developed for what he called the conscious control of the human organism. His teaching and writing on the technique brought more and more students and many famous people to study with him, including G. B. Shaw, John Dewey, and Aldous Huxley.

The Alexander technique is not a series of exercises or a talk therapy. It is a systemic approach to good and appropriate use of the body through conscious control.[56] Alexander developed a threefold pattern to implement his findings:

1. Let the neck be free (which means merely to see that you do not increase the muscle tension in any act).

2. Let the head go forward and up—forward of the neck, that is, not forward in space (which means merely to see that you do not tense the neck muscles by pulling the head back or down in any act).

3. Let the torso lengthen and widen out (which means merely to see that you do not shorten and narrow the back by arching the spine).[57]

Though these instructions sound deceptively simple, in order to carry them out clients must be fully aware of how they are using their body and how they might be able to use their body in the next moment. Old habit patterns interrupt these instructions, and the client must be able to inhibit these habitual responses and *let go* before the potential for new choices becomes available.

The Alexander technique is a means whereby the client can come to a conscious change of habits and patterns, and then integrate those changes into day-to-day living. A similar technique is called the Feldenkrais method. The originator of this method, Moshe Feldenkrais, is a physicist. He, too, came upon his method through problems with his legs and knees. Unable to find relief from doctors he consulted, Feldenkrais, a black belt in judo and a student of yoga, Freud, and Gurdjieff, turned his awareness onto himself to solve his own problems.

His primary observation was that the unity of mind and body was an objective reality that the continuity of mental functions is assured by corresponding motor functions.[58] He decided that in order to cure his knee disorder he would have to teach himself to walk anew. He studied anatomy, physiology, psychology, and anthropology in his search for clues on how to approach his problem.

Further observations led Feldenkrais to recognize the importance of gravity in human functioning:

> The bulk of stimuli arriving at the nervous system is from muscular activity constantly affected by gravity.... posture is one of the best clues not only to evolution but also to the activity of the brain.[59]

Feldenkrais has developed more than one thousand individual exercises that are designed to demonstrate to the client the process of movement. The exercises are not designed to be repeated continually to build up muscle tone. They are meant to be used as awareness facilitators, so that the client can come to experience the workings of his own body/mind system.

> The motor cortex is the common axis on which both the conscious and reflex reactions are hinged; and no permanently altered reaction to any environmental stimuli can rationally be expected without a rearranged muscular response.[60]

One of the first psychological thinkers to bring attention to the body was Wilhelm Reich. His study of character armor and the relationship between physical and emotional functioning is only recently being taken seriously. Of all the work growing from Reich's original insights, bioenergetics forms the most engaging expansion. Bioenergetics seeks to reintegrate the client through five basic realizations:

1. to reestablish the client's identification with his body;
2. to recognize the pleasure principle as a major basis for conscious experience;
3. to allow the client to be his feelings;
4. to realize that all awareness is subjective awareness;
5. to recognize ultimate human humility in the human/universe relationship.

Most of these points stem from the work of Alexander Lowen,[61] who has also developed a number of postures, positions, and exercises that he believes will facilitate the integration of such insights.

The positions include stretching backward and bending the body for-ward like a bow; arching the back over a stool; and hyperextension, where the back is arched and the hands reach under the body to touch the soles of the feet.

These passive positions are supplemented by a number of active movements. Lowen will often have clients strike a bed (women with a tennis racket, men with their fists). Other movements have the client lying on his back and kicking the bed with either flexed or extended legs. Often flailing arms accompany this kicking.

The point of these exercises and postures is to start the breathing and bioenergetic flow of the body so that that flow may then be translated into action. Lowen feels that such flow will bring about bodily pleasure which can serve as a vital source of emotional well-being.

Stanley Keleman, another practitioner of bioenergetics, views bodily experience as an experience in the present which gives biological form and identity to living. He sees three states of aliveness which he calls vibration, pulsation, and streaming.

The way in which we perceive the world depends fundamentally on the quality of aliveness in our tissue. Aliveness is instinctive intelligence. A person who is sensually alive is a very reality-oriented person who is able to do a great deal of work. A person who is alive is creative.[62]

Keleman works with a client in three stages. First, the client is brought to experience his inhibited aliveness. He is encouraged to express more movement through breathing or by hitting or kicking a mattress. In the second stage, the client will slow down so he can experience what the movement has brought about internally and emotionally. In the third stage, the transitional consciousness of the second stage is translated into a multiplicity of potentials for making contact with the world.

> If you want to know yourself stop moving. But if you want to be yourself, you must move. . . . To be yourself, to express yourself, you must allow yourself to be in the act of moving and expressing, even if that expression is lying down and going to sleep. To be who you are demands that you accept the risk of not knowing.[63]

All of these approaches to the body—Rolfing, the Alexander technique, the Feldenkrais method, and bioenergetics—share an integrative orientation in the way that they facilitate human growth and development. One element of this combination is one-to-one, therapist-to-client work; the other is an intensive group experience on a continuing basis. This demands a commitment from the client to the personal growth experience. The awareness and insights generated from the body work must be fully integrated in a therapeutic situation so that optimal functioning can be achieved.

Meditation

In addition to the growing acceptance of the body, a number of other approaches to human functioning have begun to recognize the importance of meditation, fantasy, and play in connection with personal growth. Many of these ideas come from other cultures and from disciplines outside the psychological sciences.

While Western culture has traditionally paid attention to the outside world, certain elements of Eastern culture have turned their focus toward what happens internally. This internal focus is called meditation.

The practice of meditation can be traced back through more than four thousand years of history. It is an integral part of many of the world's great religious systems: Hinduism, Taoism, Buddhism, and others. Rosenfeld describes meditation in its simplest form: sitting quietly, doing nothing.[64] White describes meditation as being

> a means of growth, both personal and transpersonal. . . . mediators claim that the best way—indeed, the only way—for people to change is by "working on themselves" from within, through meditation.
>
> The highest goal of meditation is enlightenment.[65]

Essentially, meditation is a way of doing something while doing nothing. The doing nothing is the sitting quietly; the doing something is the introspection, the inner awareness. One of the goals of meditation is to enable the meditator to experience better his or her own internal reality. The way to do this is for meditators to sit quietly and allow the environment to be around them. Alan Watts describes the listening done during meditation as being comparable to the way one would listen to music.[66]

Another important aspect of the practice of meditation is the attention that meditators pay to breathing. A common instruction given to meditators is to watch, passively, as their breath enters, circulates through, and then leaves their bodies, only to enter again and begin a new cycle.

In Zen Buddhism meditators are instructed, at the beginning of their practice, to count their inhalations and then to count their exhalations. This counting is used as a method to help the meditators focus their attention on their breathing, rather than on thoughts, fantasies, worries, or the like. Watts sums up the goal of true meditation most succinctly:[67]

Above all, don't look for a result, for some marvelous change of consciousness or *satori*: the whole essence of meditation practice is centering upon what is—not what should or might be.

Psychosynthesis

Meditation has had great effects on a number of different therapeutic approaches within the personal growth movement. The practice and approach called psychosynthesis incorporates many meditational techniques into its form of psychotherapy. Psychosynthesis was formulated through the work of Roberto Assagioli beginning as early as 1910. Assagioli trained people in his method from his home in Italy.

Psychosynthesis is both a psychological and educational approach to the human being as a creature oriented toward growth. A major addition to psychosynthesis, often lacking in the theoretical foundations of other psychotherapeutic approaches, is its inclusion of the spiritual side of human nature. Psychosynthesis integrates concepts like the will, the soul, and the imagination with standard psychological ideas such as libido, instinctual drives, and the like.

This emphasis on the spiritual nature of human beings also contributes to a basic tenet of psychosynthesis: that we can transcend our personal identities to make contact with our *overself*. As Weide observes:

Assagioli is a leader among the relatively few modern psychotherapists who work systematically with people in a detailed program of first developing, then transcending, their personal selves (1973).

Psychosynthesis uses a variety of techniques and methods. These include guided imagery, role playing, meditation, movement, journal keeping, symbolic art work and its interpretation, will training techniques, and self-identification work.

Psychosynthesis theorizes that the client has continuous but limited contact with a set of sub-personalities, inner voices, and motivations that can be examined and brought under the focus of *willful* consciousness. To do this, it incorporates and synthesizes techniques from psychodrama and gestalt therapy. Often these subpersonalities involve body feelings and are worked with through the utilization of various postures and movements.

Assagioli, through psychosynthesis, has attempted to set out a detailed map of the self. His approach utilizes and integrates material from a variety of personal growth approaches under one unitized system. Other approaches that utilize many techniques and methods are much more eclectic and are known under the common name of *growth games*.

Growth Games

Lewis and Streitfeld[69] have gathered together more than two hundred different approaches to enhancing personal growth. Most of these games come out of the personal growth movement. They describe games to take responsibility, to expand sensory sensitivity, to alter consciousness, and to enliven the body, as well as games for developing warmth and trust and for breaking through personal blocks.

Other approaches to growth games incorporate gestalt therapy,[70] sensory awareness, and encounter.[71] Many of the games are designed to allow clients to experiment with therapeutic concepts outside of the therapeutic environment. Stevens sums this up, telling the client that his approach to growth games

> does provide you with tools that you can use to explore your life, simplify and clarify your problems and confusions,

and help you discover your answers—what you want to do.[72]

A specialized kind of game is the theater game. Theater games are a mix of personal growth techniques, elements of psychodrama, and improvisational methods taken from theatrical training. Spolin describes the interplay between the theater and personal growth thus:

> Acting can be taught to the "average" as well as the "talented- if the teaching process is oriented towards making the theater techniques so intuitive that they become the students' own. A way is needed to get to intuitive knowledge. It requires an environment in which experiencing can take place, a person free to experience, and an activity that brings about spontaneity.[73]

Growth games, theater games, meditation, and psychosynthesis all share a common boundary with more formal approaches to the intensive group experience. The *sesshin* in the practice of Zen Buddhism is an example of this boundary. *Sesshin* is a week-long meditation where a group of people gather together under the guidance of a leader (usually a Zen master or head monk) to meditate for up to twenty hours a day. Even though the members of the group remain silent for most of the week, the intensive nature of this shared experience is most powerful.

The other techniques referred to above can operate in a variety of modalities, but the intensive group model tends to facilitate personal growth and the realization of individual potentialities. This makes it the mode of favor for implementing many of the approaches to improved human functioning.

Perspectives

Are these approaches, methods, and techniques of any value? Detractors and critics of the personal growth movement would say no, for a variety of reasons. Material in the *Congressional Review* and that brought out in hearings before the California State Legislature object to the personal growth movement because it tends to support life styles that conflict with traditional social standards. Other testimony compared personal growth techniques to brainwashing.[74]

Other critics have noted that only charismatic leaders of personal growth groups seem to get good results (but also casualties). They maintain that the method or technique employed in the group is secondary to the strength of the group leader's personality.[75] It has been noted in the political sphere that charismatic persons exert great power in many groups.[76]

Still others note that the aims of the personal growth movement negate any attempt to make long-range plans or to identify goals because of their *here-and-now* philosophical orientation. It has also been maintained that personal growth results are too ephemeral, too utopian, and thus escapist at their very core.

When, however, personal growth is viewed as making connections, so that something is created which did not exist before, and when process itself is considered fundamental, then such growth becomes the essence of existence. In this perspective, what are usually considered "results" can be seen as by-products of the process.

The general philosophy of the personal growth movement seeks to correct what are a variety of, essentially, epistemological errors through the increase of individual and group awareness. This process-oriented approach emphasizes that such errors must be acknowledged and experienced before any behavior change can take place, *if* such a change is desired and warranted.

Such a fundamental and basic reexamination of the nature of human behavior and experience might be criticized as being too unrealistic. Its very challenge to socially accepted norms is enough to threaten certain cherished culturally approved behaviors (e.g., the suppression of any show of aggression except war).

Certainly many people who have participated in some of the personal growth techniques have had escapist experiences or derived escapist results. Others show a decidedly different picture of the results of such contact.[77] As a young movement, personal growth will be affirmed or denied by the culture of the future.

Future Directions

Of the many future frontiers to be investigated by the practitioners of personal growth methods, the synthesis of a variety of approaches is certainly one of the most exciting developments. Psychosynthesis, which has been described above, is part of this mold and sets a high standard through its integration of fantasy, work on the will, meditation, and spiritual dimensions.

Other exciting developments occur where techniques are combined to form an expanded, holistic view of human functioning. Combinations like transactional analysis (TA)/primal therapy, TA/gestalt,[78] and gestalt/ bioenergetic are new examples of such theoretical expansion.

TA is basically an intellectual and behavioral approach, and is well complemented by the deep emotional work done in primal therapy, by gestalt therapy's emphasis on a holistic approach to organismic functioning, or by body work. Bioenergetics' use of body work, physical structure, and exercises offers fresh new material to the gestalt therapist, especially in group work.

In the combination of gestalt/TA, semantic analysis is extended to new broader limits within the scope of psychotherapy. Gestalt has always aimed at correcting basic self-perceptual errors as they are manifested in the client's language. (e.g., "I can't talk to my mother" can be changed and restated as "I won't talk to my mother." This change introduces the notion of the client's inevitable responsibility for his own actions by a simple semantic adjustment.)

TA uses such words as *parent, adult, child, game, script, stamp, and racket* to identify psychological activities, behaviors, and relationships that the client is experiencing. The advantage of this is that these words can be used by both the therapist *and* the client. By using such terms, the therapist can better share his insights with the client through the use of this common language.

Given the choice between the arcane and the open, between over complication and simplicity, I have thrown in with the "people" tossing in a big word now and then as sort of a hamburger to distract the watchdogs of the academies, while I slip in through the basement doors and say Hello to my friends.[79]

These semantic changes and identifications allow both the client and the therapist to reexamine human behavior with full perception of the construction of personal mythologies. Stories are always being told on an internal level to justify, explain, and place behavior in an acceptable context. These stories or myths can be made conscious and even discussed in therapy.

In the group situation, such use of personal mythology and synthesis of psychotherapeutic approaches yields a new perspective for the growth model of human functioning.

This becomes even clearer when comparing the *growth* model with the *medical* model.[80]

Growth Models

Our position is that *treatment* in the medical model can be considered one of many pathways to growth, which differs in some ways from others. It is of particular value for those whose personal and interpersonal functioning is impaired or those who have significant, persistent disturbances in feeling, thinking, or behavior. The approaches in both models share the goals of seeking to increase self-awareness, to improve one's relationships with others, and to increase effectiveness in functioning. The differences are largely in emphasis.

The growth approach tends to focus on developing one's potential: awareness, sensing, and feelings are highlighted; risk-taking behavior is encouraged; here-and-now experience is given prominence; significance is given to making choices and decisions; work with the body is often included; and the leader often shares his own feelings and experiences, providing a model for self-disclosure and feedback.

In the medical model, correction or removal of a defect or illness by a therapist who maintains relative distance is predominant; understanding, thinking, and talking are emphasized; repetitive patterns, past history, defenses, and resistances are examined; analyzing causes and making interpretations represent significant aspects of the treatment.

The growth approach has been described by Ernest Rossi[81] as being more humanistic, subjective, and personal, rather than the more scientific, objective, and impersonal aspects in the medical model. Our experience in recent years suggests an increasing overlap between the two, a trend which we believe will benefit both models. Many encounter group leaders have come to recognize the importance of supplementing a peak emotional experience with understanding its significance in the individual's life pattern. This can be done by connecting the here-and-now experience to other situations and behavior involving conflict, and increasing one's awareness of alternatives available for their resolution. In turn, many psychotherapists have come to value some of the newer growth approaches as useful adjuncts to their own treatment methods, either incorporating them into their own work or referring patients or clients to weekend marathon workshops to supplement ongoing therapy. We hope that the differences between these two approaches, and among those who practice both, will be used creatively to enhance each.[82]

In this chapter we have reviewed and discussed the elements and approaches to personal growth. Somewhat like the spokes of a wheel, there are many paths to the center and each person can select which ones are most appropriate to his individual growth.

References

1. H. M. Ruitenbeek, *The New Group Therapies* (New York: Avon, 1970), p. 22.

2. W. Sheldon, *Varieties of Delinquent Youth* (New York: Harper, 1949), quoted in W. C. Schutz, *Elements of Encounter* (Big Sur, Calif.: Joy Press, 1973), p. 6.

3. J. F. T. Bugental. *The Search for Authenticity.* (New York: Holt, Rinehart, & Winston, 1965).

4. E. Shostrom, *Man the Manipulator* (Nashville, Tenn.: Abingdon Press, 1967).

5. E. Berne, *Games People Play* (New York: Grove Press, 1964).

6. R. D. Laing, *The Politics of Experience* (New York: Pantheon, 1967).

7. A. Janov, *The Primal Scream* (New York: Dell, 1970).

8. H. Prather, *Notes to Myself* (Lafayette, Calif.: Real People Press, 1970).

9. M. Buber, *I and Thou* (New York: Scribner, 1958).

10. G. Land, *Grow or Die* (New York: Random House, 1973).

11. C. R. Rogers and B. Stevens, *Person to Person* (Lafayette, Calif.: Real People Press, 1967).

12. J. Gibb, in L. N. Solomon and B. Berzon, eds., *New Perspectives on Encounter Groups* (San Francisco: Jossey-Bass, 1972).

13. J. Gibb, in H. A. Otto and J. Mann, eds., *Ways of Growth* (New York: Viking Press, 1969).

14. J. Gibb, in H. A. Otto, ed., *Human Potentialities* (St. Louis: Green, 1968).

15. W. C. Schutz and C. Seashore, in L. N. Solomon and B. Berzon, eds., *New Perspectives on Encounter Groups* (San Francisco: Jossey-Bass, 1972).

16. A. H. Maslow, *Toward a Psychology of Being* (Princeton: Van Nostrand, 1962).

17. C. Moustakas, in H. A. Otto, ed., *Human Potentialities* (St. Louis: Green, 1968).

18. S. Jourard, in H. A. Otto and J. Mann, eds., *Ways of Growth* (New York: Viking Press, 1968), p. 2.

19. S. Jourard, in L. Blank, G. B. Gottsegen, and M. D. Gottsegen, eds., *Confrontation: Encounters in Self and Interpersonal Awareness* (New York: Macmillan, 1971.)

20. C. Moustakas, in H. A. Otto, ed., *Human Potentialities* (St. Louis: Green, 1968).

21. A. Watts, *The Wisdom of Insecurity* (New York: Random House, 1951; Vin-tage Books).

22. F. S. Perls, in J. Fagan and I. L. Shepherd, eds., *Gestalt Therapy Now* (New York: Science and Behavior Books, 1970.)

23. F. S. Perls, R. F. Hefferline, and P. Goodman, *Gestalt Therapy* (New York: Dell, 1965).

24. F. S. Perls, *Gestalt Therapy Verbatim* (Lafayette, Calif.: Real People Press, 1969).

25. J. F. T. Bugental, ed., *Challenges of Humanistic Psychology* (New York: Mc Graw- Hill, 1967).

26. R. Assagioli, *Psychosynthesis* (New York: Hobbs, Dorman, 1965).

27. A. Lowen, *The Betrayal of the Body* (New York: Macmillan, 1967).

28. C. Selver and C. Brooks, in H. A. Otto, ed., *Explorations in Human Potentialities* (Springfield, Ill.: Thomas, 1966), p. 493.

29. B. Gunther, in H. A. Otto, and J. Mann, eds., *Ways of Growth* (New York: Viking Press, 1968).

30. B. Gunther, *Sense Relaxation* (New York: Macmillan, 1968).

31. F. S. Perls, *Ego, Hunger, and Aggression* (New York: Random House, 1969).

32. *Ibid.*, p. 120.

33. F. S. Perls, *The Gestalt Approach and Eye Witness to Therapy* (Ben Lomond, Calif.: Science and Behavior Books, 1973), p. 114.

34. K. W. Back, *Beyond Words* (Baltimore: Penguin, 1972), p. 6.

35. J. Gibb, in H. A. Otto, ed., *Human Potentalities.*

36. J. Gibb, in L. N. Solomon and B. Berzon, eds., *New Perspectives on Encounter Groups.*

37. W. C. Schutz, *Here Comes Everybody* (New York: Harper and Row, 1971).

38. S. Jourard, in L. Blank, G. B. Gottsegen, and M. D. Gottsegen, eds., *Confrontation: Encounters in Self and Interpersonal Awareness.*

39. C. Moustakas, in H. A. Otto, ed., *Human Potentialities.*

40. Back, *Beyond Worlds*, pp. 106-116.

41. Schutz, *Here Comes Everybody*, p. 3.

42. V. V. Haigh, "Psychotherapy as Interpersonal Encounter," in J. F. T. Bugental, ed., *Challenges of Humanistic Psychology* (New York: McGraw-Hill, 1967), p. 223.

43. C. R. Rogers, "Tle Process of the Basic Encounter Group," in J. F. T. Bugental, ed., *Challenges of Humanistic Psychology*, p. 265.

44. E. J. Rosenfeld, *The Book of Highs* (New York: Quadrangle, New York Times Book Co., 1973).

45. S. Peterson, *A Catalog of the Ways People Grow* (New York: Ballantine Books, 1971).

46. W. C. Schutz, *Joy* (New York: Grove Press, 1967).

47. M. Lakin, *Interpersonal Encounter: Theory and Practice in Sensitivity Training* (New York: McGraw-Hill, 1972).

48. Maslow, *Toward a Psychology of Being.*

49. S. Kierkegaard, *Eitherlor*, vol. 1 (New York: Doubleday, 1959; Anchor Books).

50. E. E. Mintz, *Marathon Groups, Reality, and Symbol* (New York: Avon Books, 1971).

51. C. Selver and C. Brooks, "Report on Work in Sensory Awareness and Total Functioning," in H. A. Otto, ed., *Explorations in Human Potentialities*, p. 488.

52. Ibid., p. 493.

53. R. Gustaitis, *Turning On* (New York: Macmillan, 1969), pp. 253-268.

54. S. Keleman, *Sexuality, Self, and Survival* (San Francisco: Lodestar Press, 1971), p. 24.

55. I. Rolf, "Structural Integration," in *Journal of the Institute for the Compara-tive Study of History, Philosophy, and the Sciences*, vol. 1, no. 1 (1963), p. 7.

56. I. Rubenfeld and E. J. Rosenfeld, "The Alexander Technique," in B. Aaronson, *Workshops of the Mind* (New York: Anchor Press/Doubleday, in press).

57. F. M. Alexander, *The Resurrection of the Body* (New York: Delta, 1969), p. xxvi.

58. M. Feldenkrais, "Mind and Body," in *Systematics*, vol. 1, no. 4 (1964).

59. M. Feldenkrais, in *CIBA-GEIGY Journal*, no. 1 (1971).

60. M. Feldenkrais, *Body and Mature Behavior: A Study of Anxiety, Sex, Gravitation, and Learning* (New York: International Universities Press, 1949), p. 160.

61. Lowen, *The Betrayal of the Body.*

62. S. Keleman, -The Body is All," in *The Geocentric Experience: A Bulletin* (Los Gatos, Calif.: Lamplighters Roadway Press, 1972), p. 50.

63. *Ibid.*, p. 55.

64. Rosenfeld, *The Book of Highs*, sec. 10.

65. J. White, *What Is Meditation?* (New York: Anchor Press/Doubleday, 1974), p. xi.

66. Alan Watts, "The Art of Meditation," in *ibid.*

67. *Ibid.*, p. 33.

68. T. N. Weide, "Varieties of Transpersonal Therapy," in *Journal of Transpersonal Psychology*, vol. 5, no. 1 (1973), p. 9.

69. H. R. Lewis and H. S. Streitfeld, *Growth Games* (New York: Bantam, 1970).

70. J. O. Stevens, *Awareness: Exploring, Experimenting, Experiencing* (Lafayette, Calif.: Real People Press, 1971).

71. C. Hills and R. B. Stone, *Conduct Your Own Awareness Sessions* (New York: Signet, 1970).

72. Stevens, *Awareness*, p. 3.

73. V. Spolin, *Improvisation for the Theater* (Evanston, Ill.: Northwestern Uni-versity Press 1963), quoted in S. Peterson, A Catalog of the Ways People Grow (New York: Ballantine, 1971), p. 273.

74. Back, *Beyond Words*, pp. 231-232.

75. M. Lieberman, I. Yalom, and M. Miles, *Encounter Groups: First Facts* (New York: Basic Books, 1973).

76. E. Canetti, *Crowds and Power* (New York: Viking Press, 1960).

77. R. Gustaitis, *Turning On*; F. S. Perls, *In and Out of the Garbage Pail* (Lafayette, Calif.: Real People Press, 1969).

78. M. James and D. Jongeward, *Born to Win: Transactional Analysis with Gestalt Experiments* (Reading, Mass.: Addison-Wesley, 1971).

79. E. Berne, *What Do You Say After You Say Hello?* (New York: Bantam, 1972), pp. xv-xvi.

80. B. Satir, *Conjoint Family Therapy* (Palo Alto, Calif.: Science and Behavior Books, 1964).

81. E. L. Rossi, "Game and Growth: Two Dimensions of our Psychotherapeutic Zeitgeist," in *Journal of Humanistic Psychology*, vol. 7 (1967), pp. 139-154.

82. S. Miller and S. Miller, *First Report of the Project in Humanistic Medicine* (San Francisco: Esalen Institute, 1973).

Part VI

Journal Articles and Book Reviews

Accepted author manuscript version reprinted, by permission, from *The Sport Psychologist*, 2004, 18, (4), 430-444. © Human Kinetics Publishers, Inc.

Helping coaches meet their own needs: Challenges for the sport psychology consultant

Burt Giges and Albert J. Petitpas
Springfield College
Ralph A. Vernacchia
Western Washington University

Sport psychology offers many services to athletes to help them deal with the demands of competition. Although coaches are faced with many of the same types of stressors as athletes, little has been offered to help them with their own needs. The purpose of this article is to examine some of the issues that are experienced by coaches, and to stimulate interest in providing sport psychology services directly to them. These services include strategies to increase coaches' self-awareness, and to help them remove or cope more effectively with any psychological barriers (thoughts, feelings, wants, or behaviors) that interfere with their performance.

The sport psychology literature contains numerous suggestions for providing psychological services for athletes who need assistance with identity issues, challenges, transitions, time management, health, gender and racial considerations (Andersen, 2002; Cogan & Petrie, 1996; Danish, Petitpas, & Hale, 1993; Etzel, Ferrante, & Pinkney, 1996; Greenspan & Andersen, 1995). Unfortunately, the same volume of interest has not been shown in attending to similar issues and needs of coaches. Several years ago, Vernacchia, McGuire, and Cook (1996) wrote "Coaches had needs from the sport psychology profession that were not currently being addressed in a practical manner" (p. xi). Although the sport psychology literature offers programs and techniques for coaches in dealing with athletes (Anshel, 2003; Brewer, 2000; Martens, 1987; Simons, 1992; Vernacchia et al., 1996), there is relatively little about how coaches can be helped to cope with the stresses of coaching, and still meet their own needs. As Gould, Greenleaf, Guinan, and Chung (2002) pointed out, "While studying coaches and their practices has always been of interest to sport psychology researchers, seldom has the coach been viewed as a performer in his or her own right" (p. 231). Other than the many articles about coaches' stress and burnout (Dale & Weinberg, 1990; Fuoss & Troppman, 1981; Henschen, 2001; Kelley, Eklund, & Ritter-Taylor, 1999; LeUnes & Nation, 1990; Raedeke, Granzyk, & Warren, 2000; Rotella, 1985; Vernacchia, 1992), the needs of coaches before burnout occurs have not received the attention they deserve.

The purpose of this article is to provide information to sport psychology consultants who are working with coaches, to assist them in helping coaches increase awareness of their own needs and of any psychological barriers that might interfere with their performance. This approach may serve to prevent potential problems from developing, as well as help coaches cope with them if they do occur.

Psychological Needs

Coaches are performers, educators, administrators, leaders, planners, motivators, negotiators, managers, and listeners, but they are also people. As such, they bring to their roles and tasks fundamentally the same psychological needs as other people. These needs include security, self-worth, identity, autonomy, mastery, intimacy, belonging, and a sense of meaning or purpose in life (Erikson, 1950; Frankl, 1992; Maslow 1987). Deci (2002) pointed out that these innate psychological needs are necessary conditions for psychological growth, integrity, and well-being; and that satisfaction of these basic needs facilitates autonomous motivation. In describing the philosophy of former Indiana University swim coach James "Doc" Counsilman, Walton (1992) wrote "He borrowed his philosophy from Maslow's hierarchy of human needs and adapted it to the context of a coach and athlete competitive team situation" (p. 84). In working with coaches, the authors have been impressed by how significantly these basic human needs influence coaches' performance.

When a team does well, most coaches feel good about themselves, and may experience a significant increase in their self-esteem. Some coaches also find satisfaction in how they go about coaching, not just in winning (Chelladurai & Ogasawara, 2003; Sullivan & Nashman, 1993). Coach John Wooden (1988) believed that "Success in coaching or playing should not be based on the number of games won or lost, but rather on the basis of what each individual does in relation to his own ability..." (p. 14). Walton (1992) quoted former Green Bay Packer Coach Vince Lombardi as actually saying "Winning isn't everything - but making the effort to win is" (p. xi). When challenged by planning for a difficult competition, coaches have an opportunity to experience their sense of mastery. Their need to belong may be satisfied by being part of a closely-knit organization, although some coaches would not have this need high on their list of priorities. In addition, teaching athletes new skills, tactics, strategies, and values can be highly satisfying and beneficial to a coach's sense of self-worth.

Psychological needs are just as fundamental to growth as are physical needs. Unless both are met adequately, growth may be impaired. In their seminal work about problem athletes, Ogilvie and Tutko (1966) considered coaches' needs their primary concern. Although their main focus was to increase coaches' understanding of the emotional factors among problem athletes, they also explored coaches' reactions to their athletes in general, and described how these reactions could affect athletes' performance. They encouraged self-examination among coaches, noting that coaching serves the needs of coaches as well as athletes. Tutko and Richards (1971) also mentioned the need for coaches to know their own personality, because they serve as examples to their athletes. In addition, Vernacchia (1992) emphasized that coaches not only need to attend to their athletes' needs, but also their own, particularly because coaches may have many of the same concerns as those of their athletes. Specifically, performance anxiety, job insecurity, coping with stress, and time management issues are some of the problems that the authors have observed in both groups. One concept that sport psychology consultants can use to improve the experience of coaches is to help them increase their self-awareness. Improved self-awareness would also be of value to the consultants themselves in their work with coaches and others.

Self-Awareness

Self-awareness involves knowledge of one's own behavior, thoughts, feelings, needs, and wants (Giges, 1996; Goleman, 1995, 1998; Martens, 1987; Ravizza, 1998). It can lead to a fuller knowledge of oneself, and a greater appreciation of one's complexity and wholeness. In the book *Sacred hoops: Spiritual lessons of a hardwood warrior* (Jackson & Delehanty, 1995), Coach Phil Jackson of the Los Angeles Lakers basketball team emphasized the importance of self-awareness for himself as well as for his athletes. A major advantage of such knowledge is an increased ability to be in charge of oneself, enabling individuals to be less distracted by their own feelings, wants, and values, and better able to respond to others effectively. Goleman (1998) stated "Self-awareness serves as an inner barometer, gauging whether what we are doing (or are about to do) is, indeed, worthwhile" (p. 57, 58). He believed "Self-awareness pays off as a key skill in handling stress. Without careful attention, we can...be surprisingly oblivious to just how stressful our work life really is. Simply bringing simmering feelings into awareness can have salutary effects" (p. 86). He stated that "The more accurately we can monitor our emotional upsets, the sooner we can recover from distress" (p. 86).

Self-awareness can also lead to improvement in sport performance (Martin, 1999; Smoll & Smith, 1980; Vealey, 1988). Without it, feelings can surface in unexpected or undesired ways (Giges, 1996). Goleman (1995) wrote "Emotions that simmer beneath the threshold of awareness can have a powerful impact on how we perceive and react, even though we have no idea they are at work" (p. 55). For example, unawareness of fear can lead to controlling or dominating behavior. Unawareness of guilt or shame can result in defensiveness or blaming others. Consider coaches who might realize that their plan did not work, but to avoid feeling guilty about selecting a poor strategy, they blame their athletes for not trying hard enough. In this example, if the coaches were aware of their guilt feeling, they might choose to deal with the situation differently. Awareness of guilt might be difficult, however, for coaches who are unable to make an internal attribution and accept responsibility for their mistakes (Anshel, 2003; Cox, 1998). In such cases, attribution training might be helpful (Orbach, Singer, & Price 1999). In addition, if a coach is not aware of his or her wants, a feeling of powerlessness, or a self-perception as a victim can result. Specifically, coaches usually have a dream or a mission that pulls them into coaching. When they forget why they coach and what they want from coaching, they may feel trapped when they face difficult situations, and be unable to see alternative choices.

Self-awareness also provides an opportunity for change (Giges, 1996; Goleman, 1998). Most often, we become aware of a problem behavior after it occurs. When this happens, we may say "I see that I did that." With a commitment to change and repeated awareness of the behavior, awareness begins to occur earlier. When it is present during the behavior, we may say "I see that I am doing that right now." With additional time and practice, awareness moves earlier in time, until it is present before the undesired behavior occurs. At this point, we can say "I see that I am about to do that." When awareness precedes the behavior, a choice can be made to behave differently. This is an opportunity for change and is represented by the statement "I can do it differently" (Giges, 1996).

According to Murphy and Tammen (1998), self-awareness is the first step in a sequence of self-monitoring and self-regulation. Behncke (2002) described self-monitoring as a process using self-awareness to observe and modify internal psychological experience, and he views self-monitoring as the basis of self-regulation. Mascolo and Fischer (1998) wrote "Thus, self-awareness is important because the (self) system uses awareness of its own agency and identity in its own regulation" (p. 349). Goleman (1998) described self-awareness as a process of knowing our internal states and resources, and self-regulation as a process of managing them.

Unfortunately, the self-awareness that is necessary to identify and manage personal concerns is often not emphasized in traditional coach education programs. Coaches in training are occasionally introduced to the importance of self-awareness (Martens,

1987) and understanding their coping patterns (Lynch, 2001). Some coach education programs (e.g., American Coaching Effectiveness Program, 1989) even provide participants opportunities for self-examination. Self-awareness, however, is more than a one time activity or exercise. True awareness of oneself, including the advantages and disadvantages of one's personal style, is an ongoing process that requires work and effort over time (Luft, 1984). Similarly, in the world of executive coaching, an effective program requires continuing opportunities to develop self-understanding, which involves self-awareness and meaningful feedback (Kiel, Rimmer, Williams, & Doyle, 1996). To provide a background to discussing specific intervention strategies and techniques for sport psychology practitioners, the authors believe it would be useful to describe the difficulties that some coaches encounter in their coaching experience.

Understanding the World of Athletic Coaching

Coaches are involved with athletes at many different developmental levels: youth sport, high school, college, club, and professional. In addition, the competitive level at which they work ranges from beginner to intermediate to elite and world class. Furthermore, the settings for the games, meets, and matches can vary from a few teams or individuals, to regional, national, world championships, or to the Olympics. Coaches are called upon to be teachers, mentors, surrogate parents, administrators, and performers. Although the demands and pressures will vary with the circumstances and environment, what all coaches have in common are basic psychological needs. Satisfaction of these needs may provide many positive and rewarding experiences for those in the coaching profession. Specifically, coaches may experience enjoyment, gratification, competence, an increase in self-esteem, and a sense of meaning and purpose in their lives. We have selected the high performance segment of the coaching world to describe some of the issues that may, however, interfere with a coach's effectiveness and life experience, based on our professional experience and that of our colleagues. We recognize that this description may not apply to the same degree to other coaches whose livelihood is not dependent on coaching, or to those whose athletes function at a different level. At any level of coaching, however, it is important for sport psychology consultants to be mindful of the personal needs of the coaches with whom they work.

Coaches of elite and world-class teams and athletes appear to live in a "fishbowl" world of absolutes: winning and losing. The choices and decisions that affect outcomes are clearly visible to those around them. These coaches often experience a sense of urgency from the heightened expectations by the media, alumni, and fans, and the possible judgment that "you are only as good as your last game or season." For this group, it seems that no matter how well they do, it is never quite good enough. The coach who wins a championship is expected to win again next year; and if he or she wins two or three championships in a narrow time frame, demands for a "dynasty" maintains the pressure. In such a world of forced achievement and unrealistic expectations, coaches may become driven taskmasters. They spend many of their professional hours telling others what to do, and have little interest in taking the time to meet their own needs (Vernacchia, 1995). As a result, the demands and requirements of coaching lead them to neglect their own needs and those of their families. They often express the wish to change and spend more time with their families, but they continue the pattern until they retire (Naylor, 2003; Yukelson, Sullivan, Morett, & Dorenkott, 2003). This is similar to the business world, where executives rarely give priority to their own personal growth in the face of multiple competing demands for their time and energy (Kiel et al., 1996).

Dedication and commitment are the cornerstones of athletic success (Vernacchia & McGuire, 1998), and many coaches, as former athletes, are socialized into this mentality and lifestyle. It doesn't take long for them to get accustomed to this work ethic, ritual, and routine. Coaching is always on their mind, and they often experience the leadership stress of being "all things to all people" (Vernacchia, 1992). There is little down time from planning, strategizing, and working for them to gain a better understanding of themselves. Coaches are passionate about what they do, but they may not see the paradox of passion: that the endeavor that excites them the most could also exhaust them the most. Because they are focused on serving others, and are often perfectionists, they are at risk for professional burnout (Henschen, 2001). Relationship patterns learned in the past, as well as current family or marital stress, can also interfere with effective leadership, as much as the stress of the coaching position itself (Kiel et al., 1996). The additional demands of travel, administration, public relations, and fund raising may further contribute to their physical or emotional depletion. To prevent this from happening, consultations with a sport psychology practitioner may be needed to assist them in achieving and maintaining a more balanced lifestyle.

For coaches who remain in their position year after year because it is difficult for them to leave, the accumulation of job related stress becomes increasingly burdensome. They seem to be on an occupational merry-go-round, although athletes come and go. In addition, college and high school coaches may be faced with a generation gap that develops between themselves and their athletes. Coaches get older, but their athletes remain at the same age and developmental level. As a result, coaches may find that there are important differences between their interests and those of young athletes. Although coaches emphasize to athletes the importance of being focused on athletic performance, many contemporary young athletes find it difficult to stay focused on one task. Patience can wear thin for focus-oriented coaches who demand undivided attention to the means and objectives of athletic training and performance. These differences in age, interests, and focus represent potential stressors for coaches. Additional stress can come from managing relationships with their staff, administrators, or others, especially if coaches do not have managerial skills (Peterson, 1996).

In the coach's world, professional advancement and job security often depend on the performances of young and inexperienced athletes, over whom the coach has little control once the athletic contest begins. Many coaches also have relatively little control over the funds to recruit new athletes. In addition, coaches are involved in a profession that is not very cost effective. Although there are some high profile coaches who are handsomely rewarded for their efforts and accomplishments, most coaches work in a world where going to work early and coming home late are valued, regardless of financial compensation. For many of these coaches, salaries and fringe benefits are low, and work time demands are high.

We are also in the age of the "technocoach." Advances in the sport sciences and in technology have served to encourage over-coaching and over-preparation of athletes. Computers, video and digital cameras, rehabilitative methodologies and equipment, coupled with the proliferation of performance enhancing information and training methods, place an inordinate demand on coaches to keep current with the latest developments in their sport. The challenge for contemporary coaches is to maintain their feel for the art of coaching, while at the same time master the science of their sport (Vernacchia, 1992). For each of these stresses, it is important that sport psychology consultants be available to provide opportunities for coaches to cope more effectively.

Sport Psychology Interventions

Gould, Greenleaf, Guinan, and Chung (2002) emphasized that coaches, as well as athletes, need to be helped to deal with stress and distractions. Sport psychology consultants can serve as valuable resources for coaches who might neglect themselves while immersed in the pressured, achievement-oriented world of athletics. The principles of sport psychology can provide both the understanding and the strategies (educational, social, work-related, and recreational) to enable coaches to develop and maintain a healthy pursuit of athletic and personal excellence (Vernacchia, McGuire, & Cooke, 1996). A valuable means of reaching coaches regarding their professional and personal lives is through coaching education programs. For example, USA Track and Field has developed sport psychology programs and curricula that address the issues of effective and healthy coaching through various topics that include: establishing a coaching philosophy based on foundation beliefs about athletic participation; coaching ethics; and preventing and reversing coaching burnout (Vernacchia, 1999). Sportscoach UK also offers workshops on mentoring sports coaches to help them develop and improve their coaching skills (Sportscoach UK, 2003).

An additional strategy that can be effective in this process is in-house coaching roundtables that are conducted on a monthly basis by athletic departments. These roundtables are led by a sport psychology professional, and can address a variety of topics related to coaching, including coping with and managing coaching stress. Sport psychology practitioners can also provide social support (listening, emotional support, task appreciation, and personal assistance) (Rosenfeld & Richman, 1997) as another way to help coaches lead a more rewarding personal and professional life. Coaches need such support to provide a sounding board for the coaching and lifestyle decisions they face daily. An important question for them to face is: "Do they live to coach or coach to live?" (Vernacchia, 1995).

Strategies for Sport Psychology Consultants

Because of the impact coaches have on their athletes, it is important for coaches to know their own feelings, needs, and wants, in order to be able to give priority to their athletes' needs. In working with coaches, sport psychology consultants can use the following questions to assist coaches in becoming more aware of their own psychological experience in coaching. The questions are intended to identify both positive and negative thoughts, feelings, behaviors, and desires. They can be asked either as separate pairs or in one extended session. Because they represent opportunities for further exploration, it would be preferable if a trained sport psychology practitioner administered them. For each of these questions, consultants can help coaches broaden their answers with additional questions about emotions, wants, attitudes, or opinions, in order to clarify or enhance the responses given. How coaches answer the questions influences what the consultant does next. Some possible interventions are discussed after each pair of questions.

1. What were your original reasons for becoming a coach?
2. What were your hopes and expectations?

Purpose: To help coaches reconnect with their original dream about coaching. If coaches recall the original reasons, hopes, and expectations that they had when they began to coach, the consultant can encourage additional reflection to include the interest and excitement the coach may have felt. This could be useful for coaches whose work has become routine and dull. If a coach has forgotten the original desires and anticipation, the consultant can ask additional questions to help revive them.

3. What do you most want from coaching now?
4. What are your main sources of enjoyment or satisfaction at present?

Purpose: To highlight coaches' current motivation. Some coaches may feel victimized by the pressures and stresses of coaching. With these questions, the consultant can help coaches focus on their own desires, and perhaps reawaken the energy that comes from recognizing that what they are doing is connected to something they want. The consultant can also begin listening for what might be getting in the way of a coach's satisfaction or enjoyment.

5. What gives you good feelings about yourself as a coach?
6. What is most important to you in coaching? What do you do to make that a priority?

Purpose: To connect self-esteem and values to current behavior. Here, the consultant has the opportunity to underline the importance of coaches having good feelings about themselves in their work. The self-respect that comes from working in accordance with their inner values can enhance a coach's positive experience. This is especially true for coaches who do not feel in charge of their lives.

7. What interferes with you working effectively?
8. What upsets you as a coach? How do you react when you get upset?

Purpose: To identify potential psychological barriers and the resulting behaviors. From the answers coaches give, consultants can evaluate whether additional psychological work may be desirable. For example, consistent blaming of others might indicate a coach's difficulty in making internal attributions, and seeing how their own patterns of behavior could contribute to problems with others. Alternative coping techniques, e.g., relaxation or reframing, could be offered by the consultant to help coaches deal with upset.

9. What emotion do you feel when you do not get what you want?
10. What do you do when you feel that way?

Purpose: To illustrate the connection between wants, feelings, and behavior. For coaches who are not accustomed to making these connections, the consultant can clarify how emotions and desires influence behavior, and how behavior can affect emotions. This might begin to stimulate a coach's interest in internal psychological processes, and lay the groundwork for further self-exploration.

11. What might lead to your feeling: fear? guilt? embarrassment? hurt? shame?
12. What might give you bad feelings about yourself?

Purpose: To identify sources of unpleasant emotions. With these questions, the consultant gives coaches a beginning vocabulary of emotions. This could be particularly helpful for those coaches who have had little experience identifying their feelings. The answers can also be clues to difficulties that coaches may have in their work and relationships, and be used as starting points for further exploration.

13. What behaviors might result from each of these feelings?

Purpose: To identify behavioral consequences of negative emotions. Consultants can reinforce the connections between emotions and behaviors, and offer coaches the opportunity to consider alternative behaviors. Coaches can get greater control over their emotions, and cope more effectively when they have more behavioral options available.

14. What would you like to change?

Purpose: To introduce the possibility of alternative behaviors. The answers to this question allow the consultant to follow the coach's lead in initiating change (Giges, 2000).

With the increase in self-knowledge that may come from answering these questions, it may be easier for coaches to understand how some situations can become problems for them. Nonetheless, simply answering these questions is not likely to provide the depth of insight that is often necessary to motivate behavior change. Smoll and Smith (1980) also believed that awareness alone is not enough to ensure desirable behavior. Gaining information about oneself needs to be a continuous goal, but coaches, because of the position power that they hold, often do not get much direct feedback from players or their assistant coaches. As such, sport psychologist consultants can help coaches understand that gaining feedback about their interactive style can be just as valuable as any information that they gain about offensive, defensive, or performance strategies. Support for this belief can be found in a number of the classic texts from the management training literature (e.g., Hersey & Blanchard, 1982; Schein, 1969).

Managers, like coaches, have position power by virtue of their titles. Nonetheless, it is unlikely that either group would be able to motivate their people to achieve maximum results unless they were also able to earn the trust and respect of their team members. It is the ability to earn the trust and respect of others that establishes the foundation of personal power, and the most effective managers and leaders are those individuals who possess both position and personal power (Luft, 1984).

In general, management theory suggests that one of the primary sources of respect is knowledge. As such, it is no wonder that high performers in most fields seek out expert coaches to provide them with the knowledge necessary to excel. Nonetheless, knowledge alone is often not enough to motivate people to take risks or to push themselves to their limits. This extra motivation is typically dependent on trust and the quality of the relationship established between the leader and the subordinate (Petitpas, Danish, & Giges, 1999). How is trust established? One answer is that a trusting relationship is developed as a result of a process of self-disclosure and feedback. As described by Luft and Ingham in their classic Johari Window Model of awareness training (Luft, 1984), individuals who keep information about themselves hidden or private are less likely to receive support from others. In addition, it is doubtful that they would receive the feedback necessary to identify specific behaviors, attitudes, or statements that may inhibit mutual understanding and the development of a trusting relationship. On the other hand, coaches who are willing to self-disclose allow other people to get to know them better and to understand their motives. By so doing, these people are likely to spend less time trying to read the coaches' minds, and are more likely to feel safe enough to provide open and straightforward feedback. Coaches who receive feedback on their blind spots can choose to modify their behaviors or statements in ways that can reduce stress and increase their personal effectiveness. There are times, however, when something blocks self-awareness, and at these times, removing such barriers may help restore that awareness.

Psychological Barriers

The theoretical basis for the concept of psychological barriers derives from gestalt therapy (Perls, Hefferline, & Goodman, 1951), and from the growth and development model of psychological functioning (Erikson, 1950; Danish, Petitpas, & Hale, 1992). In gestalt therapy, "organismic self-regulation" refers to an internal psychological process consisting of a continuing flow of needs and satisfactions. Specifically, when a need emerges into the foreground of our experience, it can either be satisfied or interrupted. If it is satisfied, it recedes into the background, allowing another need to emerge. This process continues unless it is interrupted by a troubling thought, an uncomfortable feeling, conflicting desires, or external influences. When this happens, the need remains unsatisfied and interferes with the flow and with optimal functioning until the interruption is removed.

A basic assumption in the growth and development model is that we all have an inherent capacity for optimal functioning, and would be able to do so if nothing interfered. Danish et al., (1992) described various roadblocks that people may encounter in reaching their goals, and wrote "These individuals had to overcome their roadblocks before they were able to work toward their goal" (p. 409). Sternberg and Spear-Swerling (1998) also emphasized the importance of overcoming obstacles: "The decision one makes as to what to do about a barrier obstacle will powerfully affect whether one is able to reach one's desired destination, or perhaps, how one changes one's desired destination" (p. 225). Deci (2002) stated that interference with basic psychological needs leads to poorer performance and impaired well-being.

Optimal coaching is more likely to occur in the absence of obstacles. More specifically, whether a coach's task is preparing practice routines, planning game strategies, or becoming more self-aware, distractions diminish effectiveness. Just as physical barriers (i. e., fatigue, illness, or injury) can interfere with performance, so too can psychological barriers (Giges, 2000; Simons, 1992). When psychological barriers impair self-awareness, they can result in energy-draining distractions that interfere with focusing on important tasks. Barriers can arise from problems with family, administrators, colleagues, or athletes. In addition, barriers to self-awareness can develop from personal issues; that is, from the coach's own thoughts, feelings, behavior, or wants. For example, thinking barriers include self-doubt, self-criticism, low self-confidence, and perfectionism. Feeling barriers could be anxiety, guilt, anger, shame, sadness, and emotional hurt. Behavioral barriers are overworking, giving up, impulsiveness, and poor communication. Psychological barriers related to what we want include poor motivation, loss of desire or commitment, and conflicting interests.

Helping coaches remove or cope more effectively with psychological barriers (Giges, 2000) consists first of identifying the barriers with clarity and specificity. For example, feeling "uncomfortable" would be difficult to change without knowing what type of discomfort (i. e., fear, embarrassment, guilt, etc.) exists. Sport psychology consultants can assist coaches in self-exploration with a non-judgmental attitude, to determine what feeling, thought, want, or behavior is interfering with a coach's effectiveness. Many coaches become self-condemning or blaming if they do not achieve the results they intend. This tendency is, unfortunately, self-defeating. A self-critical pattern of thinking can undermine self-confidence, lower self-esteem, and be a distraction from the task at hand. Jackson and Delehanty (1995) wrote " The incessant accusations of the judging mind block vital energy and sabotage concentration" (p. 117). In addition, disapproval of oneself can lead to greater dependence on external approval, and an increased need to please others. It is, therefore, important that self-awareness be non-judgmental (Giges, 1996; Lynch, 2001).

Within each of us is the capacity to observe what we do, what we think, what we feel, and what we want. This observer part of us neither approves or disapproves. It merely sees. It does what has been called "neutral noticing" (Giges, 1996): no criticism, no reprimand, no disapproval, or judgment. In gestalt therapy, the awareness continuum refers to a process of observing our moment-to-moment awareness. During this full attention to present experience, judgment is suspended (Naranjo, 1970). In meditative practice, this process is described as detached observation or mindfulness: awareness in a non-judgmental form (Kabat-Zinn, 1994; Walsh, 1977; Young, 1994). In psychoanalytic theory, the "observing ego" refers to the part of our personality that merely witnesses what it sees without judgment (Ormont, 1995; Sterba, 1940).

If a coach has been abrupt or insulting to an athlete, he or she could observe that behavior without justifying it, or becoming defensive about it. If self-condemnation is triggered by the awareness, that too can be observed without further self-criticism. As described above, this type of observing can lead to a choice to behave differently in the future. In addition, this process can protect an already stressed coach from the energy draining distraction of self-criticism. "Neutral noticing" can be achieved with the help of a friend, colleague, or family member. Specifically, this can be done by listening to the coach's description of the situation, identifying those thoughts and comments that contain self-condemnation or self-disapproval, and encouraging the coach to express the thought or feeling without self-criticism. Sometimes, this level of help may be insufficient to bring about change. In these situations, additional assistance from a trained sport psychology practitioner may be useful to help coaches alter self-defeating behaviors.

The next step in removing psychological barriers involves initiating change, creating a small shift in the thinking that underlies the difficulty. The key word is "initiating." Too early an expectation of an end result can lead to new barriers, such as frustration or discouragement. Some ways to create this shift include: exploring other options in behavior or in viewpoint; clarifying the difference between what's real and what's imagined (i. e., "what is" vs. "what if"); or modifying "all-or-none" thinking (e. g., "Either my team wins this game or my life is ruined"). A small initial change can often result in a significant outcome with practice, persistence, and patience (Giges & Petitpas, 2000). Consultants can help maintain this change with follow-up sessions to review progress, new challenges, and new barriers, and to reinforce the work done previously. In some instances, where barriers are not removed, it may be necessary to help coaches cope more effectively by offering other techniques, e.g., psychological skills training.

Challenges for the Sport Psychology Consultant

When a coach's success is achieved at the expense of his/her personal health or family relationships, what can the sport psychology consultant do? Although there are several possible answers, we believe that they all begin with establishing a good working relationship with the coach. With this as a foundation, and with the coach's permission, a consultant can begin to discuss the coach's present perceptions, beliefs, attitudes, and emotions, as well as implications and consequences for the future. With greater self-awareness and a more objective assessment of the problem, the coach has a better chance to re-evaluate the situation. If the coach decides to continue the present pattern without change, the consultant can provide emotional support for the coach, and be alert to any beginning change in the coach's approach.

Some coaches may be very difficult to work with, and be almost unapproachable with regard to their personal difficulties, even if these result in problems with athletes, assistant coaches, administrators, or parents. How can sport psychology consultants engage such coaches in self-examination? Here again, the starting point is the relationship with the coach, in particular the building of trust by the coach toward the consultant. This takes time and experience, and requires that the consultant learn how the coach views his/her work situation, and what he/she cares about (Peterson, 1996). Trust may also develop as the coach observes the consultant working with athletes, assistant coaches, and other members of the athletic community. In individual meetings with the coach, the consultant can include descriptions of general psychological concepts, and illustrate them with specific examples. This might stimulate an interest in the coach, and pave the way for more personal discussions. This situation is also an excellent opportunity for consultants to obtain peer supervision, and to discuss possible difficulties and strategies with professional colleagues.

There are other coaches who may be willing and open to self-reflection and introspection, but have neither the experience nor the skills to do so. Sport psychology consultants can be helpful to these coaches by clarifying the connections between thoughts, feelings, and behaviors, by identifying different kinds of emotion, and by describing the effects of conflicting wants.

Conclusions

The purpose of this article was to open discussion about the importance of providing coaches with sport psychology services that focus on their own needs and motivations.

Coaches, like athletes, are often forced to perform under high levels of pressure, operate under intense public scrutiny, and are held to incredibly high expectations. At the same time, they may be judged on factors that are outside their direct control, namely the performance and behaviors of their athletes. As a result, coaches are often in need of consultation services to assist them in increasing their awareness of their own needs, and helping them to learn strategies to overcome barriers that inhibit their ability to achieve their desired outcomes. Sport psychology practitioners may be helpful to coaches in initiating and maintaining changes in behavior, emotions, attitudes, judgments, or wants. Hopefully, this article will motivate more sport psychology professionals to share their strategies and suggestions for working with coaches.

References

American Coaching Effectiveness Program, Level 2. (1989). *Sport psychology workbook*. Champaign, IL: Human Kinetics.

Andersen, M. B. (2002). Helping college student-athletes in and out of sport. In J. L. Van Raalte & B. W. Brewer (Eds.), *Exploring sport and exercise psychology* (2nd ed., pp. 373-393). Washington, DC: American Psychological Association.

Anshel, M. (2003). *Sport psychology: From theory to practice.* San Francisco: Benjamin-Cummings.

Behncke, L. (April, 2002). Self-regulation: A brief review. *Athletic Insight - The Online Journal of Sport Psychology, 4, (1).* Retrieved September 15, 2003 from http://www.athleticinsight.com/Vol4Iss1/SelfRegulation.htm

Brewer, B. W. (2000). Doing sport psychology in the coaching role. In M. B. Andersen (Ed.), *Doing sport psychology* (pp. 237-247). Champaign, IL: Human Kinetics.

Chelladurai, P., & Ogasawara, E. (2003). Satisfaction and commitment of American and Japanese collegiate coaches. *Journal of Sport Management, 17,* 62-73.

Cogan, K. D., & Petrie, T. A. (1996). Consultation with college student-athletes. *College Student Journal, 30,* 9-16.

Cox, R. H. (1998). *Sport Psychology: Concepts and applications.* Boston: WCB/McGraw-Hill.

Dale, J., & Weinberg, R. (1990). Burnout in sport: A review and critique. *Journal of Applied Sport Psychology, 2,* 67-83.

Danish, S. J., Petitpas, A. J., & Hale, B. D. (1992). A developmental-educational intervention model in sport psychology. *The Sport Psychologist, 6,* 403-415.

Danish, S. J., Petitpas, A. J., & Hale, B. D. (1993). Life development intervention for athletes: Life skills through sports. *The Counseling Psychologist, 21,* 352-385.

Deci, E. L. (2002). Facilitating autonomous self-regulation through support of basic psychological needs. *Journal of Sport & Exercise Psychology, 24* (Suppl.), S50.

Erikson, E. (1950). *Childhood and society.* New York: W. W. Norton.

Etzel, E. F., Ferrante, A. P., & Pinkney, J. W. (Eds.). (1996). *Counseling college student athletes: Issues and interventions* (2nd ed.). Morgantown, WV: Fitness Information Technology.

Fuoss, D. E., & Troppman, R. J. (1981). *Effective coaching: A psychological approach*. New York: Wiley.

Frankl, V. (1992). *Man's search for meaning: An introduction to logotherapy*. Boston: Beacon Press.

Giges, B. (June, 1996). *Self-awareness for sport psychologists*. Workshop conducted at the Thirteenth Annual Conference on Counseling Athletes, Springfield, MA.

Giges, B. (2000). Removing psychological barriers: Clearing the way. In M. B. Andersen (Ed.), *Doing sport psychology* (pp. 17- 31). Champaign, IL: Human Kinetics.

Giges, B., & Petitpas, A. J. (2000). Brief contact interventions in sport psychology. *The Sport Psychologist, 14,* 176-187.

Goleman, D. (1995). *Emotional intelligence.* New York: Bantam Books.

Goleman, D. (1998). *Working with emotional intelligence.* New York: Bantam Books.

Gould, D., Greenleaf, C., Guinan, D., & Chung, Y. (2002). A survey of U.S. Olympic coaches: Variables perceived to have influenced athlete performances and coach effectiveness. *The Sport Psychologist, 16,* 229-250.

Greenspan, M., & Andersen, M. B. (1995). Providing psychological services to student athletes: A developmental psychology model. In S. M. Murphy (Ed.), *Sport psychology interventions* (pp. 177-191). Champaign, IL: Human Kinetics.

Henschen, K. P. (2001). Athletic staleness and burnout: Diagnosis, prevention, and treatment. In J. M. Williams (Ed.),

Applied sport psychology: Personal growth to peak performance (4th ed., pp. 445-455). Mountain View CA: Mayfield.

Hersey, P., & Blanchard, K. (1982). *Management of organizational behavior: Utilizing human resources* (4th Ed.). Engelwood Cliffs, NJ: Prentice-Hall.

Jackson, P., & Delehanty, H. (1995). *Sacred hoops: Spiritual lessons of a hardwood warrior.* New York: Hyperion.

Kabat-Zinn, J. (1994). *Wherever you go, there you are: Mindfulness meditation in everyday life.* New York: Hyperion.

Kelley, B. C., Eklund, R. C., & Ritter-Taylor, M. (1999). Stress and burnout among collegiate tennis coaches. *Journal of Sport & Exercise Psychology, 21,* 113-130.

Kiel, F., Rimmer, E., Williams, K., & Doyle, M. (1996). Coaching at the top. *Consulting Psychology Journal, 48,* 67-77.

LeUnes, A. D., & Nation, J. R. (1990). *Sport psychology, an introduction.* Chicago: Nelson-Hall.

Luft, J. (1984). *Group processes: An introduction to group dynamics.* Palo Alto, CA: Mayfield.

Lynch, J. (2001). *Creative coaching.* Champaign, IL: Human Kinetics.

Martens, R. (1987). *Coaches' guide to sport psychology.* Champaign, IL: Human Kinetics.

Martin, J. J. (1999). A personal development model of sport psychology for athletes with disabilities. *Journal of Applied Sport Psychology, 11,* 181-193.

Mascolo, M. F., & Fischer, K. W. (1998). The development of self through the coordination of component systems. In M. Ferrari & R. J. Sternberg (Eds.), *Self-awareness: Its nature and development* (pp. 332-387). New York: Guilford Press.

Maslow, A. (1987). *Motivation and personality* (3rd ed.). New York: Harper & Row.

Murphy, S. M., & Tammen, V. (1998). In search of psychological skills. In J. L Duda (Ed.), *Advances in sport and exercise psychology measurement* (pp. 195-209). Morgantown, WV: Fitness Information Technology.

Naranjo, C. (1970). Present-centeredness: Technique, prescription, and ideal. In J. Fagan & I. L. Shepherd, (Eds.), *Gestalt therapy now: Theory, technique, and applications* (pp.47-69). New York: Science and Behavior Books.

Naylor, S. (2003, October). *Straight from the horse's mouth: What coaches really want from a sport psychology consultant.* Colloquium presented at the annual meeting of the Association for the Advancement of Applied Sport Psychology, Philadelphia, PA.

Ogilvie, B. C., & Tutko, T. A. (1966). *Problem athletes and how to handle them.* London: Pelham.

Orbach, I., Singer, R. N., & Price, S. (1999). An attribution training program and achievement in sport. *The Sport Psychologist, 13,* 69-82.

Ormont, L. R. (1995). Cultivating the observing ego in the group setting. *International Journal of Group Psychotherapy, 45,* 489-507.

Perls, F., Hefferline, R. F., & Goodman, P. (1951). *Gestalt therapy: Excitement and growth in the human personality.* New York: Dell.

Peterson, D. B. (1996). Executive coaching at work: The art of one-on-one change. *Consulting Psychology Journal, 48,* 78-86.

Petitpas, A. J., Danish, S. J., & Giges, B. (1999). The sport psychologist-athlete relationship: Implications for training. *The Sport Psychologist, 13,* 344-357.

Raedeke, T. D., Granzyk, T. L., & Warren, A. (2000). Why coaches experience burnout: A commitment perspective. *Journal of Sport & Exercise Psychology, 22,* 85-105.

Ravizza, K. (1998). Increasing awareness for sport performance. In J. M. Williams (Ed.), *Applied sport psychology: Personal growth to peak performance* (3rd ed., pp. 171-181). Mountain View, CA: Mayfield.

Rosenfeld, L. B., & Richman, J. M. (1997). Developing effective social support: Team building and the social support process. *Journal of Applied Sport Psychology, 9,* 133-153.

Rotella, R. J. (1985). The coach and stress. In L. K. Bunker, R. J. Rotella, & A. S. Reilly (Eds.), *Sport psychology* (pp. 129-135). Ann Arbor, MI: McNaughton & Gunn.

Schein, E. H. (1969). *Process consultation: Its role in organization development.* Reading, MA: Addison Wesley.

Simons, J. (1992). Psychological barriers of major competitions: Basic issues and coaching interventions. *Track and Field Quarterly, 92,* 28-31.

Smoll, F. L., & Smith, R. E. (1980). Techniques for improving self-awareness of youth sport coaches. *Journal of Physical Education and Recreation, 51,* 46-49.

Sportscoach UK (2003). A guide to mentoring sports coaches. *Sportscoach UK.* Retrieved September 29, 2003 from http:// www.sportscoachUK.org/improve/workshop/developyourcoaching.htm#msc

Sterba, R. F. (1940). The dynamics of the dissolution of the transference resistance. *Psychoanalytic Quarterly, 9,* 363-379.

Sternberg, R. J., & Spear-Swerling, L. (1998). Personal navigation. In M. Ferrari & R. J. Sternberg (Eds.), *Self-awareness: Its nature and development* (pp. 219-246). New York: Guilford Press.

Sullivan, P. A., & Nashman, H. W. (1993). The 1992 U. S. Olympic team sport coaches: Satisfactions and concerns. *Applied Research in Coaching and Athletics Annual, 8,* 1-14.

Tutko, T. A., & Richards, J. W. (1971). *Psychology of coaching.* Boston: Allyn & Bacon.

Vealey, R. S. (1988). Future directions in psychological skills training. *The Sport Psychologist, 2,* 318-336.

Vernacchia, R. A. (1992). Overcoming overcoaching: The key to beating burnout. *Track and Field Quarterly, 92,* 44-46.

Vernacchia, R. A. (1995). "They used to call me coach": Burnout and the career termination of coaches. In K. P. Henschen & W. F. Straub (Eds.), *Sport psychology: An analysis of athlete behavior* (3rd ed., pp. 361-370). Longmeadow, MA: Mouvement.

Vernacchia, R. (1999). Burnout and role conflict. *USA Track and Field coaching education curriculum: Level II sport sciences/sport psychology.* Indianapolis, IN: USA Track and Field.

Vernacchia, R. A., McGuire, R. T., & Cook, D. L. (1996). *Coaching mental excellence: "It does matter whether you win or lose."* Portola Valley, CA: Warde.

Vernacchia, R. A., & McGuire, R. (1998). What coaches want from sport psychology. *Journal of Applied Sport Psychology, 10,* (Suppl), 129-130.

Walton, G. M. (1992). *Beyond winning: The timeless wisdom of great philosopher coaches.* Champaign, IL: Leisure Press.

Walsh, R. N. (1977). Initial meditative experiences. *Journal of Transpersonal Psychology, 9,* 151-192.

Wooden, J. R. (1988). *Practical modern basketball.* Needham Heights, MA: Allyn & Bacon.

Young, S. (1994). Purpose and method of vipassana meditation. *Humanist Psychologist, 22,* 53-61.

Yukelson, D., Sullivan, B. A., Morett, C., & Dorenkott, B. (2003, October). *Coaches' perspective on applying sport psychology into their coaching.* Colloquium presented at the annual meeting of the Association for the Advancement of Applied Sport Psychology, Philadelphia, PA.

Accepted author manuscript version reprinted, by permission, from *The Sport Psychologist*, 2000, 14, (2), 176-187.

Brief Contact Interventions in Sport Psychology

Burt Giges
Springfield College and Westchester Track Club
Albert Petitpas
Springfield College

The sport psychology literature provides many examples of the use of mental skills training with athletes. Little attention, however, has been given to those brief interventions that occur frequently when working with athletes in the field. Such interventions are time limited, action oriented, and present focused. The purpose of this article is to provide a brief overview of the use of brief contact interventions with athletes in field settings. In particular, we provide a short introduction to such interventions; describe a framework for their use, and present several case examples. We believe that brief contact interventions can be made more effective by following the principles described in this article.

Although the sport psychology literature is filled with case examples using various techniques to help athletes improve their performances, little attention has been paid to managing the brief interactions that occur frequently when working with athletes in the field. Unlike traditional counseling interventions that are typically scheduled for a set period of time, sport psychology interventions in the field are often brief and action oriented. Ravizza (in Simons & Andersen, 1995) described some of the differences between scheduled and brief sport psychology interactions in the following:

> The ideal situation is to be in your office and have the athlete come in, and you've got two hours together, and you really get into it. But a lot of the work is when you're traveling with the team. It's in a hotel lobby, it's on a bus, it's five minutes here, six minutes there, and in these little blocks of time you can do a lot. I've really seen that in five minutes you can impact a person by getting them thinking and getting their thought processes going so then they can think clearly about things. (p. 459).

In the present article, brief contact refers to a single interaction of short duration (15-20 minutes) that takes place within the course of an ongoing consulting relationship. These single interactions have a lot in common with several brief therapy models, but differ in terms of the length of contact and the structure of the intervention strategies employed. Brief therapies typically range from five to 15 sessions and follow a circumscribed set of procedures (Pinkerton & Rockwell, 1994; Reich & Neenan, 1986). Brief contact interventions, however, are unplanned interactions that take place between clients and practitioners that involve "teachable moments" where clients are able to gain new perspectives on their present situations. In both brief therapy and brief contact interventions, practitioners operate within the boundaries of their clients' presenting situations and are willing to allow other important psychological issues to remain unexplored (Kottler, 1999; Talmon, 1990). In sport settings, brief contact interactions are normally focused on performance enhancement and not inter- and intrapersonal issues, psychopathology, or early childhood experience (Giges, 1998). The purpose of this article is to open discussion about the role of brief contact interventions in sport psychology consultations. In particular, we provide a short overview of brief contact interventions, describe a framework for their use, and present four case examples.

Brief Contact Interventions

Brief therapy models have a long history in both traditional and strategic therapeutic approaches. From traditional psychotherapy, brief interventions are described as strategies that are active, focused, goal-oriented, circumscribed, warmly supportive, action-oriented, and concerned with present adaptation (Barten, 1971; Talmon, 1990). A practitioner using brief strategies offers small interventions, observes the client's responses, makes adjustments to include those responses, and intervenes again (Rosenbaum, Hoyt, & Talmon, 1990). These small interventions commonly focus on one problem, use the client's strength, and maintain a present and solution-focused mind-set (Bloom, 1981). Hoyt (1995) provided an illustration of this process in his discussion of the central question in Goulding and Goulding's (I979) redecision therapy, "What are you willing to change today?"

What--specificity, target, focus
are--active verbs, present tense
you--self as agent, personal functioning
willing--choice, responsibility, initiative
to change--alter, not just "work on" or "explore"
today--now, in the moment
?--inquiry, open field, therapist receptive (p. 84-85).

Hoyt's expansion of this basic question captures the key elements that form the framework of brief contact interventions. Practitioners involved in these brief interactions are likely to benefit from the principles presented in such a parsimonious fashion. In addition, Wells (1993) suggested that by staying within the context of identifying and understanding the problem, the therapist creates a collaborative basis for interventions that are already under way. The guiding principles involve starting with the client's definition of the problem, concentrating the focus on this definition, working on it from the beginning, and continuing to refine the services delivered through evaluating the client's response to those interventions already made.

The theoretical basis for the interventions described in the present article also borrows substantially from a synthesis of principles in counseling psychology, gestalt therapy, and cognitive therapy. From counseling psychology comes an emphasis on growth and development, and using the strengths of the client to learn more effective ways to deal with challenges (Sexton & Whiston, 1994). Gestalt therapy focuses on present functioning (the "here and now"), on what is happening (rather than why), and on personal choice and responsibility (Perls, 1969). In addition to asking questions about an athlete's current experience (thoughts, feelings, wants, and behavior), gestalt therapists often use guided imagery to bring past experience into the present. Cognitive therapy gives primary importance to thoughts as the major determinant of feelings and behavior (Beck, 1967). Because maladaptive thoughts derive from one's viewpoint or perspective, an important technique in cognitive therapy is reframing. This intervention consists of helping the athlete consider alternative meanings and interpretations to given situations. Therefore, in brief interventions in sport psychology, the consultant follows the athlete's lead, builds on what is presented, stays focused on the athlete's abilities and options in the present, and assists in creating a shift in the athlete's perception of a situation.

Brief contact interventions also have much in common with the strategic, interactional approaches developed from family systems research centers such as the Mental Research Institute in Palo Alto and Family Therapy Institute in Washington, DC (e.g., Fisch, Weakland, & Segal, 1982; Watzlawick, 1983; Watzlawick, Weakland, & Fisch, 1974;). For example, strategic interactional approaches work from a "non-pathology" orientation, start with what the client brings as a presenting problem, deal with the here and now, emphasize what rather than why, use the person's own language, clearly define the problem and the goal, and frequently use reframing as a significant component of the interventions. Practitioners using brief contact interventions strive to initiate some type of change in behavior or perception because they believe that even a very small change may be all that is needed to bring about an alteration of an entire non-productive pattern of thinking or behavior (Erikson, 1974). This theoretical perspective is a systems model in which an appreciation of different levels of information and communication is necessary to understand and resolve problems that are believed to be maintained by the client's attempts at problem-solving that have become repetitive and ineffective (Watzlawick, et al., 1974).

A Framework for Brief Contact Interventions

Brief contact interventions may be effective because small changes in just a single session can have a snowballing effect that can initiate significant improvements in a person's functioning (Erikson, 1974; Kottler, 1999). Nonetheless, these brief interventions should take place within the context of an on-going consulting relationship. Kivlighan and Schmitz (1992) have argued that attempts to offer encouragement or to reframe the way a person looks at a situation can have a negative impact on adherence to treatment goals, if offered before a working alliance has been established between the practitioner and the client.

Brief contact interventions in sport psychology consultations should be grounded within the context of an established working alliance (Bordin, 1979). Sport psychology consultants who have established rapport with their athlete-clients and who have a good understanding of the nature and history of their performance problems are in the best position to intervene by taking advantage of "teachable moments" (Petitpas, Danish, & Giges, 1999). These interventions do not rely on the intuition of the practitioner, but are guided by the basic principle: follow the athlete (Orlick, 1989). By pursuing the athlete's stated goals and by following and using the athlete's specific language, the consultant demonstrates an understanding of the situation and is well positioned to facilitate the small changes that can lead to performance improvements. The goal of the consultant's interventions in such an approach is to initiate a shift in the athlete's perception of the situation, which may then lead to a change in the athlete's experience, and help remove any psychological barriers to optimal performance.

Brief contact interactions follow a set of guiding principles (Giges, in press): (a) present experience is given priority, (b) the athlete's words, gestures, facial expressions, and body posture are carefully observed, and (c) the consultant listens for "entry points." Athletes will often say something that the consultant hears as an opportunity for more in-depth exploration. Such opportunities are entry points, openings that can be used to help increase athletes' understanding of their experiences. These entry points may consist of an unexpressed feeling, an unrecognized want, or an underlying judgment or self-criticism, and can be observed in the following case examples.

Case Examples

The following examples of brief interventions are drawn from the first author's experiences with members of two track and field teams. Except for one example, these contacts occurred at track meets, prior to the athletes' events, and were each approximately 15-20 minutes in duration. The consultations described were initiated by the specific runner, the coach, or by the first author. In each case, the first author had an established relationship with the athlete in question. The athletes had also been observed by the consultant, in the course of their training and competition, and general impressions of how they functioned were formed from these observations. Although some consultants have recommended that sport psychology consultants should avoid game day or race day interventions, especially during major competitions (Henschen, 1991), the examples given here suggest that under certain circumstances such involvement may be helpful.

Runner F

F is a young woman who has been running competitively for a few years. It was always important to her to do well each time she raced, and for her this meant "finishing strong" even if she did not win. Previously, all her races were at outdoor track meets. The coach knew that this first indoor meet presented a new challenge for her, and that she was afraid of not doing well. Therefore, he suggested I talk with her. She usually sat with her teammates, but when I noticed her sitting by herself, I walked over to talk with her.

B. Hi, how are you doing?
F. I'm very nervous today.
B. Do you want to talk about it?
F. I don't know. Yeah, I guess.
B. So, what do you think is going on?
F. Well, this is my first indoor race...I'm afraid of dying out there.

In a longer interview, I might ask her more about her feelings. In this brief contact, I thought that helping her focus on what she can control would be more useful.

B. How do you think that would happen?
F. I know me. If I'm not doing well in the race I'm afraid I'll give up.
B. What would make you give up?
F. I've done it before. I can't stand the idea of not doing well.
B. What would make not doing well today so terrible?
F. I don't know...Yes I do. It would show that I'm no good.

In this brief pre-race work, I would not address any underlying difficulty, such as equating her self-worth with her performance. I kept the focus on what she could control in the present.

B. Does doing well have to do with what you're doing or what somebody else is doing?
F. I never thought about that...I guess it has more to do with what I'm doing.
B. So what would it take for you to do well?
F. Well, I think that if I could just finish the race without dying out there, I'd be OK.
B. Are you capable of doing that?
F. I don't know...Yeah, I guess...I do it most of the time outdoors.

B. How do you do it?
F. How do I do it? I don't know. I guess if I don't give up on myself...if I believe in myself and keep going, I can do it.
B. Does being indoors really change that?
F. ...Probably not...It shouldn't, although this is my first indoor meet...No, I guess it really doesn't have to.

I sensed a shift in her feeling about herself regarding the race today, and decide to check whether that was her experience.

B. How do you feel right now?
F. Well, I still fell pretty nervous, but I kind of think I'll be able to finish.
B. Do you want to talk any more about it?
F. No...Thanks. I'll let you know what happens after the race.
B. Talk to you later.

She did finish. What happened in our discussion was apparently enough of a shift in her perception of herself racing indoors to allow her to run even with the anxiety, and to allow the identity issue to recede for now. This brief contact would not be sufficient in the long term if any underlying problem persisted and caused her difficulty in the future.

Runner M

M is a middle distance runner who has been running for several years and has recently been improving her times and her race results. She is generally optimistic, and her confidence in her ability as a runner has been increasing. On this occasion, however, she seemed a bit down when she came over to talk with me before her race.

B. Hi. How are things going?
M. Well, I thought they were going well, but the last time I did a 3000 it was a disaster.

B. Is that having an effect on you now?
M. Yeah. I'm worried the same thing is going to happen today.
B. Tell me what happened last time?

Although this is a question about an event in the past, it addresses her present worry.

M. Well, I didn't go out fast enough. The lead runner got so far ahead of me, I got discouraged.
B. What were you thinking?
M. I was going, "I'll never catch her...I should have gone out faster."
B. Anything else?
M. Well, it got worse...I began to feel like I shouldn't be competing against these women...that I'm really not good enough.

This runner was not usually pessimistic or negative in her thinking. I suspected something had triggered her negative thinking about not running well.

B. You're not usually this negative. What do you think might be going on?
M. I don't really know. All I know is that since that time my hamstring tightened up, I haven't been running well.
B. Did the hamstring pull have any other effect on you?
M. Yeah...I guess...I started losing my confidence...I began to doubt whether I'm as good as the other runners.

In this brief contact, instead of exploring the self-doubt and loss of confidence, I decided to limit the questioning to her current physical condition and its effect on her performance.

B. Is your hamstring healed now?
M. I thought so, but I'm afraid to go all out.

B. In the past, when you did go all out, how did that feel?
M. Great!...I don't even have to win, as long as I don't quit inside.

The shift from comparing herself to others to getting satisfaction from her own effort is important. I decided to pick up on it.

B. So when you give it all you got, it's very satisfying.
M. And how! You know, as I look back on that last race, I think I was afraid of pulling my hamstring again, and I didn't even realize it.
B. What do you think about that now?
M. Wow! There I was thinking I'm out of my league running against them, and what was really going on was that I was holding back...I'll bet if I didn't hold back, I could run with them.
B. Do you think you will run with them this time?
M. Well, I'm not sure...I hope so. I'm definitely going to give it a try. I'll let you know.

In the race, caution again led her to go out slowly, and she was almost half a lap behind the leader after the first 1000. In the remaining five laps, she began to close on the leader bit by bit. With less than a lap to go, she caught her, and to her delight (and mine too, I confess), she passed her and won the race. Our brief talk helped her remember that her own determination was an important source of satisfaction for her. She also realized as we spoke that she had previously been holding herself back without being aware of it, and was now able to go all out. No further interventions were necessary at that time.

Runner C

C had taken a year off from running to pursue his studies. Prior to his first mile race after returning, he was extremely nervous about how he would look if he did not do well. I asked him if he would like to talk with me to about decreasing his anxiety. He welcomed the idea and, with the coach's help, we were able to use an available room in the hotel adjacent to the track. He began without waiting for any questions from me.

C. I am so nervous I'm jumping out of my skin.
B. I can see that.
C. I haven't raced in over a year...I could go out there and end up looking like an idiot...I don't think I trained enough...I don't really feel ready to race...The coach thought it would be okay if I wanted to...I really do want to, but maybe it's too soon.

He spoke rapidly, without pausing between his comments. For this brief contact, I decided not to explore his feelings further, and not to ask him what he thought was making him so nervous. My approach was to help him regain some sense of control. I decided to ask him to look at what he could do even though he felt nervous and unsure.

B. Let's assume you didn't train enough, and that you're not quite ready to race, could you imagine going out on the track and doing a hard practice run?
C. Sure, but it's not the same.
B. I know, but you might be able to make it similar.
C. How?
C. Yeah, if you think it would help. B. Would you be willing to do an exercise that I would guide you through?
B. Okay. Get yourself into a comfortable position and close your eyes...[there was a short relaxation introduction using awareness of breathing]...Now, imagine you're at the track before the other runners and audience arrive...Take a couple of warm-up laps in your sweats...Can you do that?
C. [nods]
B. [slowly] While no one is around, get ready to do a hard practice run...Something almost as hard as if you were racing... maybe 90% of maximum effort...Remove your sweats, and I'll start you off... Ready...Go!...After the first lap, as you continue running, notice that a couple of other runners are deciding to do the same thing--to go out on the track and do a hard run...

you see them and keep running...and as you're continuing, you notice some spectators beginning to trickle into the seats. About half way through, you see that there are several others on the track, and the stands are pretty full. You notice it, and don't give it much thought. You're into your own run. As you approach the end, you decide to give it all you got, and have a strong finish.

C. [takes some deep breaths]

B. What are you feeling right now?

C. Energized...Up. That was good. My nervousness feels different. I mean, it's there, but it's nowhere near as bad as it was before.

B. Do you think you want to go ahead with the race?

C. Sure!

B. Okay. Go to it.

In this case, it is difficult to know what part of the change in his nervousness was due to the relaxation brought on by the breathing exercise, what part was the fantasy experience, and what part came from the idea of running his own race. My intent was to help him see the possibility of running his own race, focus on his own participation, apart from the other runners or the spectators, and thereby decrease his preoccupation with what others might think. Even though the causal factor in the brief contact is debatable, the intervention seemed to have a beneficial effect. Because he was out of shape, he finished dead last. Instead of his anticipated shame or self-criticism, however, he seemed satisfied that he was able to give it what he had and to finish the race. He was neither irritable nor depressed, as he had been after previous races in which he had done poorly. In fact, he was able to join his teammates in the stands to support other members of the team in their races.

Runner E

E was formerly a member of the track team until she moved to another city. We had been keeping in touch with each other since her move, and the following session was conducted on the telephone prior to one of her races. She did not have a coach at the present time. Her confidence was slipping, and she had reverted to the negative thinking that usually occurred whenever she was not running well.

B. Hi, how are things going?
E. I'm not doing so hot. I'm afraid I'm not going to do well again today.

In our correspondence, she often wrote about losing interest in running, feeling pessimistic about her ability, and discouraged about her future as a runner. In this conversation prior to her race, it seemed more helpful to stay focused on her racing than on her feelings.

B. During a race, do you know when you begin to believe you're not going to do well?
E. Yeah, actually...when somebody passes me, it's like the race is over.
B. How does that work?
E. I start to think...I don't belong here...who am I kidding?... these people are all better than I am...I get so discouraged...I literally lose my courage!...The word that popped into my head about what I am was "FAILURE!"

In this brief contact, discussion about what she thinks causes her to lose courage or to see herself as a failure would not be practical. Because it is important to keep a narrow focus, I decided to use her experience of the word that "popped into her head."

B. That sounds like an important moment.
E. What do you mean?
B. I mean the moment when someone passes you.
E. And how!

B. Maybe you can use it to your advantage.
E. How?
B. Well, until now it triggers off a loss of courage and a judgment of failure.
E. It's scary. If I fail, everyone will be very disappointed, including me...I'm also being cut down to size...I start thinking I'll have to start all over...I'll never get anywhere.
B. That's what usually goes with the idea of "failure." Suppose you took being passed as a signal...like a red flag...a wake-up call that says, "Hey, someone just passed you! What are you going to do about it?"
E. What could I do about it?
B. You do surges at different times during the race?
E. Yeah, I kind of think of it as stepping on the peddle and giving it more gas. But I've never done it when someone's past me.
B. When you have done it, how have you felt?
E. Free!
B. How about replacing "Failure" with "Free," and using it as a time to surge?
E. That would be great if I could do it.
B. Would you like to do it in the race coming up later today?
E. Yeah. I think I would. I'm going to give it a try.

I felt comfortable giving her what amounted to a racing strategy because she did not have a coach at the time. If she had had a coach, then I would have suggested that she and the coach talk over such a strategy before trying it out in a race. Sport psychologists need to be mindful of when their interventions begin to cross professional boundaries.

She called later to tell me about the race. During the race, she did not exactly carry out the plan. When someone passed her, she did not think of the word "Free" and surge at that moment, but she also did not lose courage or think "Failure." Later in the race, she did initiate a surge with the new cue word "Free," and felt good about that. After that day, being passed did not have quite the same negative effect on her as it did before. Sometimes talking about a problem initiates a change, even if the intervention is not carried out exactly as intended.

Conclusions

Instead of regularly scheduled hourly appointments, many sport performance enhancement interventions take place in field settings that allow only time limited contacts. The purpose of this article was to describe several of these brief field interventions and provide a simple framework for structuring these contacts to keep them focused, active, goal-oriented, and concerned with present adaptation. Our goal was to begin an exchange of information about other frameworks that are used to structure brief contact interventions. With the ever-increasing travel requirements faced by elite athletes, more sport psychology consultations are taking place via e-mail, telephone, or intermittent brief contacts, and there is little empirical evidence to support the efficacy of these modes of service delivery. We hope this article will bring attention to brief contact interventions, and spawn future outcome research and new frameworks for practice.

References

Barten, H. (Ed.). (1971). *Brief therapies.* New York: Behavioral Publications.

Beck, A. T. (1967). *Depression: Clinical, experimental, and theoretical aspects.* New York: Hoeber.

Bloom, B. L. (1981). Focused single-session therapy: Initial development and evaluation. In S. H. Budman (Ed.), *Forms of brief therapy* (pp. 167-218). New York: Guilford Press.

Bordin, E. S. (1979). The generalizability of the psychoanalytic concept of the working alliance. *Psychotherapy: Theory, Research, and Practice, 16*, 252-260.

Erickson, M. H. (1974). Foreword. In P. Watzlawick, J. H. Weakland, & R. Fisch, *Change: Principles of problem formation and problem resolution* (p. ix). New York: W. W. Norton.

Fisch, R., Weakland, J. H., & Segal, L. (1982). *The tactics of change: Doing therapy briefly*. San Francisco: Jossey-Bass.

Giges, B. (1998). Psychodynamic concepts in sport psychology: Comment on Strean & Strean. *The Sport Psychologist, 12*, 223-227.

Giges, B. (in press). Removing psychological barriers: Clearing the way. In M. B. Andersen (Ed.), *Doing sport psychology: Process and practice*. Champaign, IL: Human Kinetics.

Goulding, M. M., & Goulding, R. L. (1979). *Changing lives through redecision therapy*. New York: Brunner/Mazel.

Henschen, K. (1991). Critical issues involving male consultants and female athletes. *The Sport Psychologist, 5*, 313-321.

Hoyt, M. F. (1995). *Brief therapy and managed care: Readings for contemporary practice*. San Francisco: Jossey-Bass.

Kivlighan, D. M., & Schmitz, P. J. (1992). Counselor technical activity in cases with improving working alliances and continuing-poor working alliances. *Journal of Counseling Psychology, 39*, 32-38.

Kottler, J. A. (1999). *Nuts & bolts of helping*. Boston: Allyn & Bacon.

Orlick, T. (1989). Reflections on sportpsych consulting with individual and team sport athletes at summer and winter Olympic games. *The Sport Psychologist, 3,* 358-365.

Perls, F. (1969). *Gestalt therapy verbatim.* Lafayette, CA: Real People Press.

Petitpas, A. J., Danish, S. J., & Giges, B. (1999). The sport psychologist-athlete relationship: Implications for training. *The Sport Psychologist 13,* 344-357.

Pinkerton, R. S., & Rockwell, W. J. K. (1994). Very brief psychological interventions with university students. *Journal of American College Health, 42,* 156-162.

Reich, J., & Neenan, P. (1986). Principles common to different short-term psychotherapies. *American Journal of Psychotherapy, 40,* 60-69.

Rosenbaum, R., Hoyt, M. F., & Talmon, M.(1990). The challenge of single-session therapies: Creating pivotal moments. In R. A. Wells & V. J. Giannetti (Eds.), *Handbook of the brief psychotherapies* (pp. 165-189). New York: Plenum Press.

Sexton, T. L., & Whiston, S. C. (1994). The status of the counseling relationship: An empirical review, theoretical implications, and research directions. *The Counseling Psychologist, 22,* 6-78.

Simons, J. P., & Andersen, M. B. (1995). The development of consulting practice in applied sport psychology: Some personal perspectives. *The Sport Psychologist, 9,* 449-468.

Talmon, M. (1990). *Single-session therapy: Maximizing the effect of the first (and often only) therapeutic encounter.* San Francisco: Jossey-Bass.

Watzlawick, P. (1983). *The situation is hopeless, but not serious: The pursuit of unhappiness.* New York: W. W. Norton.

Watzlawick, P., Weakland, J. H., Fisch, R. (1974). Change: *Principles of problem formation and problem resolution.* New York: W. W. Norton.

Wells, R. A. (1993). Clinical strategies in brief psychotherapy. In R. A. Wells & V. J. Gianetti (Eds.), *Casebook of the brief psychotherapies* (pp. 3-17). New York: Plenum Press.

The authors wish to thank Judy Van Raalte and Britt Brewer for their valuable suggestions in the preparation of this manuscript.

Accepted author manuscript version reprinted, by permission, from *The Sport Psychologist*, 1999, 13, (3), 344-357.

The Sport Psychologist-Athlete Relationship: Implications for Training

Albert J. Petitpas and Burt Giges

Springfield College

Steven J. Danish

Virginia Commonwealth University

The quality of the counseling relationship has proven to be the most significant factor in facilitating treatment adherence and positive counseling outcomes. The authors of the present article contend that the dynamics of the sport psychologist—athlete relationship are quite similar to those of counselor—client relationship. They offer suggestions for the training of sport and exercise psychology graduate students that borrow extensively from the research and training strategies used in counselor education. In particular, a possible interface between sport psychology and counseling psychology training and practice is suggested, a brief overview of research on the qualities of the counseling relationship is presented, and several training strategies are provided.

Recently, Poczwardowski, Sherman, and Henschen (1998) suggested that the field of sport psychology would benefit from an interface with counseling psychology in the areas of supervision, service philosophy, delivery models, and theoretical frameworks. They contend that sport psychology is a developing field that needs to pay careful attention to standards of service delivery in order to establish credibility with other disciplines and the general public. Ironically, the field of counseling psychology was forced to confront these same concerns in the 1970s.

Counseling psychologists had to validate the effectiveness of their services to justify reimbursement from insurance carriers, and this need prompted considerable evaluation research (Gladdings, 1992). Although the results of that research show that counseling interventions have the potential to be effective with most clients, efforts to identify the specific mechanisms responsible for successful outcomes have been inconclusive (Gelso & Fretz, 1992). Of all the techniques and variables examined, only one, the client-counselor relationship, has related to positive therapeutic outcomes consistently (Sexton & Whiston, 1994). It is our belief that the sport psychology consultant-athlete relationship is also a critical component in successful sport psychology interventions.

The purpose of this article is to examine what is known about the practitioner—client relationship and the implications of that knowledge for the training of sport psychology consultants. In particular, we address three areas: (a) the interface between sport psychology and counseling psychology practice, (b) a brief overview of research on qualities of the practitioner-client relationship, and (c) suggestions for training sport psychology consultants.

A Sport Psychology/Counseling Psychology Interface

From a philosophical perspective, counseling psychology may have more in common with sport psychology than it does with clinical psychology. Counseling psychology has traditionally been viewed as a psycho-educational approach to helping that emphasizes growth and development, and it is the emphasis on education and development that differentiates counseling psychology from clinical psychology. Super (1977) characterized these differences as follows:

It is the difference between developmental and remedial help, between education and medicine, between pathology and hygielogy. Clinical psychologists tend to look for what is wrong and how to treat it, while counseling psychologists tend to look for what is right and how to help use it. (p. 13)

Instead of the clinical model of illness diagnosis, prescription, and treatment, the counseling approach can begin with client dissatisfaction or ambition, then progress through a process of goal setting, skill development, and goal achievement (Danish, Petitpas, & Hale, 1993). The counseling approach is quite similar to that of sport psychology consultants who seek to improve individuals' existing psychological skills or to teach them new skills in order to enhance their performance (e.g., Botterill, 1990; Halliwell, 1990; Ravizza, 1988; Rotella, 1990).

Over the last decade, many leaders in the field of sport psychology (e.g., Gould, 1990; Smith, 1989; Vealey, 1998) have emphasized a need for greater professional accountability and intervention research. Although researchers have supported the effectiveness of strategies such as goal setting (e.g., Weinberg, 1994) and imagery (e.g., Murphy, 1994) in sport settings, few studies have examined the specific factors in the process of service delivery that might enhance athletes' efficacy and contribute to successful outcomes. It is an understanding of the dynamics of the practitioner—client interaction where sport psychology can gain considerable knowledge from counseling psychology.

Based on an extensive body of research in counseling psychology (Sexton & Whiston, 1994), the helping interaction consists of two basic elements: the techniques used by the helper and the relationship that exists between the parties involved. These two elements are often examined independently, but they are highly interdependent. In other words, aspects of the relationship affect how the techniques are used or adhered to, and how the techniques are used affects the relationship (Gelso & Fretz, 1992).

The relationship between practitioner and client and the techniques employed have been found to be the major factors in increasing the level of adherence, whether it be for health, injury, or, most likely, sport psychology interventions (Danish, 1985). When clients do not feel understood or when they do not find the professional concerned and competent, non-adherence is likely. Moreover, when the intervention is complex, requires considerable effort and change in terms of the client's lifestyle, and is given without client input, adherence will decrease (Meichenbaum & Turk, 1987). A key factor in any intervention is the client's readiness. Readiness must be based on what the client "wants" and "needs," and not what the client believes they "should" or "have to" do (Giges, 1991).

The phrase *have to* is synonymous with *compliance.* According to Kelman (1958), compliance is the lowest form of motivation. It occurs when the motivation to change a behavior is based on external rewards or on efforts to avoid punishment. Individuals believe they are required to or "have to" perform the new behavior. There is no understanding of why or how the behavior is beneficial, and, as a result, motivation to continue the behavior is low and unlikely to be maintained.

Kelman (1958) used the term *identification* to indicate a higher level of motivation than compliance. In identification, clients follow a behavior regimen to please the professional or to be part of the group. Satisfaction is derived from conforming. Unfortunately, maintenance and transfer of the new behavior is not likely to occur in the natural setting if the professional is not present.

According to Kelman (1958), "internalization" is the highest level of motivation. It occurs when the behavior to be performed is as relevant and important to the client as it is to the professional. It is intrinsically rewarding and done by the client for his or her own benefit. Acquiring new behaviors is a difficult process, and without internalization, it is unlikely that a person would have the motivation necessary to maintain a change effort. Change is more likely to occur when a good relationship exists between the practitioner and the client and when the client collaborates in the decision about what strategies will be employed (Meichenbaum & Turk, 1987).

Studies that have evaluated sport psychology consultations lend support to the importance of the practitioner—client relationship in predicting successful outcomes. Orlick and Partington (1987) conducted one of the first evaluation studies in sport psychology. In order to identify characteristics of effective consultants, they interviewed 75 Canadian athletes who had participated in the 1984 Olympic Games and had employed consultant services. The best consultants were described as being good listeners who were able to build rapport with individual athletes and care about what happened to them. In addition, the best consultants were knowledgeable, had something concrete to offer, and were able to provide person-specific input. These traits are in sharp contrast to the worst consultants, who had poor interpersonal skills, lacked sensitivity to individual needs, and spent little time in one-to-one interactions.

Since Orlick and Partington's (1987) original study, several practitioners (e.g., Gordon, 1990; Halliwell, 1990; Ravizza, 1990) and researchers (e.g., Gould, Murphy, Tammen, & May, 1991; Martin, Wrisberg, Beitel, & Lounsbury, 1997) have identified factors that contribute to the effectiveness of sport psychology interventions. Based on this body of work, it appears that the ability to build rapport, create a positive environment, and provide concrete suggestions are highly correlated with successful sport psychology consultations. Unfortunately, acquiring the interpersonal skills and experiences necessary to build rapport and create a positive working environment are rarely emphasized in most sport psychology training programs (Orlick & Partington). Even if one considers the counseling skills qualification required to become a certified consultant of the Association for the Advancement of Applied Sport Psychology (AAASP; Zaichkowsky & Perna, 1996), it is doubtful that one course in "basic intervention techniques in counseling" and a "supervised practicum in counseling, clinical, or industrial-organizational psychology" would provide enough training and experience to prepare individuals to consult effectively with athletes and coaches in the field. Gelso and Fretz (1992) captured the essence of appropriate training in counseling in the following quote:

> Graduate study in counseling psychology is qualitatively different from that in, for example, history, physics, or music. Becoming an effective counselor happens only by learning a great deal about yourself. It is not simply a matter of applying a set of techniques. You are the major tool—one that must be highly adaptable to be effective with a wide range of clients and interventions. To become adaptable, many of your values, assumptions, and personal styles will have to be examined. (p. 557)

The emphasis on self-knowledge and adaptability distinguishes counseling preparation from training in many fields, but it should be an integral part of preparation for any field (e.g., sport psychology) that requires the development of rapport and positive working relationships (Danish, Petitpas, & Hale, 1995). If one accepts this premise, it may be time for a paradigm shift in sport psychology training models from an emphasis on skill-based instruction to greater awareness of self and the processes involved in the sport psychologist—athlete interaction. Before we examine sonic suggestions for training, we present a brief overview of practitioner—client interaction research from counseling psychology.

Qualities of the Practitioner—Client Relationship

For the most part, researchers have focused on three main topics when examining the counseling relationship: transference relationships, facilitative conditions, and the working alliance. Although it is beyond the scope of this article to examine these topics in depth, a brief introduction to each topic, and several examples of the selected constructs are presented to set the stage for the training recommendations that follow.

Transference and Countertransference

Although the concepts of transference and countertransference are normally associated with clinical interventions from a psychodynamic perspective, several sport psychology consultants have argued that these concepts have implications for sport psychology consultations, as well (e.g., Poczwardowski et al., 1998; Strean & Strean, 1998). Traditionally, transference has been described as the process by which clients ascribe feelings and attitudes they held during early significant-other interactions (e.g., with parents, grandparents, siblings) to their current relationships with their counselors (Strean & Strean). A similar perspective suggests that individuals learn from their past interactions and tend to apply this learning to all future interpersonal encounters (Singer, Sincoff, & Kolligian, 1989). Therefore, individuals who have learned to be compliant or defiant in their relationships with authority figures are likely to continue this pattern in their interactions with counselors or sport psychologists. Understanding that athletes may sometimes react to practitioners based on past learning can help decrease misunderstandings during the process of sport psychology consultations (Giges, 1998).

Research investigating the relationship between transference and counseling outcomes is limited and should be interpreted with caution, but it suggests that understanding the dynamics of the transference relationship can have a positive effect on short-term dynamic therapy (Sexton & Whiston, 1994). Of particular interest is the work of Gelso, Hill, and Kivlighan (1991), who found that counseling relationships containing a high degree of transference (e.g., dependency on the counselor) were rated more positively if they also contained a high degree of client insight. it appears that the more both participants are aware of the dynamics of the interaction, the better the counseling outcomes.

Countertransference has been defined as the practitioner's conscious and unconscious reactions to the client (Strean & Strean, 1998). Unfortunately, there are few studies that have examined countertransference interactions (Sexton & Whiston, 1994) and none that have looked directly at the relationship between countertransference and counseling outcomes. Nonetheless, there is general support for the belief that self-awareness on the part of counselors about how they react to clients during interactions can greatly enhance the counseling relationship and facilitate positive outcomes (Gelso & Fretz, 1992). This belief has been echoed by a number of sport psychology consultants (e.g., Andersen & Williams-Rice, 1996; Poczwardowski et al., 1998). For example, Giges (1991) suggested that knowledge of one's own feelings or issues when interacting with athletes can help practitioners focus on their athletes' goals and needs rather than on their own.

Facilitative Conditions

Over 40 years ago, Carl Rogers (1957) identified six characteristics of effective counselors that he believed were necessary and sufficient to facilitate client growth and produce successful therapeutic outcomes. Rogers' seminal work spawned considerable research activity. Although the so-called facilitative conditions did not prove to be sufficient to elicit positive therapeutic outcomes, research has supported their importance in facilitating change and goal attainment (Gelso & Fretz, 1992; Sexton & Whiston, 1994). Of the six original facilitative conditions, congruence, empathy, and unconditional positive regard have received the most research attention.

Congruence is normally defined as the counselor's ability to be real, open, and honest in the relationship with the client (Gelso & Fretz, 1992). Both sport and counseling psychologists (e.g., Ravizza, 1990; Sexton & Whiston, 1994) believe that this type of genuineness and honest communication is critical in establishing a positive working relationship. Although both the counselor and the client should be open and real during their interactions, the counselor's role is more complicated than that of the client. The challenge for the counselor is to be real and consistent in the relationship while putting his or her own needs aside in order to focus on the client's needs and concerns. Buber (1958) coined the term *one-sided inclusion* to describe this challenge, and most of the research examining the relationship between congruence and counseling outcomes has focused on variables related to counselors' self-presentation and self-disclosures (Sexton & Whiston).

An example of the importance of understanding the dynamics of one-sided inclusion is illustrated in the following exchange between a counselor and an athlete who is having trouble concentrating during certain competitions:

Client: I worry about being prepared for the event. I get so nervous I can't concentrate. It is especially bad if my event is scheduled for late in the day.

Counselor: Well, I can relate. I had trouble concentrating when I participated, and competing in the afternoon was the worst.

Client: Really? What did you do?

Counselor: I would try to stay away from thinking about the event until an hour before, and then I would do some imagery.

Client: How did that work?

Counselor: Most of the time it worked well, but occasionally I would get too keyed up.

Client: Oh.

From this brief interaction, you can see that the focus has shifted from the client's concerns and feelings to the counselor's self-disclosure. This new focus provides little support or direction to the client and may have been used without thinking about possible consequences. Although the counselor's self-disclosure may have made the counselor more real in the eyes of the client, it may have also changed the dynamics of the relationship or discounted the client's feelings. When considering the use of self-disclosure, it is important to ponder who is being served by the self-disclosure (i.e., counselor or client), how the client may respond, and how the self-disclosure may affect the helping relationship.

The counselor's ability to develop empathetic understanding of the client's experience is the second facilitative condition that has received considerable research attention. Rogers (1957) described empathy as the counselor's ability "to sense the client's private world as if it were your own, but without ever losing the as if quality" (p. 98). Other researchers (e.g., Hansen, Stevic, & Warner, 1972) have suggested that empathy is not just being able to sense the client's private world but also the ability to communicate that understanding in a manner that is attuned to the client's feelings. Both definitions are based on the notion that if clients believe that their feelings and beliefs are understood and accepted by the counselor, they are apt to have more faith in their counselors and, therefore, are likely to invest more energy in efforts to reach the therapeutic goals. There is considerable research suggesting that empathetic understanding is a shared characteristic of effective counselors, independent of their theoretical orientation (e.g., Orlinsky & Howard, 1986; Sloane & Staples, 1984).

The ability to listen to, and empathetically understand, the experiences of another individual is an active process requiring a number of skills and interpersonal qualities. Empathy involves not only knowing how to reflect feelings and statements but also understanding how to give feedback, adopt the perspective of others, build rapport, help generate alternative responses, and gain a commitment to take some action

(Danish, D'Augelli, & Hauer, 1980; Egan, 1986; Ivey, 1988). A brief introduction to reflective listening will illustrate just one of the skills required to develop an empathetic understanding of the client.

Empathy is built on effective communication skills and requires an awareness of both our verbal and our nonverbal communications. If only about 10% of what a person communicates is verbal, then attention to nonverbal skills such as appropriate eye contact and body language is likely to ensure consistency between our verbal and nonverbal messages (Danish et al., 1980). In addition, counselors who use reflective-type verbal responses are likely to be more effective in developing empathy and a trusting relationship (Ivey, Ivey, & Simek-Morgan, 1993). Reflective responses not only summarize what a client has said or identify the feelings expressed but also help the client continue to talk, explore, and clarify thoughts and feelings, because they are said in a manner that communicates the counselor's willingness to help. Consider an athlete who is experiencing a loss of confidence following an injury:

Athlete: I am just not the same person I was last season. I continue to work hard, but sometimes I feel like it is all so useless. I'm just not getting any better.
Counselor A: Sounds like you think your hard work is not worth it.
Counselor B: It seems that you are feeling hopeless about your game right now.

In this example, Counselor A uses a reflective response that summarizes content, whereas Counselor B's reflective response targets the feelings being expressed. In both cases, the statements follow from the communication of the athlete and encourage further exploration and clarification on the part of the athlete. Contrast these responses to those of the counselor in the following example:

Athlete:	I just don't know if I can continue to follow this rehab program. Sometimes, I feel that I am just not ready to push my knee.
Counselor:	Perhaps you could do some imagery to help you regain your confidence.
Athlete:	Yes, but I really don't think that will be the same thing, and I don't really feel all that comfortable doing it.
Counselor:	Maybe, if I take you through it a few times, you will feel more comfortable.
Athlete:	OK, but I'm not sure I have the time right now.

In this example, the counselor did not follow the leads of the athlete. Instead, the counselor suggested an intervention (i.e., imagery) and tried to lead the athlete in that direction. Unfortunately, the athlete was not ready to try the intervention and indicated this lack of readiness by using several "yes, but" statements. In this situation, the counselor needs to use more reflective responses and take the time to explore the client's thoughts and feelings more fully before offering a possible solution. Although imagery may have proved to be an effective intervention in this situation, the athlete did not feel understood and therefore was not ready to move forward.

Another facilitative condition that has received some research attention is the counselor's ability to accept the client unconditionally. According to Rogers (1957), unconditional positive regard is the nonjudgmental acceptance of the client as a person of worth, no matter what the presenting behaviors. Unfortunately, this construct has proven to be multidimensional and quite difficult to measure (Sexton & Whiston, 1994). As a result, researchers have focused primarily on the counselor's ability to display a warm and accepting attitude toward the client. This attitude has been described as treating the client with respect and dignity, and operationalized as being attentive to clients' communications (attending skills), displaying interest in clients' experiences (focus), and trying to identify clients' personal strengths (positive asset search; Ivey et al., 1993).

Although research on the various facilitative conditions has been marked by inconsistent findings, most researchers concur that congruence, empathetic understanding, and treating the client with respect are strongly related to adherence and positive counseling outcomes (e.g., Ivey et al., 1993; Patterson, 1984). There is support for the belief that these facilitative conditions should also extend to sport psychology consultations (e.g., Gould et al., 1991), and thus, they have clear implications for training in sport and exercise psychology.

The Working Alliance

The working alliance refers to a collaborative relationship between the counselor and client in which both parties are working together to address whatever concerns are impeding the growth and healthy functioning of the client (Osachuk & Cairns, 1995). A strong working alliance is often viewed as the primary factor that accounts for clients' willingness to work through the plateaus and setbacks that frequently occur during the course of therapy (Gelso & Fretz, 1992). Therefore, the ability to establish a working alliance is likely to be related to treatment adherence and positive outcomes.

Bordin (1979) identified three factors that come together to create the working alliance: agreement on goals, agreement on tasks, and the development of an emotional bond between the counselor and the client. In order to get agreement on goals and tasks, clients need to believe in the efficacy of the strategies suggested and have faith that their counselors have the necessary skills to assist them. Without such beliefs, it is doubtful that clients would put forth the effort necessary to achieve the desired results (Danish et al., 1993). On the other side of this interactive process, counselors need to present themselves in a manner that demonstrates their empathetic understanding and positive regard for their clients. When a relationship based on trust and mutual respect is established between the client and the counselor, agreement on goals and tasks is more likely to occur (Bordin).

Research supports a strong relationship between the quality of the working alliance and successful counseling outcomes (Horvath & Greenberg, 1989). It is important to point out, however, that this relationship is quite complex, may change over time, and may be viewed differently by the client and the counselor (Sexton & Whiston, 1994). For example, even though the quality of the working alliance is likely to be established within the first three sessions of the counseling relation-ship, the working alliance cannot be forced (Horvath & Symonds, 1991). It develops over a period of time and is built on the participants' willingness and abilities to trust and understand each other. As discussed earlier in the section on facilitative conditions, counselors foster the development of a working alliance by using reflective responses to follow clients' leads, by demonstrating empathetic understanding, and by communicating respect and acceptance (Ivey et al., 1993). Because the working alliance is a collaborative process, counselors must be mindful of individual differences (e.g., gender, age, cultural background), be sensitive to the clients' concerns about trusting others and taking risks, and proceed at their clients' pace (Petitpas & Danish, 1995). Counselors' supportiveness and willingness to develop collaborative working relationships account for about 50% of outcome variance from the client's perspective (Bachelor, 1991).

Counselors should invite clients to engage in intervention strategies, but they should never attempt to force clients to participate. For example, Kivlighan and Schmitz (1992) found that counselors who offered encouragement or focused on emotions before the working alliance was established placed their clients in passive roles that negatively influenced agreements on goals and tasks. Collaborative problem solving requires that counselors take the time to understand issues from their clients' perspectives and then check to see if their clients understand and accept any information that has been provided to them. Understanding and acceptance can be verified through the use of reflective responses and other attending skills such as paraphrasing and summarization (Ivey et al„ 1993).

Although a large number of sport and exercise consultants define their role as that of teacher or educator only (e.g., Ravizza, 1990; Rotella, 1990), it is not unusual for them to assume the role of support person, as well as to develop an emotional bond with their athlete-clients (Singer, 1996). Sport psychologists and athletic counselors were identified as second only to parents as sources of emotional support to a group of athletes who were rehabilitating from injuries (Izzo, 1994). If the development of an emotional bond is also an important aspect in creating positive working relationships in sport psychology interventions, it follows that sport and exercise psychology training programs should place more emphasis on understanding the dynamics inherent in an interactive helping relationship.

Suggestions for Training

In reviewing various theories and approaches to counseling, it becomes apparent that it is difficult to make a case for the efficacy of one helping strategy over any other. There is considerable support, however, for the belief that positive counseling outcomes are more a factor of the quality of the counselor—client relationship than the specific counseling strategies used (Sexton & Whiston, 1994). There is also support for the belief that the quality of the practitioner—athlete relationship is important to the success of sport psychology consultations (Gould et al., 1991; Orlick & Partington, 1987). If the relationship between the practitioner and the athlete is important, training in sport psychology should include opportunities for students to gain self-knowledge and an understanding of the processes involved in creating a positive helping relationship. Self-knowledge is viewed as critical in acquiring the level of self-understanding necessary to build effective working alliances in counseling (Okun, 1987). An awareness of processes such as power is-sues, control battles, stages of treatment, and working alliances helps provide counselors with a plan for what should be done, when, and why (Burlingame, Fuhriman, Paul, & Ogles, 1989).

In order to gain the basic counseling and listening skills necessary for certification as an AAASP-certified consultant, students must not only understand what they do with athletes but also how they do it. For example, a graduate student might consider his enthusiasm and willingness to go out and engage athletes who need assistance as a major strength, but if these qualities are perceived as intrusive by others, it is doubtful that he would be successful in creating positive working relationships. Students need to get feedback about the advantages and disadvantages of their interpersonal styles in order to eliminate potential "blind spots." There are a large number of structured self-awareness, values-clarification, and needs-assessment training programs that are helpful in providing information and feedback about one's self-presentation (e.g., Crace & Hardy, 1998; Giges, 1991).

In addition to self-awareness programs, counselor education training relies on a number of strategies to promote self-awareness and a better understanding of the dynamics of the counselor—client interaction. Many of these strategies could be easily incorporated into the training of sport psychology consultants. Although it is beyond the scope of this article to describe all of these strategies in depth, some brief descriptions are provided.

Being a Client

Many counseling psychology programs encourage their graduate students to become clients themselves. This can take place in the form of participating in role-plays in which students act as clients or through an actual counseling relationship at a private or university-based counseling center. By becoming clients, graduate students not only gain a better understanding of the dynamics of the counselor—client interaction and working alliance but also gain considerable self-understanding and an awareness of their own values, needs, and concerns. Students in sport psychology programs are also likely to benefit from this self-knowledge and, at a minimum, should try out for themselves any of the sport psychology interventions they intend to use with their athletes. By going through the process of goal setting or by using imagery to improve aspects of one's own performance, individuals often gain an appreciation for the importance of getting agreement on goals and tasks and acquire a greater awareness of potential roadblocks to goal attainment.

Videotaping and Live Supervision Models

By videotaping intervention work with athletes, graduate students gain opportunities to observe their nonverbal behaviors and to track their ability to follow the leads of their clients. Training programs that have interview labs are able to videotape actual or role-playing sessions and then provide immediate feedback to the counselor trainee. In addition, many counseling programs use live supervision models where students working with clients can be observed through viewing mirrors. This model has the advantage of allowing classmates and supervisors to discuss the dynamics of the interaction as they occur. Student counselors can also be provided with instant feedback on their performance and suggestions for alter-native strategies if a new approach is deemed necessary.

Verbatim

A "verbatim" is another vehicle for providing feedback about one's counseling skills and information about the dynamics of the counselor—client interaction. The verbatim is particularly helpful in situations in which videotaping is not feasible or appropriate but in which counselor—client interactions can be recorded on audiotape. The verbatim is created by student counselors who transcribe from a videotaped or audiotaped session everything that is said during a segment of the interaction. By recording the verbal interactions during segments of sessions that are going well and comparing what is said to segments that are not going well, students are able to gain insight into their response tendencies, the dynamics of the interactions, and other information related to the process of service delivery. In particular, the verbatim is an excellent tool to evaluate one's use of reflective responses and to identify skills and attending behaviors that may enhance the establishment of an effective working alliance.

Training Logs

Training logs are forms of diaries that enable counselors in training to monitor their feelings, values, and beliefs as they interact with different clients and manage different types of problems. Information recorded in training logs can be open-ended self-reflections, or it can be structured around a series of specific questions. Sample questions include (a) What feelings came up for me during my interactions with clients today? (b) What issues caused me the most concern today? (c) What did I learn about myself as a counselor today? and (d) How did my thoughts and emotional reactions foster or impede goal attainment in my sessions today?

The Trainee—Supervisor Relationship

Another way of gaining insight into the counseling process and obtaining feedback about one's personal style is often provided through the interactions that take place during the course of supervision. It is not unusual for the trainee—supervisor relationship to mirror that of a client—counselor interaction. Counseling trainees frequently defer to the knowledge of their supervisors during the early stages of their training. As they began to trust the supervisor and gain confidence in their own abilities, the relationship evolves from one of teacher and student to a more collaborative or consultative interaction (Berger & Graff, 1995). By examining the dynamics that occur during the course of supervision, counselors in training can gain considerable information about process dynamics such as roles, power differentials, and dependence—independence issues that provide insight into the processes inherent in the client—counselor relationship.

Process versus Content Supervision

Although there, are a number of supervision models available, a focus on the process of counseling sessions is likely to be more informative to the student trainee. Process supervision provides direct feedback on the pattern of interactions that take place between the counselor and client. Consider the following vignette.

Mary, a soccer player, comes to see a sport psychologist because she feels she has lost confidence in her game (content). During the initial session, Mary discloses her fear of making mistakes and frequently uses negative self-statements in the hope of getting some reassurance from the sport psychologist (process). The sport psychologist fails to attend or acknowledge her subtle requests for support and reassurance (process). Mary then shifts the focus to her coach, complaining that her coach does not listen to her or care about her as a player (content). Ironically, from a process supervision perspective, Mary's perceived communication problem with her coach was just re-created with her sport psychologist (process). A similar scenario could also play out directly in the trainee—supervisor relation-ship by substituting the trainee for Mary and the supervisor for the sport psychologist. Supervision that provides both content and process feedback is apt to increase student counselors' knowledge and enhance their awareness of the dynamics of the client—counselor relationship.

Conclusions

Both sport and counseling psychology have benefited from an interface with social psychology (Brawley, 1993; Strong, Welsh, Corcoran, & Hoyt, 1992), and now may be an appropriate time for these two disciplines to benefit from an inter-face with each other. The purpose of this article was to extend the suggestions of Poczwardowski et al. (1998) to examine how sport psychology training might benefit from counseling psychology's extensive research on the importance of the client-counselor relationship in facilitating adherence and positive intervention outcomes. To that end, we have provided a brief overview of research on several of the key variables in the client-counselor relationship and outlined a small number of training strategies that are designed to foster self-knowledge and enhance graduate students' understanding of the dynamics of the counseling relationship. Our hope is that this article spawns considerable debate about current training practices in sport and exercise psychology in order for the field to continue to grow.

References

Andersen, M.B., & Williams-Rice, B.T. (1996). Supervision in the education and training of sport psychology service providers. *The Sport Psychologist*, **10**, 278-290.

Bachelor, A. (1991). Comparison and relationship to outcome of diverse dimensions of the helping alliance as seen by client and therapist. *Psychotherapy*, **28**, 534-549.

Berger, N., & Graff, L. (1995). Making good use of supervision. In D.G. Martin & A.D. Moore (Eds.), *First steps in the art of intervention: A guidebook for trainees in the helping professions* (pp. 408-432). Pacific Grove, CA: Brooks/Cole.

Bordin, E.S. (1979). The generalizability of the psychoanalytic concept of the working alliance. *Psychotherapy: Theory, research, and practice*, **16**, 252-260.

Botterill, C. (1990). Sport psychology and professional hockey. *The Sport Psychologist*, **4**, 358-368.

Brawley, L.R. (1993). Introduction to the special issues: Application of social psychological theories to health and exercise behavior. *Journal of Applied Sport Psychology*, **5**, 95-98.

Buber, M. (1958). *Between 1 and thou*. New York: Scribner.

Burlingame, G.M., Fuhriman, A., Paul, S., & Ogles, B.M. (1989). Implementing a time-limited therapy program: Differential effects of training and experience. *Psychotherapy*, **26**, 303-313.

Crace, K., & Hardy, C. (1998, May). *A values-based approach to optimal performance*. Workshop presented at the Fifteenth Annual Conference on Counseling Athletes, Springfield, MA.

Danish, S.J. (1985). Psychological aspects in the care and treatment of athletic injuries. In P.F. Vinger & E.F. Hoerner (Eds.), *Sports injuries: The unthwarted epidemic* (2nd ed., pp. 345-353). Boston: John Wright PSG.

Danish, S.J., D'Augelli, A.R., & Hauer, A.L. (1980). *Helping skills: A basic training program* (2nd ed.). New York: Human Sciences Press.

Danish, S.J., Petitpas, A.J., & Hale, B.D. (1993). Life developmental interventions for athletes: Life skills through sports. *The Counseling Psychologist*, **21**, 352-385.

Danish, S.J., Petitpas, A.J., & Hale, B.D. (1995). Psychological interventions: A life development model. In S.M. Murphy (Ed.), *Sport psychology interventions* (pp. 19-38). Champaign, IL: Human Kinetics.

Egan, G. (1986). *The skilled helper: A systematic approach to effective helping* (3rd ed.). Monterey, CA: Brooks/Cole.

Gelso, C.J., & Fretz, B.R. (1992). *Counseling psychology.* Fort Worth, TX: Harcourt Brace Jovanovich.

Gelso, C.J., Hill, C.E,, & Kivlighan, D.M. (1991). Transference, insight, and the counselor's intentions during a counseling hour. *Journal of Counseling and Development,* **69**, 428-433.

Giges, B. (1991, April). *Self-awareness for sport psychologists.* Workshop at the University of Utah Sport Psychology Symposium, Salt Lake City, UT.

Giges, B. (1998). Psychodynamic concepts in sport psychology: Comment on Strean and Strean. *The Sport Psychologist,* **12**, 223-227.

Gladdings, S.T. (1992). *Counseling: A comprehensive profession* (2nd ed.). New York: Macmillan.

Gordon, S. (1990). A mental skills training program for the Western Australian State cricket team. *The Sport Psychologist,* **4**, 386-399.

Gould, D. (1990). AAASP: A vision for the 1990s. *Journal of Applied Sport Psychology,* **2**, 99-116.

Gould, D., Murphy, S., Tammen, V., & May, J. (1991). An evaluation of U.S. Olympic sport psychology consultant effectiveness. *The Sport Psychologist,* **5**, 111-127.

Halliwell, W. (1990). Providing sport psychology consulting services in professional hockey. *The Sport Psychologist*, **4**, 369-377.

Hansen, J.C., Stevic, R.R., & Warner, R.W., Jr. (1972). *Counseling: Theory and process*. Boston: Allyn & Bacon.

Horvath, A.O., & Greenberg, L.S. (1989). Development and validation of the Working Alliance Inventory. *Journal of Counseling Psychology*, **36**, 223-233.

Horvath, A.O., & Symonds, B.D. (1991). Relation between working alliance and outcome in psychotherapy: A meta-analysis. *Journal of Counseling Psychology*, **38**, 139-149.

Ivey, A.E. (1988). *Intentional interviewing and counseling: Facilitating client development* (2nd ed.). Pacific Grove, CA: Brooks/Cole.

Ivey, A, E., Ivey, M.B., & Simek-Morgan, L. (1993). *Counseling and psychotherapy: A multicultural perspective* (3rd ed.). Needham Heights, MA: Allyn & Bacon.

Izzo, C.M. (1994). *The relationship between social support and adherence to sport injury rehabilitation*. Unpublished master's thesis, Springfield College, Springfield, MA.

Kelman, H.C. (1958). Compliance, identification, and internalization: Three processes of opinion change. *Journal of Conflict Resolution*, **2**, 51-60.

Kivlighan, D.M., & Schmitz, P.J. (1992). Counselor technical activity in cases with improving working alliances and continuing-poor working alliances. *Journal of Counseling Psychology*, **39**, 32-38.

Martin, S.B., Wrisberg, C.A., Beitel, & Lounsbury, J. (1997). NCAA Division I athletes' attitudes toward seeking sport psychology consultation: The development of an objective instrument. *The Sport Psychologist*, **11**, 201-218.

Meichenbaum, D., & Turk, D.C. (1987). *Facilitating treatment adherence: A practitioner's guidebook.* New York: Plenum.

Murphy, S.M. (1994). Imagery interventions in sport. *Medicine and Science in Sports and Exercise*, **26**, 486-494.

Okun, B.F. (1987). *Effective helping: Interviewing and counseling techniques* (3rd ed.). Monterey, CA: Brooks/Cole.

Orlick, T., & Partington, J. (1987). The sport psychology consultant: Analysis of critical components as viewed by Canadian Olympic athletes. *The Sport Psychologist*, **1**, 4-17.

Orlinsky, D.E., & Howard, K.L. (1986). Process and outcome in psychotherapy. In S.L. Garfield & A.E. Bergin (Eds.), *Handbook of psychotherapy and behavior change* (pp. 311-381). New York: Wiley.

Osachuk, T.A., & Cairns, S.L. (1995). Relationship issues. In D.G. Martin & A.D. Moore (Eds.), *First steps in the art of interventions: A guidebook for trainees in the helping professions* (pp. 19-43). Pacific Grove, CA: Brooks/Cole.

Patterson, C.H. (1984). Empathy, warmth, and genuineness in psychotherapy: A review of reviews. *Psychotherapy*, **21**, 431-438.

Petitpas, A., & Danish, S. (1995). Caring for injured athletes. In S.M. Murphy (Ed.), *Sport psychology interventions* (pp. 255-282). Champaign, IL: Human Kinetics.

Poczwardowski, A., Sherman, C.P., & Henschen, K.P. (1998), A sport psychology service delivery heuristic: Building on theory and practice. *The Sport Psychologist*, **12**, 191-207.

Ravizza, K. (1988). Gaining entry with athletic personnel for season-long consulting. *The Sport Psychologist*, **2**, 243-254.

Ravizza, K. (1990). SportPsych consultation issues in professional baseball. *The Sport Psychologist*, **4**, 330-340.

Rogers, C. (1957). The necessary and sufficient conditions of therapeutic personality change. *Journal of Consulting Psychology*, **21**, 95-103.

Rotella, R.J. (1990). Providing sport psychology consulting services to professional athletes. The Sport Psychologist, **4**, 409-417.

Sexton, T.L., & Whiston, S.C. (1994). The status of the counseling relationship: An empirical review, theoretical implications, and research directions. *The Counseling Psychologist*, **22**, 6-78.

Singer, J.L., Sincoff, J.B., & Kolligan, J. (1989). Countertransference and cognition: Studying the psychotherapist's distortions as consequences of normal information processing. *Psychotherapy*, **26**, 344-355.

Singer, R.N. (1996). Future of sport and exercise psychology. In J.L. Van Raalte & B.W. Brewer (Eds.), *Exploring sport and exercise psychology* (pp. 451-468). Washington, DC: American Psychological Association.

Sloane, R., & Staples, F. (1984). Psychotherapy versus behavior change: Implications for future psychotherapy research. In J. Williams & R. Spitzer (Eds.), Psychotherapy research: Where are we and where should we go? (pp. 203-215). New York: Guil ford.

Smith, R.E. (1989). Applied sport psychology in an age of accountability. *Journal of Applied Sport Psychology*, **1**, 166-180.

Strean, W.B., & Strean, H.S. (1998). Applying psychodynamic concepts to sport psychology practice. *The Sport Psychologist*, **12**, 208-222,

Strong, S.R., Welsh, J.A., Corcoran, J.L., & Hoyt, W.T. (1992). Social psychology and counseling psychology: The history, products, and promise of an interface. *Journal of Counseling Psychology*, **39**, 139-157.

Super, D.E. (1977). The identity crisis of counseling psychologists. *The Counseling Psychologist*, **7**, 13-15.

Vealey, R. (1998, September). Toward inclusive exclusiveness: Let's take sport psychology for a spin. Presidential address presented at the annual meeting of the Association for the Advancement of Applied Sport Psychology, Hyannis, MA.

Weinberg, R.S. (1994). Goal setting and performance in sport and exercise settings: A synthesis and critique. Medicine and Science in Sports and Exercise, **26**, 469-477.

Zaichkowsky, L., & Perna, F. (1996). Certification in sport and exercise psychology. In J.L. Van Raalte & B.W. Brewer (Eds.), *Exploring sport and exercise psychology* (pp. 395-412). Washington, DC: American Psychological Association.

Accepted author manuscript version reprinted, by permission, from *The Sport Psychologist*, 1998, 12, (2), 223-227. © Human Kinetics Publishers, Inc.

Psychodynamic Concepts in Sport Psychology: Comment on Strean and Strean (1998)

Burt Giges
Springfield College

Many athletes, during the course of their career as competitors, experience performance impairment caused by psychological factors. At such times, it is important that sport psychology consultants understand these issues in order to help athletes deal with them more effectively. Psychodynamic theory is one approach that can provide a basis for obtaining this knowledge. Previous articles on this subject have addressed individual case histories and treatment of psychopathology in athletes, or the benefits of a psychodynamic perspective in understanding behavior in sport, or described particular sports from a psychodynamic viewpoint (Apitsch, 1995; Begel, 1992; Beisser, 1967; Hanna, 1993; Perry & Sacks, 1981; Sachs & Buffone, 1984; Sacks, 1980, 1990). None of these articles, however, addressed how sport psychology consultants who are not clinically trained can use psychodynamic concepts to help athletes perform better. The current article by Strean and Strean (1998) in this issue, in addressing this point, opens an important dialogue.

Concepts of Psychodynamic Theory

Strean and Strean's (1998) description of the theoretical underpinnings for understanding normal development and personality is based predominantly on classical Freudian psychoanalytic theory. They summarize the essential concepts of psychodynamic or psychoanalytic theory as follows: Unconscious processes affect behavior; past history influences present functioning; all behavior has meaning; and defense mechanisms exist to handle conflict. These ideas imply that the children we once were remain active in the adult we now are. However, we must not equate the child's wishes with those that we consciously recognize. Moreover, the existence of unconscious thought does not necessarily mean that it is the predominant motivating factor behind a particular behavior. [Sometimes, the wish to sleep, after the alarm clock rings comes from physical fatigue, and is a conscious choice for needed rest]. Furthermore, understanding how unconscious processes operate does not determine which intervention is most appropriate or effective (Giges, 1996a). In addition, by defining psychodynamic theory as both a theory and a form of therapeutic intervention, Strean and Strean create an ambiguity that may cause difficulty for practitioners who are not clinically trained.

Sport Psychology Consultants

How can psychodynamic concepts enhance the performance of sport psychology consultants? In their attempt to answer this question, Strean and Strean address treatment of athletes with obsession, phobia, depression or uncontrollable anger, or other symptoms. Although most of the clients are athletes, who can develop symptoms, the described treatment process is psychodynamic psychotherapy, and not sport psychology consultation. Furthermore, the section Therapeutic Intervention" addresses techniques that are part of psychotherapy practice. For example, most sport psychology consultants would not consider "free association" a "fundamental rule." The authors state, "For athletes to develop more confidence, they must first learn to enjoy their mental contents (i.e., free associations)" (p. 214). This is not a prerequisite to increased self-confidence. It can also come from developing new skills, mastering challenges, or attaining difficult goals, especially in sport.

What can sport psychology consultants who have not had training and supervised experience in psychotherapy be realistically expected to do with understanding gained from psychodynamic theory? How do such consultants analyze transference, interpret resistance, and assess ego strengths? Can they be expected to make an interpretation, which the authors say, "make the athlete aware of the unconscious meaning...or cause of a given psychic event" (p. 2419? Is digging out significant details from the past necessary or even desirable in addressing an athlete's performance issues? These interventions are not just concepts or techniques; they are considerations that are integral to the complex process of psychotherapy. Such treatment is significantly different from sport psychology consulting (Giges, 1996b).

Strean and Strean state, "According to psychodynamic theory, professional assistants help clients see how and why they experience the helping person in a certain way" (p. 215). This would not apply to performance enhancement consulting. Further, "In psychodynamically oriented intervention, counselors primarily focus on how the athlete responds to questions, confrontations, clarifications, and interpretations, rather than on whether the content is correct" (p. 220). Is this appropriate for sport psychology consultants? Imagine a consultant giving an athlete incorrect information, then later trying to analyze why the athlete got upset when it led to negative consequences. Again, the authors describe how a psychodynamic therapist might work, without clearly distinguishing this from sport psychology consulting. Although the authors intended to demonstrate how concepts and treatment procedures from psychoanalysis can be adapted to sport psychology consulting, they do not clearly demonstrate how that can be done. In their conclusion, they acknowledge existing differences, but throughout the text these are never clearly identified. The authors have left that to the individual practitioner.

Applying Psychodynamic Theory

Psychodynamic theory can be useful to the sport psychology consultant by helping to explain behaviors that are significantly influenced by unconscious factors. This is quite different from psychodynamically oriented practice, however, which requires specialized training and supervised experience. If these are acquired, a more direct application of these interventions may be appropriate (Giges, 1993). By focusing on psychopathology and treatment, Strean and Strean limit the usefulness of their ideas in sport psychology practice. Furthermore, to describe performing poorly as unconsciously arranging to fail blurs the distinction between conscious and unconscious. The phrase "arranging to" implies some deliberate planned action, although "unconsciously" means not in the person's awareness. If a thought is unconscious, it is not available for conscious arranging. This point has additional significance in dealing with recurrent injury, which is sometimes incorrectly described as *malingering*. Moreover, applying concepts (developed for understanding individual behavior) to an entire team is also questionable. For example, the authors wonder "why the New York Knickerbockers consistently seem to arrange to be defeated by inferior teams" (p. 211).

Care must be taken not to discuss psychodynamic understanding outside the privacy and confidentiality implicit in individual consultation. Commenting about Michael Jordan, the authors risked subjecting the athlete's inner experience to unnecessary public exposure. They write, "Without Jordan's deeper thoughts on the matter, we would be speculating from any perspective" (p. 211). Nevertheless, they proceed to do exactly that. "Yet, from a psychodynamic view, we might suppose that what motivated Michael Jordan to become a 'minor league' player in baseball was partially a reaction to his father's death" (p. 211). Given that Strean and Strean do not have a consultative relationship with Jordan, such speculation may damage credibility of serious psychological exploration, whether their supposition is correct or not.

An important issue that does apply to both psychodynamic psychotherapists and sport psychologists is the authors' discussions of transference and countertransference. Understanding whether an athlete perceives a practitioner more in terms of past relationships than current reality can help decrease misunderstanding, frustration, and disappointment. This does not, however, require that the transference reaction be directly interpreted for the athlete. Practitioners should also know about their own issues when helping athletes, to assure that their work addresses the athlete's goals and needs rather than their own. Increased self-awareness can be a significant step in that direction (Giges, 1991).

To further help sport psychology consultants find value in concepts drawn from psychodynamic theory, Strean and Strean could shift from a treatment to an educational perspective, from a psychopathology focus to learning emphasis, and from the medical model of illness to a growth and developmental model. Danish, Petitpas, and Hale (1993) described a developmental model in sport psychology practice. I illustrated the shift by changing the perception of psychological "symptoms" to "removable barriers" in the pursuit of personal goals (Giges, 1997). Some examples of this approach in consultation with athletes include the following:

A runner, who felt ashamed and dropped out of races when someone passed her, was able to change the behavior after guided imagery in which she continued running;

A tennis player, who felt anxiety about losing, improved after using guided imagery to recreate a match he lost, and adding nurturing friends to the audience;

A runner who felt discouraged about being behind the leader in a race, became more determined as she realized the satisfaction of 'giving it everything she's got';

A motorcyclist's prerace anxiety decreased, after he learned a relaxation method that he could use at the starting line, and subsequently shift his focus to "Go! Go! Go!"

A swimmer, whose practice times were better than in competition, was able to reverse this trend after experiments giving maximum effort earlier in practice races.

Many of these athletes had deeper psychological issues, which did not require intensive exploration in order to deal with their performance problems. Understanding these issues, however, helped me (as a sport psychology consultant) create interventions which included this understanding, thereby increasing their meaning to the athlete. The process can be seen in consultation with a golfer who broke golf clubs and threw golf balls into the woods after making poor shots. He was a tense, perfectionistic, well educated businessman, whose self-esteem was tied to his golf score. From the psychodynamic perspective, his behavior demonstrated strong aggressive drives (id), poor impulse control (ego), and harsh self-criticism (superego). He unconsciously disowned the "bad" parts of himself, and attributed them to the clubs and balls (projection). He then destroyed or eliminated them (uncontrolled aggression). His perfectionism also led him to value learning and intellect very highly; it was this point that guided my approach. I helped him shift from condemnation of himself for poor performance in golf to appreciating himself for his interest and ability in learning. I asked him how he knows when he hasn't hit the ball well. He looked at me with a curious expression and said, "It slices off to the right." I then suggested that the ball was informing him of an improper swing, and could, therefore, be seen as his teacher.

Furthermore, to apply what he learned, he would need his clubs, which could then be viewed as his allies. He reacted with laughter, and described a sense of excitement and eagerness to get out on the course with his new teacher and buddies. The next time out, he again had the urge to throw his golf ball and break his golf club. Thinking back to his sessions, he did not do so, and was surprised to feel self-satisfaction as an excellent student of the game. He called a few months later to report that his troublesome behavior had not recurred, and that urges to break the clubs and throw the balls had subsided. Direct interpretation of his unconscious issues, and analysis of transference and resistance were not necessary to help him achieve his desired results. Instead, my approach was primarily cognitive restructuring technique with psychodynamic understanding. Of course, some athletes may require more directly examining their issues through psychotherapy.

Summary

Psychodynamic theory can be useful in sport psychology practice if it is translated into techniques that are within the province of sport psychology consultants. Directly applying procedures drawn from psychodynamic psychotherapy may not be appropriate, unless the practitioner has received such training and supervised experience. The presence of unconscious issues does not always require that they be handled directly. They can, however, be used to shape interventions to fit individual needs more effectively.

References

Apitzsch, E. (1995). Psychodynamic theory of personality and sport performance. In S. Biddle (Ed.), *European perspectives on sport psychology* (pp. 111-127). Champaign, IL: Human Kinetics.

Begel, D. (1992). An overview of sport psychiatry. *American Journal of Psychiatry,* **149**, 606-614.

Beisser, A. R. (1967). *The madness in sports.* New York:Appleton-Century-Crofts.

Danish, S.J., Petitpas, A.J., & Hale, B.D. (1993). Life development intervention for athletes: Life skills through sports. *The Counseling Psychologist,* **21**, 352-385.

Giges, B. (1991). *Self-awareness for sport psychologists.* Salt Lake City: University of Utah Sport Psychology Symposium.

Giges, B. (1993). Keynote address: *Reflections on career, counseling, and credentials.* Springfield, MA: Springfield College Tenth Annual Conference on Counseling Athletes.

Giges, B. (1996). *Beyond psychopathology: An alternative to the medical model in sport.* New York: International Society for Sport Psychiatry. American Psychiatric Association Annual Meeting.

Giges, B. (1996). Commentary. *Newsletter of the Association for the Advancement of Applied Sport Psychology,* **11**, (3), 24, 27.

Giges, B. (1997). *Psychological barriers to excellence in sport performance,* Keynote address at the Southeastern Region Sport and Exercise Psychology Student Symposium, Morgantown, WV.

Hanna, E. (1993). The psychodynamically oriented clinical social worker as sports

consultant: A preliminary report. *Clinical Social Work Journal,* **21**, 283-300.

Perry, S. W. & Sacks, M. H. (1981). Psychodynamics of running. In M. H. Sacks & M. L. Sachs (Eds.), *Psychology of running* (pp. 69-79). Champaign, IL: Human Kinetics.

Sachs, M. L. & Buffone, G. W. (1984). *Running as therapy: An integrated approach*. Lincoln, NE:University of Nebraska.

Sacks, M. H. (Ed.) (1980). Psychological aspects of sports. *Psychiatric Annals,_* **10** (3), 11-53.

Sacks, M. H. (1990). Psychiatry and sport. *Annals of Sports Medicine*, **5**, 47-52.

Strean, W. B. & Strean, H. S. (1998). Applying psychodynamic concepts to sport psychology practice .*The Sport Psychologist*, **12**, 208-222.

Book Reviews

Accepted author manuscript version reprinted, by permission, from the *Journal of Sport & Exercise Psychology*, 2000, 22, (32), 273-276. © Human Kinetics Publishers, Inc.

Sport Psychiatry: Theory and Practice

Daniel Begel and Robert W. Burton, Editors

Reviewed by Burt Giges, Springfield College

"Sport Psychiatry: Theory and Practice," consists of a series of chapters, written by the editors themselves or by others, to represent their view of sport psychiatry at the present time. Most of the discussions about the theory and practice of psychiatry in sport are interesting and informative.

In the Introduction, Begel writes, "It is the sport psychiatrist's job to ease the journey by caring for the athlete when he is confused, uncertain, and fighting with himself" (p.xiv). In reviewing the slow development of sport psychiatry, he says, "It may be that even with all the evidence to the contrary, psychiatrists have succumbed to the widespread tendency to idealize athletics in such a way as to blind them to instances of pathology" (p. xv). These two statements taken together establish the search for pathology and its treatment as the primary focus of the sport psychiatrist. This is quite consistent with the physician's perspective in medical practice in general.

In Chapter 1, "The Psychologic Development of the Athlete," Begel offers an intriguing discussion, from a predominantly psychodynamic perspective, of how an athlete's early development influences later attitudes and behavior in sport participation.

In Chapter 2, "The Psychobiology of Athletic Training," Murray Allen gives an erudite and rather technical description of endogenous neurochemicals. The technical aspects may prove difficult for the reader with no previous exposure to neuroendocrine biochemistry. Although the title implies a broad discussion of psychobiologic areas that relate to the training of athletes, the chapter does not include motor development, motor control, biomechanics, visual search, or nutrition.

Chapter 3, "The Athlete's Role," written by Begel and Antonia Baum, emphasizes the importance of gender and racial issues in sport, and also presents an interesting discussion of the problems facing an athlete when cast in the role of hero.

Chapter 4, "Mental Illness in Athletes," contains discussions of different diagnostic syndromes seen in athletes. Under the heading "mental illness," Burton includes such conditions as anxiety disorders, eating disorders, adjustment disorders, attention deficit disorders, and substance-related disorders.

In Chapter 5, "The Psychopathology of Everyday Athletic Life," Begel gives some good examples of how both biologic and psychological factors can interfere with sport performance. I would add that sometimes a psychological issue can be present and not be the cause of the performance difficulty. He wisely cautions against giving premature reassurance or advice without an understanding of these factors. The chapter title illustrates that everyday problems of participation in sport are considered psychopathology. Begel writes, "Although these problems of everyday athletic life may not qualify as mental illnesses according to strict nosological definitions, they are psychopathologic in their departure from optimal states of functioning, and will tax the psychological resources of any athlete who suffers them" (p. 83). Hence, "Sport Psychiatry" includes them in the section on Clinical Issues. Five types of psychological problems that frequently interfere with training and competition are listed and discussed briefly ("choke," "slump," injury, interpersonal problem with coaches and teammates, and training dilemma). The chapter does not include many other psychological barriers to optimal athletic performance, such as self-doubt and low self-confidence, negative thinking patterns, low motivation or loss of interest, anxiety, anger, and other unpleasant emotions. Except for training issues, no references are made to the relevant sport psychology literature.

In Chapter 6, "The Dilemma of Youth Sports," Begel offers a good discussion of the benefits and risks of youth sports, and makes specific recommendations for improvement.

Chapter 7, "Substance Abuse and Athletes," written by Gregory Collins, is an informative overview of problems of drug use, and presents an impressive program to cope with these problems in a professional football team. The author also demonstrates how this program can be extended to schools.

Chapter 8, "Athletes' Use of Performance-Enhancing Drugs," written by Todd Hendrickson and Burton, offers a very good summary of athletes' use of a number of performance-enhancing drugs.

In Chapter 9, "The Sport Psychiatry Examination," Ronald Kamm provides a detailed outline for a comprehensive psychiatric examination in sport. The author mentions that, ".the interview format presented is tailored to the more typical situation encountered by the sport psychiatrist: that of the child or adolescent athlete referred for a private office consultation"

(p. 161). Although this limits its applicability in many sport situations, the underlying principles on which it is based are important.

In Chapter 10, "Psychotherapy with the Performing Athlete," Begel presents an interesting blend of psychotherapy and performance enhancing psychological skills training. He cites some examples and mentions possible difficulties with this approach. He also discusses brief therapy, transference, and countertransference issues in treating athletes. In Chapter 13, "Psychopharmacology in Athletes," Baum supplements the discussion of treatment of the individual athlete with a condensed summary of medications used by sport psychiatrists.

Chapter 11, "Family Systems-Based Treatment of the Athlete Family," written by Jon Hellstedt, is an excellent discussion of family involvement in athletes' functioning, skillfully blending theory with practice. The author gives specific examples of dysfunctional families and the management of their problems.

In Chapter 12, "Psychiatric Consultation to Athletic Teams," Burton utilizes a model based on consultation/liason psychiatry, and discusses stages of consultation, examples of consultant interventions, and potential obstacles to effective consulting. In commenting on why there may be "outright opposition, suspicion, and fear" of psychiatrists' work, he states, "The important thing for the consultant to remain cognizant of is that ultimately these attitudes are defensive and based upon indviduals' fears about their own mental health" (p. 244). It is likely, however, that some opposition or fear comes from unsatisfactory consulting experiences, such as those quoted on pages xvi, 203, and 204.

A significant drawback of the book is the tendency of the editors, in their own chapters, to make deprecating comments about sport psychology. In my opinion, these comments are unwarranted and misleading. In the Introduction, for example, Begel acknowledges the intentional non-clinical stance of sport psychology, then writes,

> Thus, the treatment recommended in a vignette of a drug-abusing athlete is 'career-planning assistance,' while 'attribution retraining' is recommended for an adolescent gymnast with complex concerns about her body and her emotions. The developmental and clinical perspectives we have come to take for granted in psychiatry appear to be quite neglected in sport psychology, even where they would seem to be essential (p. xvii-xviii).

Although some clinical psychologists doing sport psychology may be trained to treat drug abuse, sport psychology is not intended to do so. Furthermore, career-planning assistance can be an integral part of an athlete's rehabilitation program that is well within the purview of most sport psychologists. Although from a psychiatrist's point of view, treatment is offered after pathology is diagnosed; the goals and tasks of the sport psychologist are not usually diagnosis or treatment of pathology. The task can, however, be to help athletes improve their coping skills or plan for future career transitions. The clinical perspective is not neglected; it is a different focus of practice than most sport psychology consultation. For the adolescent gymnast, attribution retraining may be quite valuable in helping her change some of her perceptions and reactions. If indicated, a referral for clinical intervention can be made; or clinical services can be also provided by those in sport psychology qualified to do so. As far as the developmental perspective being neglected in sport psychology, the available scientific literature in sport psychology makes this statement inaccurate.

In Chapter 4, Burton states that, "denial is often promoted as a cognitive strategy by coaches and others, including sport psychologists, camouflaged in the name of the power of positive thinking or self-talk" (p. 76). The implication here is that sport psychologists engage in deception and encourage athletes to avoid coping with reality. Further, in discussing the incidence and prevalence of various psychiatric disorders, he asks, "Why isn't our data better? Why haven't better studies been done" (p. 78)? As part of his answer to these questions, he writes, "Another reason that good data are not available is the decidedly 'anti-pathologizing' stance of sport psychologists. As a group they have been reticent to diagnose athletes..." (p. 79). Burton is implying that sport psychologists should be diagnosing pathology; but many do not have the requisite clinical training. Furthermore, many psychologists in sport psychology who do have such training have a different perspective about athletes' difficulties than that of psychopathology. Again, sport psychology is intentionally not involved with diagnosis of mental illness, nor its incidence and prevalence. It is not appropriate, therefore, to criticize those in sport psychology for not doing clinical work.

In Chapter 5, Begel discounts the contributions of sport psychology in his discussion of sources of performance problems. He writes, "Our psychologic explanations identify emotional conflicts or self-defeating thinking, and our psychosocial explanations elucidate the stresses of playing a particular role or roles" (p. 88). Although he implies that these ideas originate with sport psychiatry, there is an abundant sport psychology literature on the subjects of negative self-talk and the stresses of being an athlete. Psychiatry does have unique contributions to offer to sport: to evaluate biological factors; to intervene when health or life is in danger (e.g., serious eating disorder, suicide potential, drug abuse, violence or homicide); or to provide medication or hospitalization when needed for treatment. Sport psychiatrists can also provide valuable services to athletes in offering psychodynamic psychotherapy. However, psychiatry is not unique in its interest in preventing individual, family, and social problems in sport, in being concerned about the sport environment for children, or in understanding the processes that affect groups in sport.

In Chapter 12, Burton stresses the importance of selling teams on the value of mental health principles, and writes,

> An alternative approach, and one that is favored by many sport psychologists, is convincing the same people in power that the consultant possesses special knowledge concerning human athletic performance that he or she can impart to the team in a uniquely effective manner (p. 237).

The implication here is that psychiatrists sell the right ideas, and sport psychologists sell themselves. He then adds, "Ironically, the special knowledge of applied sport psychology tends to be quite generic in appearance and routinized, especially to the clinician used to working clinically with individuals or groups in psychodynamically informed ways." There is an extensive body of scientific knowledge in applied sport psychology that challenges the perception that it is generic and routinized. His discussions of team-building, cohesion, communication, and transitions, however, make no reference to the numerous publications on these subjects in the sport psychology literature. Furthermore, there is a gratuitous implication that sport psychologists do not address individual needs of athletes. Later in the chapter, after mentioning the inadvisability of setting expectations of specific performance gains for teams or individual players, he writes,

> The area of 'performance enhancement,' as coined by sport psychologists, is probably the most problematic. Teams may have a difficult time grasping the concept that as psychiatrists, performance enhancement is something that we practice with each and every one of our patients. In our psychotherapy and other work, we are constantly striving to help our patients reach their potential (p. 245).

In sport psychology, performance enhancement is not psychotherapy.

By discounting or minimizing the substantial contributions of sport psychology, the editors, in their individual chapters, display a regrettable condescension toward their professional colleagues. Taken as a whole, however, the book provides many stimulating discussions that can serve as a good foundation on which to build the future of sport psychiatry.

Accepted author manuscript version reprinted, by permission, from *The Sport Psychologist*, 1996, 10, (3), pp. 300-301.

Reflections on the Mental Side of Sports

Marie Dalloway
Reviewed by Burt Giges, Department of Psychology, Springfield College

Reflections on the Mental Side of Sports by Marie Dalloway is mostly a collection of self-help articles that were previously published in sports magazines for the public during the past 12 years. *(Tennis Talk, Arizona Road Racers, Arizona Running News, Sports Week USA, Women's Sports and Fitness, and Southwest Exercise and Training).* It includes discussions of relevant topics in mental training in a nontechnical language, addressed mostly to athletes seeking a general introduction to the field. The specific material covers relaxation, visualization, goal-setting, concentration, confidence, risk-taking, performance anxiety, internal dialogue, and the ideal performance state.

Included is a good discussion evaluating the effectiveness of different methods used to deal with performance anxiety. Importance is also given to the effect of one's beliefs on performance, and how to change them for the better. The article on "Athletes and Their Heroes" presents an interesting summary of the values and limits of athlete hero worship. The author also gives attention to how mental training techniques can become part of improving one's quality of life.

This collection of articles, however, needs diligent editing. A major disadvantage of republishing articles in book form is unedited repetition. The same sentences appeared in different articles several times, and occasionally, whole paragraphs were word-for-word repetitions of earlier discussions. Another difficulty in using introductory material from the past decade is that much of it seems familiar. The discussion would therefore be of less interest to the informed athlete, and of little value to the experienced coach or sport psychology consultant. It is also not really accurate to describe "optimal performance training" as a "new method" for improving athletic performance, when its techniques of goal-setting, visualization, and risk-taking have been available for over 20 years.

Further indications of the need for editing are the absence of an index at the back of the book and inconsistency in giving references at the end of some articles and not others. In addition, *stress* and *anxiety* are used interchangeably. Since they are not synonyms, this may be confusing for the beginning reader.

More importantly, some of the points the author makes should be changed. First, "The *promise* with mental training is to have an athlete play up to his or her level of ability "*consistently*" (p. 14, italics mine). It is not good practice to promise consistent results with any particular approach to improvement. Second, "you can create the Ideal Performance State at will' (p. 124); and, in the guidelines for immediately before competition, it is advised, "Enter your Ideal Performance State" (p. 128). Both statements change the meaning of ideal performance state from an experience during performance to a *preparation* for it. Finally, the author lists "drug use" under "Questionable Strategies" for enhancing performance. The point should be made much more clearly that drug use is not just questionable, it is unacceptable.

This book, as published, may be misleading for the uninformed beginner and not particularly useful for those who have previously been exposed.

Part VII

Newsletter Reports

AASP Newsletter, 22, 1, p. 2, Spring 2007
Report on the Joint Commission on Sports Medicine & Science Meeting

Burt Giges really caught the attention of attendees with his session. In his humble, gracious but compelling manner, Burt gave a presentation on "Common Ground: Where Sport Psychology and Sports Medicine Meet." Because his co-presenters were unable to join him (due to last minute emergencies) despite his careful planning, Burt responded like the flexible, resilient "champion" that he is. He filled the open slot by conducting a "live interview with an injured athlete." In this session, Burt, center stage with his client, showcased his brilliant interviewing and counseling skills. It was done in an "unconditional positive regard" highly effective manner. The contrast between stimulating but didactic presentations on the physical aspects of sports (injury, equipment, heat stroke, etc) or discussion of programs (concussion, drugs in sport, etc.) and Burt's psychosocial assessment and relationship building skills, illuminated our "profession at its best." Kirsten and I were so proud to remind the enthralled attendees that this capable physician, psychiatrist and sport psychologist "extraordinaire" is AASP's President-Elect!

Aynsley Smith, Research Director,
Sports Medicine Clinic, Mayo Clinic
AASP Professional Standards Division Head

* * *

British Psychological Society, Division of Sport and Exercise Psychology, Sport and Exercise Psychology Review, Vol. 2, No. 1 February 2006, Report on the AASP Conference, Vancouver, 2005

Burt Giges, Clinical Professor of Psychology at Springfield College, is something of an AASP legend – who not only provides thought-provoking workshops, which regularly explore sport psychology consultancy practice issues through the use of real life examples, but is also often seen getting down on the dance floor at the conference banquet each year! During this year's conference, he worked with a volunteer from the audience to explore the consultant's self-awareness during consultancy. Working with the volunteer through a personal issue they had identified, Professor Giges offered personal self-reflections at intervals during the consultancy through verbalized thoughts and feelings. This approach allowed the audience to walk with the consultant along the path of the consultancy, making connections between the volunteer's remarks and the consultant's responses, and in so doing gaining an insight into why a consultant had chosen the interventions strategies adopted.

Kate Goodger

* * *

International Society for Sport Psychiatry Newsletter, January 1996. Report on the AASP Conference, New Orleans, 1995

Burt Giges is a fellow sport psychiatrist from Westchester County, NY, an avuncular former psychoanalytic psychotherapist and researcher, now preferring cognitive-affective interventions. He gave a superb Keynote Address on "How People Change." It was a wonderful synthesis of his own ideas, filtered through the concepts and theories of others, to provide a blueprint for the field of performance enhancement. Giges would prefer to emphasize a more general improvement, avoiding the one dimensional quality of the previous term; and thereby including alternative, equally successful outcomes, such as personal satisfaction, enjoyment, or even less involvement in sport, if this is a positive change for the individual.

His lecture dealt with five aspects of intentional change, which was defined as change that was not of a developmental nature, and not dependent on external factors. These included the content, timing, and process of change, as well as resistance to change, or the "why not" of change. In the fifth aspect, he described his own thoughtful approach to helping sport psychologist consultants help others achieve their goals. He believes that, as a process, paradoxically, "changing is fundamentally similar to staying the same." That is, if any pattern of behavior requires continuous reinforcement, then the ability to maintain sameness can automatically hone powerful skills which may be harnessed for change. Another useful concept for sport psychology consultants that he imparted was a quote from psychoanalyst Allen Wheelis, "If responsibility for change is attributed to others, then what we are left with that is ours is resistance."

Ian Tofler

* * *

Performance Excellence Movement
AASP's Student Newsletter, 6, 1, p. 2, Dec. 2009: Increasing Awareness of Sport Psychology in Other Performance-Related Contexts, Excerpt from Introduction, Jessica Lutkenhouse Psy. D.

Dr. Burt Giges humbly portrayed this perspective during his Presidential Address at the 2007 AASP Annual Conference when he spoke about the importance of working together as an organization in order to achieve our main goal of improving the physical health, mental health, and well-being of our clients through sport and exercise. His wisdom was brilliantly portrayed when he said, "this means we need to pull together toward common goals, support each other by listening with an open mind, and communicate in ways that accept our differences even when we disagree, and work toward resolving whatever problems interfere with our performance." His words set a wonderful example for future students interested in the field of sport and exercise psychology. My main goal for this newsletter was to emulate this same perspective by involving students from different disciplines to foster the member collaboration and connectedness Burt spoke about. The students that contributed did an amazing job working together with both me and my co-editor to disseminate exciting articles about their sport and exercise psychology-related interests. I hope you enjoy this newsletter, and that you too will follow Burt's lead.

Part VIII

Letters from Colleagues

Letter from Sean McCann, AASP President, Sept. 2009

I have been so lucky to be able to serve with you on the Executive Board. Having you as a mentor, colleague, and friend, I could not ask for more. You are a treasure for the field and pure gold for me. You are one of my favorite people in the world Burt, and I'm glad this time has brought us together. I know what you have done for us. Thank you doesn't capture it.

* * *

Letter from Jack Lesyk, AASP Public Relations & Outreach Division Head, Oct. 2009

I want you to know, Burt, that more than anyone else, you contributed significantly to my enjoyment as well as to my personal growth...I have especially appreciated your ability to create an environment in which everyone is listened to with patience, respect, and understanding. Yet, when the time came, you were able to stand strong for your values and convictions, and express them in a firm, yet always in a polite and respectful manner. I have appreciated your moments of lightheartedness and sense of humor as well.

* * *

Letter from Michelle Magyar, AASP Scientific Program Division Head, Sept. 2009

I truly believe that the conference was a tremendous success because you have reached out to so many members, in particular, the students. Due to your leadership, our planning committee made the best decisions because you always put the members first. Every single scheduling conflict was handled with grace, and because of your recommendations, our members benefited every time. You have taught me the importance of being patient and considerate; when the easiest thing to do is to make a quick fix and be done with it (I was tempted to do this many times!). And because of your diligence and attention to detail, we were able to produce a product that was impressive and memorable for the AASP membership. I will miss working with you Burt, and I consider this opportunity to collaborate with you to be one of the best experiences of my life. Thank you and a big hug to you!

Part IX

Publications and Videos

Giges, B. (2014). Becoming a sportpsych practitioner. In *Becoming a sport psychologist* (pp. 9-18). P. J. McCarthy & M.J. Jones, Eds. Oxon, UK: Routledge.

Giges, B. (2000). Removing psychological barriers: Clearing the way. Chapter in *Doing Sport Psychology* (pp.17-31), M. B. Andersen, Ed. Champaign, IL: Human Kinetics.

Giges, B. (1998). Psychodynamic concepts in sport psychology: Comment on Strean and Strean. *The Sport Psychologist*, **12**, 223-227.

Giges, B. (Fall, 1996). Clinical and Sport Psychology. Commentary, *AASP Newsletter*, **11**, (3), 24, 27.

Giges, B. (Winter, 1995). Clinicians and educators, Commentary, *AASP Newsletter*, **10**, (1), 17.

Giges, B. (October 1977). Stoking: Criticism at its best, *Transactional Analysis Journal*, **7**, (4), 342.

Giges, B. (July 1975). Using your head: Notes on nodding, *Transactional Analysis Journal*, **5**, (3), 264-266.

Giges, B. & McCarthy, P. (2014). Understanding Athletes' Psychological Needs. In *Routledge Companion to Sport and Exercise: Global Perspectives and Fundamental Concepts.* (pp. 907-921). A.G. Papaioannou & D. Hackfort, Eds. Oxon UK: Routledge.

Giges, B. and Petitpas, A. J. (2000). Brief contact interventions in sport psychology. *The Sport Psychologist*, **14**, 176-187.

Giges, B., Petitpas, A. J., Vernacchia, R. A. (2004). Helping coaches meet their own needs: Challenges for the sport psychology consultant. *The Sport Psychologist*, **18**, 430-444.

Giges, B. & Reid, G. (2016). Awareness, self-awareness and mindfulness: The application of theory to practice. In *Mindfulness and performance.* Current Perspectives in Social and Behavioral Sciences (pp. 488-514). A. L. Baltzell, Ed. New York: Cambridge University Press.

Giges, B. & Rosenfeld, E. (1976). Personal growth, encounter, and self-awareness groups. In *The Intensive Group Experience* (87-110), M. Rosenbaum and A. Snadowsky, Eds. New York: Free Press, Macmillan.

McCarthy, P. & Giges, B. (In press). Helping coaches meet their psychological needs. In *The psychology of sports coaching: Research and practice.* R.Thelwell, C. Harwood, & I. Greenlees, Eds. Oxon, UK: Routledge.

Petitpas, A.J., Giges, B., & Danish, S.J. (1999). The sport psychologist-athlete relationship: Implications for training. *The Sport Psychologist*, **13**, 344-357.

Videos

Giges, B. Self Awareness in Sport Psychology Consulting (2011). Wilbraham MA: Virtual Brands. Available from Virtual Brands. http://www.vbvideo.com/products/self-awareness_sports.html

Giges, B., Ravizza, K., & Murphy, S. (2000). Three approaches to sport psychology consulting. Wilbraham MA: Virtual Brands. Available from Virtual Brands. http://www.vbvideo.com/products/three_approaches.html

Giges, B., Ravizza, K., Van Raalte, J., & Zaichkowsky, L. (2002). Brief Contact Interventions in Sport Psychology. Wilbraham MA: Virtual Brands. Available from Virtual Brands. http://www.vbvideo.com/products/brief_contact.html

Part X

Presentations

1991-2015 ***Workshops***: "Self-Awareness for Sport

Psychologists" at:
- University of Maryland, College Park, MD
- University of Buffalo, Buffalo, NY
- University of Utah, Salt Lake City, Utah
- University of North Carolina, Greensboro, NC
- Springfield College, Springfield, MA
- California State University, Fullerton, CA -
- University of Virginia, Charlottesville, VA
- Florida State University, Tallahassee, FL
- Boston University, Boston, MA
- University of Ottawa, Ottawa, Canada
- Temple University, Philadelphia, PA
- University of New Mexico, Albuquerque, NM

Oct. 2014 ***Workshop***: "Theory as the Basis of Practice," AASP Conference, Las Vegas, NV

Oct. 2012 ***Workshop***: "An Eclectic Approach to Sport Psychology Consulting," AASP Conference, Atlanta, GA

Oct. 2010 ***Continuing Education Workshop***: "Self-Awareness for Sport Psychology Practitioners," with Ken Ravizza, AASP Conference, Providence, RI

Sept. 2010 ***Lecture***: "Coaches Have Their Own Needs," Hudson Valley Women's Athletic Conference, Sarah Lawrence College, Bronxville, NY

Sept. 2008 ***Workshop***: "Self-Reflection in Presenting a Workshop and Conducting an Interview," with A. Poczwardowski, L. Lauer, & Y. Chung, AASP Conference, St. Louis, MO

April 2008 ***Workshop***: "Consultant's Self-Awareness in Sport Psychology Consultation," Northeast Atlantic Sport Psychology Conference, Philadelphia, PA

June 2007 ***Workshop***: "The Meaning of Trust in Mentoring, Sport, and Life," Conference on Counseling Athletes, Springfield College, Springfield, MA

Feb. 2007 ***Workshop***: "Common Ground: Where Sport Psychology and Sports Medicine Meet," Joint Commission on Sports Medicine and Science Annual Meeting, Grapevine, TX

Sept. 2006 ***Workshop***: "When Words are Not Enough: Non-Verbal Approaches to Team Self-Awareness," AASP Conference, Miami, FL

Oct. 2005 ***Workshop***: "Consultant's Self-Awareness in Sport Psychology Consultation," AASP Conference, Vancouver, CA

Oct. 2004 ***Workshop***: "Working with Athletes' Emotions: Responding in the Moment," AASP Conference, Minneapolis, MN

Oct. 2004 ***Symposium***: "Marathons from Start to Finish: Research and Practice," with M.P. Buman, K.F. Hays, and J.L. Brown, AASP Conference, Minneapolis, MN

Oct. 2003 ***Symposium***: "Professional Development of Sport Psychology Consultants across the Developmental Spectrum," with N. Webber, B.H. Jackson, and W. Moore, AASP Conference, Philadelphia, PA

June 2003 **Workshop**: "Transitions: Endings and Beginnings in Sport and Life," Conference on Counseling Athletes, Springfield College, Springfield, MA

July 2002 ***Invited*** Lecture: "Interview with an Athlete," Conference on Sport Psychology, U.N.E.D., Madrid, Spain

July 2002 ***Invited Lecture***: "A Counseling Approach to Performance Enhancement," Course in Sport Psychology, U.N.E.D., Denia, Spain

June 2002 **Workshop**: "How Can I Win If I Don't Come In First?" Conference on Counseling Athletes, Springfield College, Springfield, MA

April 2002 **Lecture**: "A Counseling Approach to Performance Enhancement," Sport Psychology Conference, Springdale, UT

Oct. 2001 **Lecture**: "Brief Interventions in Sport Psychology: Theory and Practice," with A. Petitpas, AASP Conference, Orlando, FL

Oct. 2001 **Lecture**: "Working Effectively with Athletes' Emotions: Different but Converging Approaches," with S. Foster, AASP Conference, Orlando, FL

June 2001 **Workshop**: "Consultant's Self-Awareness in Sport Psychology Consultation," Conference on Counseling Athletes, Springfield, MA

Nov. 2000 **Lecture**: "Psychological Considerations in Helping Injured Athletes: A Mind-Body Connection," with D. Yukelson, Annual Meeting, NY Regional Chapter, American College of Sports Medicine, NY

Oct. 2000 **Workshop**: "Virtual Supervision of Sport Psychology Consulting: A Live Demonstration," with K. D. Cogan, R. J. Harmison, K. Peterson, & A. Meyers, AASP Conference, Nashville, TN

March 2000 **Lecture**: "Concentration Issues in Performance: Case Study Session," with M. Thompson,

Conference on Excellence in Performance, Pfeiffer University, Misenheimer, NC

March 2000 ***Symposium***: "Psychological Barriers to Performance," with G. Balague, K. Henschen, & D. Yukelson, Conference on Excellence in Performance, Pfeiffer University, Misenheimer, NC

1997-2000 ***Workshops:*** "Psychological Barriers to Excellence in Sport Performance" at:

- NY Chapter, American College of Sports Medicine, NY
- Conference on Counseling Athletes, Springfield College, MA
- World Congress on Mental Training Salt Lake City, UT
- AASP Conference, Cape Cod. MA
- Temple University, Philadelphia, PA
- University of Ottawa, Canada
- Boston University, Boston, MA
- Conference on Counseling Athletes, Springfield College, MA

Sept. 1999 ***Workshop***: "Finding Stability in Transitions: A Challenge for Athletes," with R. McGowan, AASP Conference, Banff, Canada

Sept. 1999 ***Workshop***: "Professional Philosophy in Conceptualization of the Athlete's Concerns and Potential Interventions," with G. Balague, K. Henschen, S. Portenga, & D. Yukelson, AASP Conference, Banff, Canada

May 1999 ***Workshop***: "Interventions with Athletes in Sport Psychology Consultation," with L. Zaichkowsky, Conference on Counseling Athletes, Springfield College, MA

Sept. 1998 ***Lecture***: "Performance Enhancement x 2: A Unique Collaboration between Sport Psychology Practitioners," with K. Ravizza, AASP Conference, Cape Cod, MA

Sept. 1998 **Workshop**: "Personal and Social Implications of Sensitive Gender Issues," with C. Zientek, J. Yambor, & K.Diffenbach, AASP Conference, Cape Cod, MA

June 1998 **Workshop**: "Developing the Complete Sport Psychologist through Life Skills Training," with R. McGowan & S. Danish, Conference on Counseling Athletes, Springfield, MA

Feb. 1997 **Keynote Address**: "Psychological Barriers to Excellence in Sport Performance," Southeastern Sport and Exercise Psychology Student Symposium, West Virginia University, Morgantown, WV

Feb. 1997 **Lecture**: "Current Experiences in Sport Psychology Consultation," Sport Behavior Graduate Seminar, West Virginia University, Morgantown, WV

1994- 1997 **Lectures**: "Psychological Issues for Injured Athletes" at:

- School of Physical Education, West Virginia University, Morgantown, WV
- Sport Psychology Seminar, Athletic Dept., Pace University, Pleasantville, NY
- Sport Psychology Mini-Conference, N.Y. Chapter, American College of Sports Medicine, New York, NY
- Institute for Sports Medicine, Lenox Hill Hospital, NY

Oct. 1996 **Symposium**: "Case Reviews in Sport Psychology," with R. McGowan, K. Henschen, B. Ogilvie, & V. Bacon, AASP Conference, Williamsburg, VA

Oct. 1996 **Workshop**: "A Demonstration by Experienced Sport Psychologists," with M. A. Kane, C. Adams, G. Balague, & W. Thierfelder, AASP Conference, Williamsburg, VA

May 1996 **Lecture**: "Needs of Sport Psychologists," Sport Psychology Meeting, Temple, N.H.

May 1996 **Lecture**: "Beyond Psychopathology: An Alternative to the Medical Model in Sport," Annual Meeting, International Society for Sport Psychiatry, New York

April 1996 **Lecture**: "Performance Enhancement," Athletic Dept, Pace University, Pleasantville, N.Y.

Sept. 1995 **Keynote Address**: "How People Change," Intervention/Performance Enhancement, AASP Conference, New Orleans, LA

Sept. 1995 **Workshop**: "Artistic and Creative Aspects of Sport Psychology Consulting," with T. Orlick, G. Balague, & P. Bach, AASP Conference, New Orleans, LA

March 1995 **Lecture**: "Philosophical Issues in Sport Psychology Consulting," California State University at Fullerton, CA

July 1994 **Lecture**: "Clinical Assessment of Athletes in Crisis," Sport Psychology Meeting, Temple, NH

Oct. 1993 **Workshop**: "Contrasting Styles in Effective Consultation with Athletes," with W. Sime, K. Ravizza, K. Henschen, & J. Loehr, AASP Conference, Montreal, Canada

April 1993 **Keynote Address**: "Reflections on Career, Counseling, and Credentials," Conference on Counseling Athletes, Springfield College, Springfield, MA

Oct 1992 **Workshop**: "Examining the Process of Sport Psychology Consulting," with D. Gould, K. Ravizza, & R. Gordin, AASP Conference, Colorado Springs, CO

Index

About the Author

Burt Giges M.D. is clinical professor in the Athletic Counseling Program, Department of Psychology at Springfield College, MA, past president of the Association for Applied Sport Psychology, and a Distinguished Life Fellow of the American Psychiatric Association. He serves as special consultant to the Psychological Services Subcommittee, USA Track and Field, is on the Editorial Board of *The Sport Psychologist,* and was a guest co-editor of a special issue for case studies. Formerly, he was a consultant to the Westchester Track Club in NY, and the women's track and field team at Springfield College, and was team physician for a high school football team in NY.

Dr. Giges earned his bachelor's degree at City College of NY, where he was a member of the fencing team, was elected to Phi Beta Kappa, and graduated magna cum laude. He received his MD degree from New York University College of Medicine, won first prize for the highest scholastic standing at graduation, and was president of the Honor Medical Fraternity. He conducted research at The Rockefeller Institute for Medical Research in NY, and at the Walter Reed Hospital Research and Graduate School in Washington prior to entering psychiatry. His training in psychiatry was at The Albert Einstein College of Medicine, Department of Psychiatry in NY, where he was appointed Chief Resident, and then served on the faculty for many years. He later served as director of community mental health Services in Westchester County, and was a member of the Board of the Gestalt Center of Long Island. He has been in private practice for over 50 years.

His special interests in sport psychology include: consultant's self-awareness, psychological barriers to performance excellence, and brief contact interventions. He has conducted workshops on these issues at universities around the country, has been a keynote speaker at sport psychology conferences, and for many years taught a Lab in Counseling Athletes to graduate students at Springfield College.

Dr. Giges lives in New Rochelle, New York, with his wife of 60 years, Ilka. He is the proud father of Elinor and Julie, and loving grandfather of Jennifer, Kayla, and Zachary.

Printed in Great Britain
by Amazon

63284070R00231